Acknowledgements

My wife Ellen

Without you none of this would have been possible. You've given me more than two amazing daughters. More than love and encouragement. You've given me family.
I love you.

Wendy B

It's no secret I'd not be here if it wasn't for you. You put everything into perspective for me and I'll be forever grateful. Thanks for being the light.

Nigel M

My therapist and my friend. I love and miss you dearly. You were an inspiration.

Lee C

Miss you daily my friend. Thanks for the memories. I stay strong because of you.

Melorna

When I got over confident you knocked me back into place. When I didn't have the strength to stand you dragged me back up whether I wanted you to or not. Thank you! Much love.

Shirley

You trusted me when I didn't even trust myself. Forever grateful.

George & Shirley C

The only couple I'd ever have let take the place of my parents. Thank you.

Mark S

The only social worker I ever trusted.

Julia M

You're a tribute to your faith. Thank you, not only did you teach me maths. You taught me self respect.

Rose D

One session, one meeting, one of the most inspirational people I have ever met. I am honoured to know you. You changed my life completely.

David L

I may still be stuck in a very bad situation if it wasn't for your contributions David. Thank you.

Miss Whalen

Writing those twenty eight pages that day made me realise I could create anything and so I created this.
Thank you for your guidance.

Mum

Until we meet again.

www.samm.org.uk

Tracie's Story & Checkmate

Tracie's Story began in Macclesfield in 1982 and details the sequence of abuse by a psychopath father up until the age of ten, where his father then killed his mother.

Having weaved his way through three foster placements, four schools and struggling with identity, trust and self harm issues Tracie grapples with responsibility and blame.

At fifteen when *Tracie's Story* comes to an end he's just returned to his father, with a new person taking the place of mum and new faces in the place of his siblings.

The weight of his grandfather's death lay heavily on him and confidence was low.

It was another slap to another woman that had another outcome. It was then that *Tracie's Story* began again and *Checkmate* was born.

With little in the way of role models. Huge choices had to be made. The biggest being.

Who would he become?

Checkmate.

Checkmate

Chapter 1

Cass was great! As time had gone on we'd had a lot of chats about how they met and the story was the same but never quite lined up with Wenzel's. I'd not figured out why yet. "Why is her hair so short?" I'd asked Wenzel in the car on the way to school. It was odd she'd be prettier with it longer and I liked long hair. "She was beaten by her ex once so bad he pulled a lot of her hair out. Now she's scared to have it long" he said. I believed it. A car had stopped suddenly in front of us but we'd missed it by a good two feet. "Wait here" he said chucking his car door open. He had the lad out of the car and threw him half across his own boot before I knew what was happening. The lad was terrified. Wenzel had a word nose to nose and the lad got back in the car all the while holding his hands up and shaking his head and then the car moved off. "What just happened?" I asked Wenzel as he got back in. "Little fucker stopped dead in front of me" He said slamming his door. "Did you have to hit him?" I asked. "Oh, that was nothing. you keep truanting off school you'll get a lot worse, what? You thought I didn't know about that. I know fucking everything and if you ever look at me like you did the other night" He glanced at me but then looked back to the road he didn't finish the sentence but he didn't have to. I didn't reply.

I wasn't going to school. I'd made the decision somewhere between him threatening to kill me and him trying to replace mum. I couldn't pinpoint the logic but I knew it had to be done. I was different and if he hit Cass I'd kill him. I kept silence all the way there. "There's Caroline" he said. pointing to her heading towards school as we drove passed in the car. "Don't be late, we have somewhere special to go tomorrow" he said. I got out of the car and slammed the door as I headed straight towards Keel. "Woah you're pissed" he said hearing the door slam. "What if he gets out man he's just sat there?" Keel said waving his ciggy around. "Fuck him, he gets out you leg it and I deal with him" I said loud enough for him to hear me. My head was starting to hurt from the pressure building up inside me. Wenzel sped off and Keel asked me "What's up man?"

"How soon can Stoppy be ready?" I asked in reply.

"Anytime man. He really likes you" Keel said.

"Cool, Thanks man." I said hugging him.

Keel and I spent the day truanting playing football right there on the school field in the blistering heat in nothing but our boxer shorts. Fuck everyone. Wenzel picked me up and we went back to his flat. I went straight to my room and played Streets of rage all night. Fuck everyone, I had no plan, fuck dad, fuck Brenda, fuck Cass, fuck God and fuck family. How could I tell them? Hey Jonathon come live with dad and his new family. He's a violent killer and you'll love it!? No chance. How could I go back to Brenda's? "Hey you know, you were right! He's nuts and I'm just like him. Last night I stayed alive by truanting and then stayed awake all night pretending he was every mother fucker on a game where I stab people. Aren't I a good boy?" When I'd calmed down I asked myself what Nigel would do? "Do what you want, fuck everyone else lad" his words rang out. I'd join the army like my uncle Karl. No ties, no family, nobody to hurt, but how?

I was doing kickboxing again, this time the English version. I'd had to tell Pete that we visited a lot of Wenzel's friends and I needed to be at home to pull it off but it worked. Truth was I didn't want to be around Wenzel when he was with Cass. He was more like old Wenzel then and if I did have to defend myself I didn't want Cass hurt either.

Wenzel was driving and smoking one after another. I was dying for a fag. "What? Does it bother you?"He asked lighting another. "They are your lungs not mine" I replied. "You really hate smoking don't you?" He asked.

"Yeah it's terrible" I said.

"Okay, I'll stop" he told me.

"Really?" I asked surprised.

"No, not really dickhead" he told me blowing smoke in my face just as I recognised where we were. "This is Alderley Edge" I said. "Clever boy" he replied. It was where mum was killed. "Why are we here?" I queried.

"To see some old friends and go for a hike and you better be on your best behaviour - right?" He pulling up outside a big house and prodding me hard in the chest. Had he just hit me? I didn't like this game. My brain was screaming run, get out, leg it! Something was very, very wrong. I walked around a large hedge and recognised the house immediately. Winnie and Phil . Jonathon and Jodie's first foster placement. He knocked on the door and they let us in. Wenzel told them how great my life was now and I sat there like a good boy and laid on a little less charm than Wenzel had. They showed me pictures of when Jonathon and Jodie went on holiday with them. I looked and tried not to remember them. It hurt too much. I'd had Jonathon outside in a wheelbarrow in that garden back when I thought it would all be okay until my family were back together. I felt so strong and protective of them. Now what was I? An animal. My family gone. My charming father actually a manipulative psychopath. I looked it up. He fit the description perfectly.

We left and Wenzel swung a left instead of a right turn like we should have. "Another one for the book, won't be long now" he said getting excited. I'd never seen him like this. He was literally bobbing up and down getting a sexual thrill. "Oh you'll like this. You'll like this a lot" he said pulling into Alderley Edge caves. I'd visited mum and dad just once in the caravan and I was hopeless with directions, but I remember pictures and tree's very well."I've been here before" I said recalling the caravan site less than forty feet away behind a building. I realised I shouldn't have said anything. "Ah you do remember, yeah. long time ago. Follow me" he said grabbing a policeman's torch from his boot and some rope. I didn't move. Something wasn't right. I was searching my memory and came up with a scene. I was in the caravan and I'd visited from the foster placement I was first in, I didn't recall it when I was younger but through some sort of flashback it was returning. I could see the inside of the caravan. I'd moved a pillow and found condoms. "What are these?" I asked. "Balloons" Wenzel had laughed. I'd known he was lying but hadn't known what they were. Mum was sat holding her knee's up to her chest on the bed. Her hair was over her face. "Balloons aren't they love?" He said tapping her leg then rubbing his hand up it. She only had a nightgown on. "Erm, yeah" she said uninterested. Her eyes didn't meet ours and her head didn't move. She was very sad. As I stood there remembering that scene I realised I knew how she felt. She'd known something bad would happen but not what. She was feeling the same thing I was right now stood in a field next to a rock face with Wenzel.

"A wizard lived here" he said "Look" he added. I walked over to where he had gone but kept a good fifteen feet between us. I was ready to run but felt any attempt would be hopeless. He pointed down a large drop filled with jagged rock and greenery. "Never find a body down there" he said smiling. Was this his plan? Kill mum and bury her down there? Why was I here? This was surreal. "Big drop" I said stepping way back as he came closer. He stopped at the edge a while and then walked over to a grated over cave entrance, after inspecting it for several seconds which somehow looked fake he moved around the corner "come on" he said beckoning me towards a huge hole the size of five of me side by side and at least six feet high. "No" I said. "Come on, It'll be fun!" He said. "What's that for?" I asked pointing at the rope. "This? This is in case we get lost. Yeah we can leave a trail and find our way out he added as though making up a story on the spot, and this?" He said holding up the torch "is so I can see where we are going, you coming or not?" He was lying. I shook my head "suit yourself" he said going inside the large hole. He shouted random shit about me coming in but it was echoing and I was busy looking around. If I had to run it would be to closest building and my line wasn't hard to remember. "Help! He killed my mum and now he wants me dead!" should do it. I hoped. I saw one other person walking a dog and tried to catch his eye so he'd remember me. No luck. Wenzel popped his head around the entrance. "last chance? It doesn't go back far at all. Just twenty paces? Come on! Chicken!" I walked back to the car and ignored him. "Okay, okay" he said following me.

To this day I'll never know whether he planned to off me or was just getting a huge rise out of taking me back to where he killed my mother. Perhaps he intended to teach me a lesson and tie me up in the cave, gag me and leave me there for an hour to convince me he could kill me if he wanted to, or perhaps he was genuine and wanted to have a laugh and a joke around the caves in the only way he knew how - by being a complete idiot. I have no idea however at the time it all felt very real and his intentions about killing me genuine or not he was definitely getting a kick out of being back where he killed my mother.

Wenzel and I were in the flat for the last visit from Patrick Benson my social worker. Wenzel was telling him he needed more money and what a great time him and I have had. "You got anything to contribute?" He asked me. "Nah, I'll say goodbye outside man" I said walking down the stairs with him. "What's on your mind?" He said taking his sunglasses off. "Turn around" I said making sure my back and his were to the flat's window. I didn't look up. I knew he'd be watching us. We were stood in the carpark and it was warm out. "You can't do anything - agreed?" I told him. "I can't promise that. It depends on what you're going to tell me" he said.

"Fuck that, write this down" I said. He pulled his pad out. "If anything happens to me, you need to know this" I said.

"Has he hit you?" Patrick asked me straight away. I met his eyes. "No, write." I said pointing at the pad. "Wenzel has a girlfriend called Cassandra Charleston she lives at 303 Chaplain Street, St Helens, Mereseyside. Blue door, near a field." I said.

"Why are you telling me this" Patrick asked me.

"You wrote it down?" I asked.

"Yeah, you're worried" he asked me. "I'll be fine, but yeah, shit's turned bad" I said.

"I can.." he began as I cut him off.

"No, no, you do nothing, there's more that can get hurt than just me. Promise me, not until I say?" I asked.

"Okay, be careful" He said.

"Always" I replied and headed inside I knew Wenzel would ask so headed straight in the living room.

"What was that all about?" He said as soon as we'd watched Patricks car leave.

"Ah usual shit, Caroline says hi but won't see you, probation is over so we only see ginger nut Patrick once every six months now" I lied.

"Good" He said.

Chapter 2

The post had just arrived at Cass's, I wasn't thinking and wouldn't have thought too much about it if Wenzel hadn't of snatched it out of my hands. I let it slide as though I'd not even noticed but I was only bringing it in what was the problem? He was on another job so I was to stay with Cass whilst Larry and Judy went to school. Cass talked about my birthday which was nice because it's more than Wenzel had done I'd soon be fifteen even though I'd been saying I was fifteen for about eight months. "What do you want?" she asked me as we walked side by side towards the town centre. "Dunno" I said and I didn't. "Why?" she asked looking slightly up at me in her trademark white top with tight blue jeans. "Nobody ever cared to ask before" I said honestly. "Name it" she said. "Okay, I want a CD player for my room. I want to listen to Lola" I told her. "Okay" she said with a sly grin, she didn't ask why Lola. "Look. I like you...but...this doesn't mean you're mum...okay? Sorry. I do like you" I said. She put her arms around me it was nice "I like you too" she said. "How did you meet dad?" I asked her. "After he came out of hospital" she said as if quoted from a book and for the hundredth time. "I'm not stupid" I said still walking. "Okay, our secret?" she said "Meaning?" I asked. "Wenzel doesn't know I told you" she said. "Good with me" I replied. "We met at hospital, I was a nurse there. Before that, well before that doesn't matter but I was a nurse there and well I still am actually" she said. "So, you work in a prison?" I asked her as we crossed a quiet road just before the town centre. "A prison hospital" she corrected me and continued "Wenzel, your dad came in. He played up a bit and wouldn't talk to anyone. Not for days, they'd all sit playing games the others and he'd just sit there staring into space. I asked him to play scrabble and he said he didn't know how, so I showed him. Then we became friends then we'd have day release so we'd go back to my place and watch a film. He missed you a lot. When he got out we became a couple" She was lying. I'd already put the pieces together. He was either with mum and knocking Cass at the same time or did meet her in the hospital and used her vulnerability to help himself get out quicker. He remained quiet for so long because he was looking for the weaker staff. He needed to know who he could use. I knew Wenzel, I knew his mind. She was vulnerable and that's a huge turn on for a psychopath, easily manipulated. He would have started off making her feel special by being the first and or only person he'd talk to and then he'd progress to letting her know it was okay to be weak sometimes and probably share some stories about himself to show how well he relates to her tales. Perhaps he'd go as far saying no therapist could help him, how he hasn't had an emotional connection in so long he values her real life stories. Anything to get the edge he needs. Then he'd make her feel strong, powerful, confident and all of a sudden it would be her idea to help him out of there. The situation was ideal. She could never tell anyone about their relationship because she'd lose her job and potentially the children. So once Wenzel was out he really could do what he wanted with her. He'd think nothing of telling her "You can't leave me. I'll tell everyone. I have nothing to lose. You'll lose your job, the kids and me" he'd use her kindness against her and make her feel guilty. She was the one in a position of power after all and so she should have known better. I suddenly felt very sorry for her. All of her happiness was fake. "What's your real name?" I asked her. "Nothing gets past you does it?" she asked. "I get that a lot" I replied. We both laughed.

"Rachel call me Ray but around Wenzel it has to be Cass he's quite protective." she said although in my head I heard paranoid. "Yeah, he is" I agreed. We had burger and chips that night and I played Sgt peppers lonely hearts club CD on repeat as I took ages washing up because I loved the music and hearing children in a house again where a woman had done the cooking that wasn't my mother but wasn't a bad lass. I would have been totally happy had Wenzel not been there. I got to thinking about Cass and that if I could get her on side I could find out more about Wenzel. Maybe she'd ditch him and then look after me, Caroline, Jodie, Jonathon, Larry and Judy? I know it's a lot but I'd help. I imagined them all playing together behind the field by her house. I imagined the children running into the garden asking me to come and play as I was washing up. I'd run out picking up a bin lid and a stick and we were play fighting when Wenzel appeared in the doorway. Somehow his image swallowed the whole scene.

Cass went to work and Wenzel tried to embarrass me by putting Barbedwire on the T.V. I didn't react when she stripped or when he said "Cor I'd fuck that, wouldn't you?" Nor when he said "You're no fucking fun you know that". Larry and Judy were just being kids and making a noise upstairs. Wenzel ran up and I heard a multitude of slaps rain down as the kids began screaming. I froze. I was back in Macclesfield instantly against the wall being pushed. Then upstairs whilst he beat Caroline and me. He came down smiling "Now don't make me come back up there". I could hear sobbing. "What?" He said. I was in shock and just stared hopelessly. That didn't just happen I told myself over and over. That didn't happen. I knew it had but my brain wouldn't compute it. The following day Wenzel made fat jokes at Judy all day. Cass didn't defend her. I felt sick "Happy Birthday dear Tracie two!" came from the kitchen as Cass carried out a large box and Wenzel changed "Tracie two" to "Little dick" in the song. It was my radio cassette player with CD player. I loved it! I hugged Cass and whispered "Thank you". I took it back to Wenzel's and moved my bedside cabinet into the middle of the room. It could sit right there where I could play it whenever I wanted from anywhere in the bedroom in just two steps. Cass was okay. I just had to find a way to stay away from Wenzel. He'd opened his post when we got back. "Darts?" he said walking in and closing the door so the board was visible. "Guess so" I said "Come on have a game with your ole dad" he said grabbing the darts from in front of Oscar's vivarium. He was being far too nice. He chucked his last dart and as I bent to write down the score he grabbed me and pinned me to the wall by my neck. I hit the wall hard and he held me there off the ground. "If you fucking ever skive off school again!!!" He screamed pulling his arm back into a fist. I was certain he'd swing. I didn't move. I met his eyes with mine. He didn't move and I realised despite all my self defence, all my concerns with the knife and all my attempts at getting the family back, I didn't care. He could kill me. I had nothing left. We kept eye contact for a long time.

I'd like to say saw something from the past. I felt sorry for Joseph and Jade or I saw Alan die again or anything to make me mad and fight. I'd accept fear or crying or hitting him back but no. I felt absolutely nothing. "Do it" I murmured. My eyes hadn't left his. I wasn't angry I just didn't care. My lips moved but I don't know if he didn't hear me. He let me go after a while of holding his punch to hit me then dropped his arm to his side turned on his heel and walked out. I didn't know what to feel. I looked around "I need music" I thought and turned the radio on. It was playing Eternal Flame by the bangles, my mother's favourite song. I lost it completely. How dare I like Cass? How dare she love Wenzel? He killed his wife! How dare he hit me! How dare I betray mum!, Mum!, Mum! The word was chanting in my head and heart and I could feel it unfortunately along with it and each word of the song my anger got worse, rising like a thermometer I could feel the adrenaline. I took a step back and chopped the CD players with my hand "Heya!" As hard as I could. I'd split the CD player lid clean in half along the top and my little finger was bleeding quite badly where the plastic had cut me. Wenzel opened my bedroom door. "What the hell are" he began "Get out!, Get out!, Get out!" I screamed hitting the CD player again and then kicked the bedside cabinet over and sending it across the room before turning back to him in the doorway "Get out!"

I stood there arms by my sides bolt upright tense as fuck and angrier than I'd ever been. "Fine, ungrateful little shit" he said slamming the front door behind him. In the morning he said "About last night, we've both been through a lot. Let's leave it at that. I meant what I said though. If you're not in school today. I won't be there when you come out" I ignored him. I'd spent the night thinking, and looking at my broken C.D player. Who was I kidding? I couldn't make this work. Cass wasn't mum and Wenzel wasn't my dad no matter what the DNA test said.

I had no intention of going to school. My knives, my money, my change of clothes were already packed. If he doesn't pick me up then he really doesn't care. *Fuck him.*

I told Keel as soon as I saw him "Fuuuuck" he said exhaling from a fag right there on the school grounds. "Yeah, so I need a place to stay like yesterday if he doesn't show up"

"What if he does?" Keel asked his black quiff dropping down ever so slightly in front of his face.

"Then I go home until Stoppy is ready for me, I'll live" I joked.

"Maybe" Keel said seriously "Or you could come to school? I'll join you?" He offered.

"No mate. Thanks but no." I said normally, "I need to know for sure if he gives a shit" I said and my voice almost broke.

"What if, like, you go home and he, you know?" Keel said all carefully and concerned almost hopping foot to foot.

"Kills me?" I asked my voice normal again.

"Yeah" He said his voice cracking.

"Then he kills me" I replied and turned away to face the countryside.

Chapter 3

Stoppy was a diamond, we were sat in his front room instead of at school. He was sat on some kind of chest in front of the window and moving some toy soldiers around. His enormous frame made the chest look like a matchbox. "You can sleep on the sofa or on the floor in the bedroom it's your choice mate. Get food in when you can other than that I don't give a shit." He said. "Oh and don't use my phone" he added nodding his big bald head as far as it would reach on his broad shoulders. I remained quiet "why would this guy help me?" But fuck it - at least someone was willing to help I'd take it. What did I have to lose? "If I see you tonight you move in if I don't let's say two weeks or I'll give it someone else" he said. I was cool with that and waited around whilst Kap and Keel turned up then we all walked back to school to be picked up or sign in before heading home. Stoppy stayed at his ground floor flat. He was a good few years older than us however he had the mental age of a sixteen year old. "That's really decent of him, hey thanks man" I said punching Keels arm playfully. "He's lonely" Kap answered for everyone.

I waited forty five minutes after school time had finished when my mobile buzzed. It was Patrick Benson "Stay there! I'm on my way" he told me "OK mate" I replied flatly. I knew he wouldn't show I thought meaning Wenzel. Now I was truly alone, I was fifteen and as much as I was scared I felt more free than I'd ever done before. A really weird feeling. It was time to make my own decisions. I ignored the red Honda estate turning the corner and pulling up a few feet behind me. I'd checked nobody was in it apart from Patrick as he went around the corner my field of vision was now taking in the surrounding areas. Did any car pull up further down the road? Had he dropped someone off to watch me before he pulled up? My thought's were everywhere. I trusted nobody and at the same time so what if I was to be grabbed? How much did I really care? I lit another smoke. Not much.

"Hey" Pat said getting out of the vehicle. "Sorry" he added "Wenzel called earlier and said he'd had enough. He's not coming. What happened?" He asked.

"What else did he say?" I asked him realising for the first time that not only was I free I could say and do as I pleased.

"Well, he said he couldn't handle you. You were flying off the handle and he was washing his hands of you" Pat was stood about four feet in front of me and trying to keep his body language as relaxed as possible but I could tell he was nervous. Whatever had been said Pat wasn't happy but wasn't blaming me either. He looked like he'd just had a proper roasting. "I see" I replied and turned my back on him as I took another lung full of nicotine. Wenzel had a way of hurting everyone he came into contact with. Even those just doing their job.

"You okay?" He asked taking one step closer. "Yeah, strangely I am" I said putting my phone away and lighting a ready made roll up from the fag I'd had in my mouth. I now had two. I looked at them and wondered - who'd give a shit anyway? "Fuck it, right?" I said. "Want to sit?" He asked walking to the passenger side door and opening it then walking around to the drivers side and getting in. He closed the drivers side door once in. I got in but kept both feet on the floor outside. Without my tie on I looked like I was just enjoying a smoke after work with a colleague. I told Pat about Cass but left out the bits about the kids. "That's why I'm here. He refused to pick me up if I was truanting You can't say anything. She'll lose the kids. I can't do that to her. I've been in care. It ain't pretty. He's an ass but they aren't" I told him. A choice I didn't know then but would impact a lot of people's lives through my lack of action.

"Okay, I get it but right now we have to sort you out" he said.

I waved my arms questioningly.

"We have a place ready for you" he began.

"No, I'm not going back to Brenda's so she can say how right she was" I stood up so I was out of the car and looked around quickly.

"It's not like that" he started again getting out of the car.

"It's exactly like that. You don't live there. You don't see the shit. Sorry Patrick you have a good heart but you know fuck all. He wanted me dead!" I said turning to eyeball him for a couple of seconds longer than I should have before I turned away.

"What do you mean?" He asked. I could feel the honesty in his voice.

"Figure of speech, forget it. Sorry" I replied as relaxed as I could manage.

"You can't just say that and then clam up Tracie" he asked.

"Yes I can. Tell me about what you were saying earlier?" I asked him changing the subject.

"Okay, have it your way. It's in Knutsford. A nice old couple" He started explaining as I'd requested.

"I've heard enough" I interrupted walking away.

"Where you going?" His head shot up I ignored him and carried on going "wait!" He shouted. I lit another smoke as he followed a few steps behind. "Knutsford? like near Macclesfield Knutsford?" I started my voice beginning to raise "fuck off Patrick, An old couple? Worked well with Tony and Pip didn't it?" I didn't bother looking back at him as I walked. "You're right. I don't know shit. So tell me? let me help you!" He tried. I turned to face him and stepped forwards. "All I can say about him is Brenda was right..and then some. I fucked up! Okay!? There - Now you have it" I turned away and started jogging. "Don't make it worse by running" he said catching up with me in the car. "Pat if I don't pick you up I have to tell the police you ran away. Then they will come bring you to me. Then what?" He said. I kept running they will have to find me first I thought. I ran for maybe five minutes but my heart wasn't in it. I turned to Patrick who was sat in the car looking paler than usual as I jogged alongside. "I have a place with a mate" I told him stopping to make a roll up. "Where? We need to check it's safe" he said. "Seriously?" I asked full of sarcasm. "Okay, okay, you win but call me, okay?" He asked. I nodded and my respect for him grew. He'd tried okay it was his job but he'd tried. I went to Stoppy's checking behind me the entire way to make sure I hadn't been followed. I'd find out years later he'd followed me to Stoppy's and noted the address down. How he'd done it to this day I don't know but the address was in my social services records.

There was a weights bench in Stoppy's bedroom at the end of a huge double divan bed. Stoppy filled most of it. He'd had a single bed put in at the opposing end of the room which I don't remember being there last time. The floor although littered with guy, gun and circus magazines had a thick carpet and felt safer than the single bed. I wasn't worried about Stoppy. He seemed harmless enough I just had the impression that if someone did come in looking for me and they had intentions of kicking off they would check the bed's first. I didn't want to be that guy. I was much happier with the floor. I knew it wasn't forever but it was warm and more importantly I trusted the guy so it felt as safe as I could allow myself to feel. The living room had a battered sofa with a cheap dartboard over the gas fire. A leather chair by a huge single pane window on the opposite wall. The floor there was brushed not hoovered. "You okay mate?, Good to see you" Stoppy had said taking up the entire door frame as I'd knocked on. I nodded and walked in. It was first time I'd been in without being a guest and I immediately felt at home. I had Kap's word and that was good enough for me. "You look tired" Stoppy said. "I'm alright, thanks for this man I'll square it with you one day.

I got fuck all at the moment" I replied. "Relax, get some sleep" he said. "Nah not yet man. Brain's fried mate. Brain's fried" I said feeling the shock of recent events start to kick in. "Darts?" he asked picking up the three laying on the council's gas fire.

"Hell yeah" I replied.

We played a few games of killer where you hit the other guys number taking lives of him. Some nights I slept on the sofa most nights on the floor in his room. I washed but never took a bath the whole time. It felt like I'd be taking the piss if I did. I ate very little by choice. I couldn't pay my way so I took only what I needed to survive. I kept well hidden only going to Keel's, Kap's and Stoppy's houses. I saw them after school and on lunch breaks. I knew social services would be looking for me and knew the police would too. I got to know Keel's family a little better during this time. I was at his house with little Kathy his sister, Stoppy, Keel, Kap and Keel's sister who's name I can't remember when Stoppy asked me if I wanted anything from the chip shop. I'd replied that I wasn't hungry when in fact I was starving. He brought me back a battered sausage. I felt bad but wolfed it down "have a chip" he said holding the pack out to me. "I'm okay thanks mate. you've done enough" I said sat like a lemon on the edge of Kap's sofa just wanting the world to swallow me up. "Come on for fucks sake have a chip" Stoppy said leaning against the wall and holding the packet out to me. I got up and took a chip. I wasn't being sarcastic. I was well into the habit of Wenzel's ways and my brain did what it thought was safest. By taking a chip I was abiding by the rules and although it was probably safe to take more I wasn't risking the bullshit for being a taker off my friend. In my head that chip was all important for many reasons. For Stoppy it was just a bag of chips. "Take a handful man" he said leaning forwards. By now people were tittering and I lost it "What's fucking wrong with you?" I snapped pushing him in the chest sending chips everywhere. "I don't want a fucking chip I'm fine!" I continued.

"Okay man, Chill. No biggy" Stoppy said palms towards me at head height.

"No Biggy? You've got no fucking idea!" I screamed into his face. He walked out. I looked around to see the others looking at me. I'd fucked up again and I knew it. So did they. "Go talk to him man. He'll get it" Keel said softly. "No, you go. If I go he'll get defensive and I'll hit him or I'll apologise and he'll think it's just for somewhere to stay. Either way I fucked up it's not his fault." I said immediately calm. "Shit!" I swore kicking the remaining chips through the back door.

Stoppy returned about an hour later with Keel and Kap in tow. Stoppy was second through the door behind Keel. I stood up arms out wide and low palms towards him. "Want a chip?" He said smiling at me. I creased up "Yeah man, gimme your chips" I said hugging him. I had to tip my toe to reach around his shoulders and my hands were a long way from meeting behind him. He was huge.

Little Kathy was dancing to Barbie girl by Aqua with Keel's sister. I relaxed watching them dance together as Keel tapped his fingers on a beer can with his legs slung across the sofa and Kap tapped his foot in the middle of the room. Kap started singing and I slung my head back laughing simultaneously kicking my can across the floor onto his rug. "Shit sorry mate" I jumped up to rescue it as Kap appeared with a rag and started cleaning. Not the first time someone else has cleaned up my mess I thought sombrely Kelly and Jeanne went to the shop whilst us boys talked about girls and our dick sizes. Kap got a major headache out of nowhere and explained he was a haemophiliac I had no idea what that was until he explained that if he got cut then he'd bleed more than most as his cut's don't heal like a normal persons. He showed me how to calm his headaches with a forehead massage. I did that for hi until he was better and it felt good to be helping someone for a change until Keel's sister ran into the living room in tears and Kathy followed with red faced. She'd obviously been crying. "What's up?" Keel asked. "Followed from shop. This lad hit Kathy, we ran off. He's outside!" she said panting. "I'll go check it out" Keel said calmly "No!" I replied calm and loud. "Keel take care of your sister, Kap look after yours" I said as I headed through the door. "Need me?" Stoppy said seeing me bolt out the door past the hall. I saw his chips hit the floor as he tried to raise his huge body from sitting to standing. I was in the garden before he'd stood up. I looked to my right as the garden went straight onto a pathway. There was nobody there. I looked left which was also empty but a shorter path. I heard rustling to my far left and took off at a sprint. A small lad was stood eating chips in the middle of the patch of grass. "Oi mate?" I shouted as I reached him from the side. He turned just as I socked him in the face. How he stayed standing I don't know but he did "What the?" he got out before I jabbed and crossed him hard. This time he went down "Like hitting girls do you? Get up!" I growled dragging him upwards by his hair. "Not me man, not me" He said holding his chips to his chest. A huge paw landed on my shoulder as Stoppy said "not him mate" pointing to Kathy stood watching me by the hedge. "Who? Where did he go?" I asked the boy. "I don't know, but you're dead! My brother will kill you!" He said standing up straight and not at all scared. I was really fucking impressed but I had also been threatened again and couldn't let that go. "Go and get him" I said pointing past him. "You don't want to do that mate" Keel said from about eight feet away. "Why not?" I asked not taking my eyes off the short lad. "It's Stubbo, remember the guy who whacked Keechie and the blonde?" Keel said. "Yeah dickhead I'm Stubbo's brother. You're dead!" He said again this time leaning his head back to spit on me. Fuck it I was dead anyway if Wenzel got a hold of me or if the police took me back to him, either way I was fucked. I grabbed chip boy by the shirt and half lifted half dragged him four feet into the middle of the patch of grass. "Now listen you little shit. I'm not scared of you or your piss ant brother. Tell him to come armed because if he hits any of these" I gestured with my free hand then slapped him with it hard. He started crying "I'll cut his fucking head off so he better kill me. You got it?" He nodded like his life depended on it. I let him go and a split second later there was a pile of a chips where he previously stood.

"You don't fuck about do you?" Stoppy asked. It was the first time he'd seen me hit anyone. "No mate, but it's all good because now he either has to tell his brother who gets angry and does something stupid or he's too scared to tell him. Either way it's best result I could have got after whacking him. People fight worse when they are pissed off. They don't think. It's all anger" Stoppy looked confused and impressed. Keel was rolling a smoke "No mate, that was stupid. He tells stubbo and he will come for you mate. He won't screw around. How is that a result?" He was genuinely concerned about my future. I wasn't. "Because he won't be looking for her" I said pointing straight at Kathy. Keel took a few seconds for it to sink in then added. "Yeah, well...it was still dumb man!" He said.

I'd gone to throw my empty can in the bin in the kitchen when Kathy followed me in. She was tiny both in height and weight "Can I ask you something?" She said. I had my back to her and made out to be washing my hands in the sink "Anything, but you might not like the answer" I told her as I looked into the night sky. "Why did you protect me?" She asked innocently only looking to know the truth. I was fifteen she was a year or two younger. "Kap and your mum have been good to me. I can't give them money but this I can do" I replied.

"People say things, can I ask you a question? You don't have to answer it's just. They say you're crazy and I, I don't think you are" she said. I didn't turn around but I didn't make out I was washing my hands any more either. I just stood there. "I act crazy when I need to." I said honestly. "What's the question?" I asked turning around to face her but leaning against the sink. She looked so vulnerable "what happened to your mum?"

"Are you sure you want to know?" I replied looking through her eyes but knowing in a few short seconds they would be registering pain and her opinion of me would be altered forever. "Yeah, if you want to tell me" She said. "My father killed her, stabbed her to death" I said as though reciting the days weather. The moment I'd finished the word death her face exploded into tears and she ran out of the kitchen. I followed slowly "What happened?" Keel said appearing at the door the instant Kathy had left. I threw my hands up "never touched her man, she asked about my mum. I told her and she ran off crying" I replied. "Fuck" Keel said knowing something I didn't. I left with Stoppy and headed over to his place. He sat on the sofa me on the chair leaning on my arms. "I didn't touch her man" I said "I know, she's young she'll cry at anything" Stoppy told me. "Did I do wrong telling her? She asked? Should I have lied?" I asked him. "You did nothing wrong mate" He told me rather than answered. "Guys man. I can do that shit like tonight all day man. I don't like it. I don't want to but I can. It's where I'm from. It's what I've seen. I get it. I know how it works. I hate it but I can do it all fucking day man. It's in my blood fuck it may even be a part of Wenzel but I've never hit a bird man. Never....that's it...she's scared of me isn't she? She thinks I'd hurt her? like my dad killed my mum...well fuck he killed her...she doesn't think I'd? I broke down sobbing. It was too much. I couldn't control it my arms bobbed up and down and I caught my breath repeatedly in my chest. The tears burnt my face so much it felt permanent. Stoppy tried to put his arm around me "Don't touch me!, Don't touch me!" I screamed staring at him as my head boiled with anger and pain. At that moment I'd of given anything to beat the Wenzel out of me via whoever was closest. "Shit dude, relax mate, seriously...relax" I wasn't moving. I was just staring at him as my body went through it's process of removing shit from my system and letting me know in a big way it was doing it. I was so angry and hated myself for it which just fuelled the anger even more. "I'll kill him, I hate him. I'll kill him. I got nothing. I lost the lot. Jonathon, Jodie, Caroline,

Wenzel, mum,Cass, Pat, Alan and now my friends are scared of me?" I asked stone cold. I grabbed the darts from the table and launched all three at the board at once as hard as I could just as the living room door opened. "Shit!" I screamed as they landed a foot Northwest of Kathy's head. She looked at me tear drenched and angry then she scarpered. "Great man, just fucking great" I said to Stoppy.

Keel came in where Kathy would have been if she'd stayed. "She came to apologise for upsetting you" he said and walked out. Everything I touched turned to shit. I slept on the floor that night in Stoppy's room next to the weight bench. Halfway through the night I woke up half asleep. Stoppy was sat on the edge of the bed and a figure was stood over him. I reached for a metal weights bar thinking it was so dark the intruder wouldn't be able to see me and half thinking I was having maybe another bad dream when the figure said "stay down lad, I know who you are". I definitely wasn't dreaming. My hand wrapped around the bar. I ignored the cold. Police? I thought. How many? "It's okay, it's Keel's dad. Don't!" Stoppy said with a voice trembling in fear. I couldn't whack Keel's dad. Besides what the fucks he doing here? I'd never met Keel's dad. I figured I must be dreaming and went back to sleep. In the morning Stoppy told me Keel's dad had popped around and everything I'd said had happened had. He filled in the blanks for me. Apparently he found out Keel had been truanting so he came around to give Stoppy a slap and to tell him not to allow Keel in any more I apologised for not doing anything but told him I couldn't drop Keel's dad. It's not right.

Keel turned up which was unusual as since his dad's visit he may have truanted but not at Stoppy's. "You okay?" Stoppy asked Keel. Keel ignored him and turned to me. "You've got to leave mate. Police have been at school looking for you. I'm sorry I had to tell them something so I told them I saw you with Louise last week" He looked really sad .

"No worries mate you did the right thing thanks for letting me know. Guys" I said turning to face both of them. "I gotta disappear it's been great but they probably followed Keel." I knew it would happen, Patrick Benson had tried tried getting me back into care once again and I'd ignored his request. I'd received £15 from him to live on and given £10 straight to Stoppy. He'd obviously called the cops.

I was halfway through the window when Stoppy grabbed my arm. I looked at him. "Need anything?" He asked. "Got matches? A torch? Bin bags?" I said reeling off my survival hike list from scouts. "Sorry dude no torch" he said handing me a box of swan matches and a half roll of bin bags. "Hey....Thanks" I said making sure to look both of them in the eye. Then I turned and hopped out the kitchen window.

Chapter 4

I kept low to the fence as soon as I'd landed I was wearing two sets of clothing, a tracksuit and beneath them my jeans. I never wore tracksuits so made sure I had the full kit on with a jumper beneath. I also had my school rucksack I couldn't change how that looked but I figured if I was seen I'd leg and ditch the top layer of clothes and keep going. Thank fuck for all those military books I'd read at the library. I walked slowly not because I wanted to, I felt like running but because I had to. A running lad would be obvious, the eye is drawn to it and it's always suspicious. I walked a big square two roads around the school so as not to pass it. I told Stoppy and Keel I had a place in Pettypool that I'd go to if this happened. I described it to them in depth and it was where I wanted to be as it was beautiful and I knew the area well enough to walk around blindfolded so the lie came easily. If they spoke at all then that's where the police would be headed. Add to that Tony had been there once before so he could show them exactly where to go. Sure they'd look? I asked myself. I couldn't go to Louise's or Brenda's. Nigel would grass me up in a second and Baconegg was too scared of his dad to help. Where is the last place I should go? It hit me like a bad smell. Chester... I'm scared of Wenzel. If Patrick told the police I said Wenzel wants me dead then there's no way they would be looking for me in Chester.

I walked to Chester hiding in the woodland in the day and hiking the roads at night where I'd put the shell suit in my bag so it didn't reflect any light. I could do the trip in a day but I was in no hurry. I got as far as the Tarvin sign and decided to see Anne and Mark. Their mums words rang out in my head from the tarot reading "You'll not see us again" but I ignored it. I'd been gone what, a year? Maybe a little over. I stood on my old road Hockenhull avenue a good ten minutes pondering the what ifs. What if I brought the police to their door? What if they hate me? What if they moved? Fuck it I'd not find out stood here like a twat drawing attention to myself. I walked off around the corner to Mark and Anne's house. It looked the same but different somehow. What had changed? I'd got the route right. It wasn't far from Tony and Pip's place. Pip's place...how I'd love to have Geordie with me right now. Yeah what you going to feed him nob head? You can't even feed yourself. Wenzel's voice echoed around my head. He had a point. What use was I to Anne or Mark? Then my voice "Did you come here for nothing?" I approached the door and knocked. A thin black gentleman answered "Yes?"

"Erm, Sorry I am looking for Mark and Anne?" I asked.

"Wrong address I'm afraid" He said.

"No, no it's not" I said "I used to visit here a lot. They are good friends I'm trying to find" I added. Then he said something that blew me away. "I've lived here fifteen years lad and it's not this house I can assure you". I stepped back "oh, okay.. thanks" I said walking backwards still looking at the house. I retraced my steps to Pip's house and then back to where Anne and Mark should have lived. I then tried two roads before and after in case I'd made a wrong turning. The only house similar was the one with the black man in it. "They've moved" I said to myself feeling a large hit. "Wales" I sighed recalling the conversation. "Fifteen years?" I questioned...he has to be lying. Either way I couldn't find it anywhere. I spent over an hour in the field I used to walk Geordie in then realised Pip or Tony may walk him and see me so I headed off to Chester. I walked the streets that day and slept sat up against the Roman walls with a tree next to it. There was a bridge close by but I didn't want to go beneath it in case homeless people had the same idea. I figured my spot was in enough shelter for one person and with the bridge they would be more tempted to group there than around the tree. Nobody turned up that night but I watched numerous late night dog walkers pass me. I stayed the following night too having spent the day walking the only roads I knew - the Roman ones and to and from my old work place. Never close enough to be seen. Memories were starting to get to me. I could see myself walking into the hair dressers I used to go in with Wenzel. I hated him and didn't want to be that lad but I wanted to know who I was. How I could be there one minute and here the next? Why here felt so good but so difficult on my feet and body through hunger but how that life with him could be so bad and yet I could have a bath or get a sandwich. I kicked myself for thinking about food. I'd told myself earlier I didn't need it. I walked down the river and then back towards the walls.

I kipped back at my tree and had to move around it every time a drunk group approached. I never made the connection that certain days meant more party goers. I was too young to understand or perhaps not educated enough. All I knew was my tree was no longer safe and my feet hurt so running was pretty much out of the question. Walking was getting troublesome. I'd not removed my shoes since leaving Wenzel's. I woke up and some coins had been placed beside me I took them at first not realising someone had given them willingly and thinking they'd perhaps fallen out of someone's pocket. Then I realised they thought I was a homeless person and donated some money. I realised just how low I'd become. I headed back to the town centre. Somehow the sunshine had made me feel better and I didn't care how people saw me any more I saw a tall lad with short golden hair who I'd seen talking with Ghost before. He was in a group sat on the wall out of view of the rest of the town centre. The shopper's didn't seem to notice six lads just sat there on the wall and I realised if I didn't know their faces thanks to Ghost I'd not know they were homeless either. "Excuse me mate seen Ghost?" I asked him. "Who?" he said looking around like I would if someone approached me. I let him look and stayed in front of him quiet. "Who?" He said again gently. I didn't want him to think I was tipping anyone off so kept my arms still and eyes on him "Ghost a little smaller than me dark eyes, white, carries a green sleeping bag" I said. "No, don't know her. Got a smoke?" he asked lying. His little chubby friend jumped down off the wall "What's up?

I know her, Says you're cool" he said "Sorry no smokes mate, Well. Looks like I'm homeless. Need to speak to her" I told Chunky. "No problem, here take this" he said handing me an unopened pouch of tobacco. "No mate, no cash" I said handing it straight back. If I took it I'd owe him something. "It's cool friend of ghost's is a friend of ours right lads?" they nodded and grunted and for some reason reminded me of dim lights on a Xmas tree fading in and out view. The fat lad gave me directions to a doss house he said ghost was staying at and asked if I wanted him to show me. I declined. I knew ghost but not them. They seemed genuine enough but why take the chance? If ghost was at a doss and knew this many people what were they involved in? How does a homeless guy just whip out fifty grams of tobacco and give it away? This wasn't Macclesfield. Here the homeless were polite and decent but I didn't know what else they could do. I didn't trust it and I was hurting. It was time to head back to Stoppy's. I'd been gone for around four or five days and it felt like forever.

It was weird being back in Winsford. Everyone had a home, a family except me. The family thing I was used to and loved camping but not whilst I had to constantly look over my shoulder. I needed a bath, food. drink but mostly socks. My feet really hurt badly and my socks were so hard it was unreal. I didn't pack spares when leaving Wenzel's. My scout leader entered my head "protect your feet!" I envisioned myself in an eight man tent my bare feed stuck out of the bottom. The breeze heaven on them. In reality I was stood at over square and Keel was in front of me. I'd not even seen him approach. "You okay mate? What you doing to do now?" He said looking concerned apparently I'd been speaking to him. "Stoppy will take you in mate but it's matter of time before police find you. You could stay with me or Kap but don't think my parents would do it whilst police are involved man. Sorry" He continued. I just stood there. I mean I did care and he was right and I did appreciate everything he was saying but I was out of it. My priorities were all messed up. I just wanted some socks. To have clean socks for an hour or somewhere safe to walk around in bare feet I'd of done anything. "I need socks" I said pulling my shoes off very slowly and delicately. "I can get you socks man" He said touching my arm. "No mate, not what I meant. Let me finish. I need socks, I'm going back to care" my shoe flipped off and it hurt and I stank. "I don't mind man. I can get you socks" he said squeezing my arm a little. "Nah man, I have to do this but it has to be on my terms. Not theirs" I said meeting his eyes with mine.

"What do you need?" He said immediately.

I told him and he dug out some change. I gave him half my tobacco in exchange. I chunked some coins in the slot "Patrick Benson please" I said. He wasn't happy but he did as I asked. He pulled up in his red Honda less than an hour later without police and closed the car door. I had Keel stood in plain sight on the road to check the car was empty and that there was only a ginger guy knocking around. I was behind a hedge in someone's garden on the other side of the road. If they grabbed Keel he'd just say he was on his way to Kap's and stopped for a ciggy the last he'd heard I was in Chester. Keel gave the thumbs up and I came out of my hiding hedge. I walked over to Patrick in as straight a line as I could manage. I didn't want him seeing I was in pain. "HI thanks for coming" I said lighting up a smoke. "Well you're here now get in, I've been waiting ages" he said. "No, you've been here five minutes. We talk here. We agree on what's happening with me and where I'm going or I walk" I said faking confidence badly "You're hurt" he said seeing my face curl up as I took a step backwards. "I'm fine" I said exhaling. "OK what can I do for you? We do care you know. We've been worried. Everyone has" He said.

"Everyone?" I asked sarcastically. "You? Your job. Caroline, Jonathon and Jodie don't know I exist. Brenda? Oh please"

"I'm not here to argue, please sit down" He said opening the car door. "No way, so you can slam the door and drive off?" I said.

"Tracie I don't know who you think I am but I'm here to help. I'm not your father" He said. Which kind of hit me but I wasn't sure how to feel about it. He was right I was treating every male as though they were my father but I also didn't know how a real father was supposed to be. I just knew my father wasn't it.

"Yeah well, neither is he" I replied.

"I'm not going back to Brenda's" I said. Patrick tried to talk numerous times but I didn't let him finish. "I want my own room. To be left alone. No parents. No bullshit. No call me mum crap. I'm not going to bed at 8pm. I've seen more than most adults I know. I can look after myself. In when I want and out when I want. No ties, no family stuff. I'll clean and do my own washing. I'll eat in my room. No family meals and I smoke. Like it or not I'm a smoker. I smoke." I said taking a huge drag of my roll up because I'd said the word family a few times and each time it was like putting a nail in my heart. "If I can get you somewhere this short notice will you go just until I find somewhere better?" Patrick asked me carefully. I stood up and started walking "No, call me when you have a place" He grabbed my arm and I turned as he let go. He'd immediately stepped back. He wasn't trying to hurt me he was just trying to get my attention. "Work with me. Let me help you. Let me make some calls now and we'll see what we can do" I could see from his face he meant it. Weather it was for his job's sake or mine I didn't know. "No police" I said. "If I see police I'll get in the car and you can take me to care then I'll leave and you'll never see me again" I added calmly. "Okay, okay, no police. I promise" He said heading to the car. Keel was brilliant whenever he saw someone he coughed. He waited for me all the while Patrick made his calls. "OK, we have a place in Knutsford for you" he started "Near Marc?" I asked "yes but you don't have to see anyone from Marc, they are an older couple who agree you have your own room and can come and go as you like as long as you're home by 10pm. They said you'll only ever have to call them Stephanie and George. Okay?" I felt sad. If it was as nice as that I'd love it. I felt hollow inside. Everyone else wanted a games console or a car and I just wanted a fucking bath. Secretly I wanted a family but that dream was dead and whenever it did rear it's ugly head I told it straight "they are gone, you're not worth it. you hurt them" I stood on the opposite side of the road to Keel with my social worker four paces away from me and I had nowhere in between to head to. "What about the smokes?" I asked lighting another. "I can't fix everything Tracie, What are your choices right now?" He said. I shot him a look and he shut up but he did have a point. He knew as well as I did push me too far and I was off. I'd die cold and alone before I'd be controlled again. "I'll be in the car" he said. I thanked Keel and hugged him then got in beside Patrick. "If it's shit. I'm off" I said gingerly placing my foot on the car's floor. It hurt.

Chapter 5

The house was a three bedroom semi hidden behind a large hedge. I liked that it couldn't be seen from the roadside. I walked in with Patrick and was lead into the living room by George. He was tall and thin with an edge of caution about him. He was reading me from the get go but wasn't intrusive or abrasive with it. Stephanie was in the living room stood up playing with her fingers. She looked a little nervous. George's hair was slicked back and light. He wore jeans and a cowboy style shirt with brown shoes. Stephanie was nearly as tall but appeared shorter as though gravity was doing her no favours. She had dark hair in a bob I noticed George's eyes were friendly even though his face was on edge. I felt he wanted to keep me at arms length for a while. He stuck his hand out "I'm George, call me whatever you like but I like George" he said smiling. I looked at Pat and shook George's hand. It was soft. Stephanie stepped forwards "Stephanie" she said her eyes briefly hitting mine and then darting around the room and settling on her hands again. What had they been told? "Questions?" Pat asked me. "Well hi, I'm Tracie," I said glancing at Stephanie and then meeting George's eyes and sitting down on the sofa as George had indicated. "I'm sure Stephanie and George will tell me?" I added thinking it was better for me if the ball was in their court and at least I knew them better than they knew me. Stephanie stepped up. "OK, we know you want space but haven't been told much about you. You have your own room...." Stephanie ran through what Patrick and I had agreed and then she added "we eat at the table but it's not essential. You don't have to join us. If you're in when we are then we'll offer to make you something. Otherwise it's up to you to help yourself. No food or drink upstairs but kitchen, garden and dining room is fine with us isn't it George?" she said. He nodded. I had no reason to dislike them and my feet were throbbing. "I need a bath guys, can I see the room?" They showed me up the stairs and it was perfect. A single bed with a duvet, bedside cabinet and a wardrobe A small desk with a pc chair by it and it was fully carpeted with clean windows. Yeah, I could get used to this I thought. "We'll known every morning but otherwise won't disturb you unless you say it's OK to come in. You're responsible for keeping the room clean and tidy and that's how you earn pocket money. You don't need to do more than that but if you do help out we'll give you more" George said. Money? I thought wow I was impressed. "How much did you get before?" George asked "£2:50 a week when I got in care and £3:50 a week when I left but I later got a paper round so had £7:50 a week for that too" I replied.

"I think we can stretch to £5 a week for doing your room then" George said. I went back downstairs with them and took my place on the sofa. "Questions for Tracie?" Patrick asked. "Do you think you could like it here?" Stephanie asked throwing me completely off guard it was the first time I'd heard a genuine question about my happiness. "Or at least stay here until you're old enough to get your own place or whatever you decide to do?" She added mistaking my shock for concern. I hadn't thought that far ahead and stayed quiet but I'd never appreciated a question more in my life. They genuinely wanted to know if I could be happy there and that's all that was important to them. "We don't want you to run away but we won't stop you either. If you're unhappy please do tell us" she added. I liked her "today everything is perfect, you seem good people. Tomorrow, who knows? I can't make promises I'm sorry" I said. "That's a man answer, I like that. You'll be just fine lad" George said leaning forwards on his arms. I liked him too. "Do you smoke?" Stephanie asked with no trace of animosity in her voice. I looked at Patrick who nodded. "Yeah, I smoke" I said "So do we and we smoke outside in the garden only. Of a night your cigarettes go on the windowsill with ours. We won't touch them and appreciate you don't touch ours either" She said. Had I just been told I could smoke in the garden? "Sorry?" I asked. "You smoke in the garden. No fags upstairs" George said. I turned to Patrick "You can go, these guys are sound" I told him. Stephanie's head lifted up a little and George let out a little laugh. "Told you" Patrick said heading to the door. I followed him. "Patrick" I called hobbling behind him. "They do seem genuine and probably are, Thanks at same time I meant what I said any shit and I'm off" He nodded. I went in and got upstairs to sort my feet out. George gave me a pair of his socks until I got some the next day. I stood barefoot with him outside as he sat on a bench not to tower over me. "Smoke?" he asked offering me one of his. I pulled my tobacco out and made one up.

During the next two weeks Stephanie and George kept their word and I grew to like and respect them. They were honest people and as long as I was honest with them then they were to me. They kitted me out with school clothes and my own clothes. This time I was asked what I liked. It wasn't like anywhere else where the items were just bought and you were expected to accept everything. There was another girl there who was only young and stayed during the day. I didn't talk to her nor her me. During a chat with Stephanie she asked me "Do you feel comfortable with me Trace?"

"Yeah, why?" I asked her stepping back. I didn't think she was about to go sick on me but I'd learnt the hard way when people start asking emotional questions it's usually safer to put some distance between them and myself.

"I think people might be wrong about you, you know" she said curiously

"You mean Patrick, what's he said? Let me tell you, Patrick knows what I want him to know and nothing more"

"We were told you didn't relate well to women. You saw them as a threat. Do you feel threatened by me?" She asked me genuinely.

"No Stephanie" I said laughing "The two previous female carers I had....let's say they weren't good. They weren't like you guys. One ran the house like a sergeant and didn't have time for anyone. It was all fake. Her way or no way. We didn't get along. The other...well she'd lost a kid and it turned her head. She wanted me to replace him and well...I can't..you know?" I said realising that she was the first person since Nigel I'd been honest with. "My turn" I said "How do you guys feel about me?" I asked.

"You're alright, we like you" she said.

"And George?" I asked.

"Yeah him too, George is George, you'll have to ask him" she told me.

"Thanks" I said.

"What for?" she asked.

"Being honest" I replied heading to the kitchen. I was trying make sure she couldn't see my face. I was about four seconds from crying. I wanted to stay. They were good people who treated me right. Why hadn't I been put here first? I thought with a combination of anger and numbness at being so used to anger and the pointlessness of it all running through me.

Every morning I would come downstairs and George would be setting the table. He'd always say morning and I'd reply and head out for a smoke. He'd always join me for one after he'd made a brew and then I'd go into the kitchen and make breakfast whilst they ate at the table. It was still too much like a family for me to be able to eat with them. I'd watch them sometimes eating together. Stephanie would sit by the window with George opposite her as one of the girls would be sat facing the window on the longer side of a narrow table. Sometimes they would talk but often they sat in peaceful silence and just ate. It was beautiful and I longed to be a part of that lifestyle. I'd start to reminisce and pretend Stephanie was mum and George was still George but he was my George and not like Wenzel at all and I was where the girl was sat and it was all perfect like the garden outside but then it hurt because it was fake and bullshit and never going to happen and so I'd walk away.

One morning after our ritual smoke I noticed George had put some bags I hadn't seen before out in the garden "what you want done?" I asked him. "Well, you don't have to help, but if you want you can?" He asked me. The tasks were general gardening work usually, weeding, hedge trimming, edging and the like. Although one day I woke up to there being a noisy van on our drive. I thought there was a problem because in Macclesfield a van outside usually meant a load of people were getting out and someone was getting a slap. I flew downstairs my protective nature coming out against my will "George you alright!? What's going on!?" I said eyeing the van driver suspiciously.

"Moving these, you can help if you want to but you don't have to" George told me. I was listening but busy looking into the cab of the truck. I wanted to know who else was around and if someone was parked outside? Connected with Wenzel? Nobody was there it was just how my mind was working "You don't have to" I caught again as George repeated himself. I spent the next hour moving slabs to the back garden and telling myself over and over "It's safe here, it's not Macclesfield". I helped George lay his patio that day and thoroughly enjoyed the manual labour and feeling as though I was making a difference for both George and Stephanie. It was getting cooler as George handed me a twenty pound note. "I don't want that" I said "ERM, I mean.. I'm doing this" I added waving around like a fish out of water indicating the whole garden "because I want to" George smiled "Take it anyway" he said. That's the type of people they were. Good people.

I called Patrick to arrange contact, no luck. Caroline said she'd see me at school and Jonathon and Jodie weren't interested because I could still be in touch with Wenzel. I explained to Patrick that I wasn't but they were having none of it. I was convinced Jonathon and Jodie wanted nothing to do with me and that for some reason I was to blame for what Wenzel had done with my mum. I was also convinced Caroline plain hated me for leaving Brenda's. "I want my stuff from Wenzel's" I told Patrick. He said He'd call him. "He's not to know where I am" I told him. "We can't stop him. He's your dad" Patrick told me. "He finds out, I leave, your choice?" I fired back. He promised not to say and would get back to me later in the day.

I spent the next few hours smoking on the bench in the garden and imagining what it would be like to belong to a family like Stephanie and George's where they didn't have any of the bullshit I was used to living through, or what it would be like to be Louise for a day. Would I turn to drink like she had? Or would I just fuck off and be done with it? Perhaps I'd love it because I'd seen the things I'd seen. I didn't know I just knew whilst I was thinking about other people I wasn't concentrating on the things I was going through and I definitely wasn't waiting for a call from Pat to tell me my father hated me and my family couldn't give a toss.

George had called me from somewhere in the house as I'd received a phone call. It was Patrick "He said he'll only talk to you" Pat told me regarding Wenzel. I called Wenzel straight away "What do you want?" he said "Patrick said you'd only talk to me. I want my stuff" I said.

I could hear him take an inhale of a cigarette and heard the click as it lit up and he breathed in quickly. "Yeah that's right you snivelling shit, you want your stuff?" He'd thrown his lighter on the side in the kitchen. I heard it click. "Who do you think you are? You were a mistake when you were born. You're all mistakes, after all I've done for you" He sneered. I hung up and waited thirty seconds. I needed time to digest that. I knew he'd be an ass, I knew he'd be angry but didn't realise he'd actually tell the truth and he was totally telling the truth. In his mind we were all mistakes. I wasn't angry that he'd called me a mistake. I knew that mother loved us and knew that I was loved by my nan and granddad I knew Wenzel wasn't a decent parent and really didn't care about me and that was fine. That I was getting used to but to call my brother and sister's mistakes? That hurt me in ways that I didn't realise I could feel. I was becoming defensive and as I was on the brink of a destructive path anyway it made more sense for me to hang up. Besides.. I wasn't going to let him know he could get to me. He knew the buttons to push but I knew how he thinks and when he feels in control he gets a sexual buzz from it. There's no way I was giving him that satisfaction. I called him back after counting to thirty. "Did you fucking hand up on me?" He stormed.

I laughed part nerves part fuck it I hope his head explodes. "You've got my keys when I get my keys you get stuff got it!?" He shouted and cut me off. I called Patrick and explained the conversation. "What now?" He asked. "let him cool off then you call him. Tell him his attitude is abusive. I'm very happy where I am and he can happily have his keys when my stuff is delivered until then they are my keys". I told him. Pat promised to sort it. I'd actually forgot I had them until then. It got me wondering though. Why was he so worried I had his keys? What was he afraid of?

Chapter 6

Back at school I'd fit in easily again with my circle of friends. Kap and
Keel had been amazing and totally understood when I said I wanted
to stay out of trouble for a while. I needed time to sort my shit out
and that meant just keeping a low profile for a while.

I'd walked downstairs expecting my brew and smoke when I saw
George was lay on the floor in front of the sofa which was strange.
He had his head leaning against it and his legs out in front of him.
The table was set ready for breakfast and his arms were across his
chest like my granddad's used to be when he was sleeping. This was
totally not like George, he was always up with a brew and a smile. I
went from zero to ninety in less than two seconds as images of Andy
slamming into the floor went through my head. "George, George!" I
said prodding his shoulder. He turned and rubbed his eyes "You
okay? Breathing okay?" I asked him. "Yeah, I was sleeping lad" he
said. "You alright?" He added as I stood up and walked out of the
back door. I ignored him and lit up a smoke on the bench. George
followed and sat down beside me. We were both sat with our fore
arms on our knee's leaning forwards looking at the garden "I'm
alright lad, relax" he said. I gave it a few seconds thinking of what to
say and then just blurted out "I thought....well..it doesn't matter
what I thought" I told him pushing images of Alan out of my head
again and realising I actually really cared about George.

I'd gone to Knutsford and got lost so I called Stephanie for directions
but she insisted she'd pick me up. It was nice because she then took
me shopping to register for my fourth doctors in fourteen years. I
was pissed that social services were paying for my clothes again so
would act like I owed them something like Brenda had but a part of
me knew Stephanie and George were not like that and hell if they
could get something back from the social services for providing for
me then why not? Who was I to argue. "Ever thought of adopting?"
I asked her as we walked past another rail of socks. "What a curious

question" She said. "Yeah we've thought about it in the past" she added. "What stopped you?" I asked feeling slightly intrusive but all the more intrigued. "Well it's a long process and then there's the not knowing if the child would be a match. We wanted to though" She confided. "You'd make great parents, Would you ever consider it again say....now?" I let it hang there like a guillotine waiting to fall. "Oh heavens no we are way too old now" she said. I'd heard enough. She was polite but I got it. Nobody wanted me. Why would a decent family want me? "We love having you here, you can stay as long as you like" she said. I just nodded as I inspected a pair of socks I'd never buy. "And you and George seem to be getting on really well" she added. "Yeah he's cool" I said leaving the socks for some other kid to have. When we got home I asked for a paper and pen. I needed to make a list but my head wasn't clear. I drew graphic pictures of people killed instead and then burnt the lot at the bottom of the garden. I knew I wasn't right but I wasn't quite sure what was wrong either. Usually the art therapy stuff helped but not this time. Pictures wouldn't solve anything.

A new girl was coming to stay here name was Carla and she was a little younger than me. I only knew because Stephanie had asked me to be nice as she was new. I had no interest in speaking to anyone really. I was halfway through ignoring my homework and pretending I was living in the forest at Winsford when there was a knock on my door. I knew it wasn't Stephanie or George so I did the polite thing and ignored it. Perhaps she'd go away. She didn't, "Helloo" I heard her call loud enough that I had to answer it. That hello seemed to say "I know you're in there and know you're ignoring me but we both know you're too polite to ignore me if I say hello because it will be too much hassle to explain if I go and get the carers because I'm worried about you so just answer the damn door already". I opened the door and a little pale face with dark hair looked at me from behind a big bag. "Hi I'm Carla I'm new. Look I could get in trouble here...can I trust you?" She asked me. "Depends. What is it?" I replied as she pulled two bottles of Vodka from her bag. "I need to get rid of these, my dad owns a pub I worked there with him. Can you get rid of them?" She asked. I laughed. "Hell yeah, what you want for them?" I said. "Nothing just get rid of them" She whispered as she pulled another bag from her room. "And these" she added passing me a bottle of Gin, Dark rum and Brandy. "Thanks I owe you one" she said before disappearing behind her bedroom door. I knew just the way to say thanks to Keel and Kap for all their help.

Keel and Kap were waiting for me at 8am as arranged however when the lads discovered beer was involved a few turned up I didn't even know. Stoppy couldn't make it because he was working but Kap, Keep, Lee the comedian, Simon a little pale lad who was really thin and looked like a matchstick dipped in ink on a count of his jet black hair, we called him Woody, Michael and my friend Fordy who's mum was dead all turned up as did Richard I played rugby with. We all went over to the fields behind the school and tried a drink. I soon discovered that Gin was vile. I was fifteen. My first taste of drink was Lamb's navy rum at Rachael's with Gilbert. Gilbert had downed his and then looked at me. I downed mine and we did the same with another. As time went on so did the drinking and my hands became numb. That's what I noticed first anyway. I figured it because as Gilbert was making snide comments about Rachael was tapping the stone wall beside the fireplace with my first and finding it strange how usually the pain would help me ignore him however I could feel nothing even though my hand was red. I decided if I could make him laugh then I'd distract him from being abusive to Rachael. I slid off the chair and got into my green sleeping bag. "I'm a caterpillar!" I said over and over rolling around like an idiot. Rachael found it hilarious and creased up. Gilbert wasn't amused but it lightened the atmosphere and he stopped having a go at her. The good memory stung so I downed another two mouth fulls of Gin. "Yuck, needs something" I said "Lemonade or Dr Pepper?" Keel asked pulling two bottles from his bag. I gave him the "You're a hero" nod of respect and he got to work mixing all the drinks into two pop bottles. How he managed it I don't know but we ended up passing around two very dangerous mixtures. Then we headed to the town centre where we stole or bought ourselves some lunch by which time we were all either tipsy or wasted. Keel managed to knock over a stand outside Greggs which had a board on complete with cakes and doughnuts We picked him up and did a runner at which point Keel could suddenly walk absolutely fine and we saw an old lady, looking through her shopping leaning forwards with a cigarette in her mouth. Keel took the lit cigarette said "thanks" and immediately placed it in his mouth and carried on walking! I was gob-smacked but turned to look at the woman who was so stunned she hadn't moved from her position. Complete with pursed lips and everything. I cracked up laughing. As cruel as it was it remains one of the funniest things I've ever seen. It's how we were, one of the lads was eyeing a car and got to talking about car badges being worth quite a bit. I didn't know. I had no interest in cars nor wanted to drive. I didn't know where today was going to take me let alone years down the line. We ended up in a shop which sold tools so we nicked a few and headed back to the multi story car park. We took anything we could from Mercedes badges to Skoda's. One lad even came back with a wing mirror, how he'd got it removed I don't know. It wasn't long before we heard shouting and legged it to the top floor. Keel was very drunk by this time and had taken to lying on the floor and waving his arms around like he was making snow angels despite it being a sunny day. "This I'll never forget man!" He shouted laughing and wiggling around. I was drunk too and jumped up on the corner of the railing above Keel. I wasn't usually a fan of heights but the combination of drink and lack of care about my safety meant I wasn't worried. If I fell I fell and that was the end to any fear. "No mate, this you'll never forget" I said unzipping my trousers and removing my member where I proceeded to piss all over him from a great height. Why I did it I don't know. It seemed funny at the time but was a pretty stupid thing to do. Keel just carried on making sun angels and shouting "It's raining!" I jumped down next to Lee as I could see he wanted to talk to me "What if they tell the school?" he said. He had a point as half of us were in uniform. "No problem" I told him "we go back to school and act normal if anyone's seen then it can't have been us can it? We were at school the whole time". I added. It was in no way a genius plan but it was all part of the seemed a good idea at the time mentality.

We sat outside school passing the bottles around until they'd almost gone. I knew I had maths with Mrs Lourne, Louise would be in lesson as would Fordy who was tipsy but not drunk. I thought I was fine so said I'd take half the badges and Lee would take the other half because he has an innocent face. He was never stopped by anyone, ever. I kind of envied him in a way. I only had to walk into a shop and security guards were looking at me like I'd stolen something. I could almost feel them knowing I was a care kid. Lee and I would return the badges to their rightful owners after school. It would be fine. What could go wrong? As soon as I got into the hall a teacher collared me. At the same time the warm air and large amounts of alcohol hit me and I swayed a little as the hall span. "What's this?" The male teacher said taking my fags from my shirt pocket. "Shigarets shir!" I said cracking up. "You can have one if you give them back?" I said leaning on the wall laughing. "Have you been drinking?" He asked. I stood bolt upright "Me sir! No sir!" then I bust out laughing again because involuntarily I'd given him the best salute I could muster as though I really was in the army and had no worries. "Wait here!" he said as he disappeared around the corner at the end of the corridor as did my smokes. I didn't know much but I knew that firstly I was in the shit and secondly I was definitely not waiting there for it to come and bite me in the ass. I did the first thing that entered my head "inform the others!" my mind screamed. I had to warn them. I ran down the hall bumping into the wall numerous times and scrambled for the stairs my coat with the badges in banging into the railings on the way up and then stopped at the top to catch my breath. "Keep going!" my mind screamed have, to, tell, Fordy. I knew Fordy knew the drill. His mum was dead too. He'd understand. He'd know what to do.

I flung the maths room door open and shouted "Fordy they are on to us we gotta run!" The room was full of students all sat awaiting Mrs Lourne who I presumed was late because she usually was. I put my coat on the peg behind the door and wobbled over to his desk "You okay?" he asked as my head landed on his desk and I stayed there looking up at him sideways. "Nah, I'm fucked. They know about the drink. Had to tell ya, leg it!" I screamed. "Tracie, wait outside" Mrs Lourne said from behind me "Oh fuck off you fat cow" I said just as Mr Fourth and Mr James entered the doorway. I tried dragging Fordy our of the chair but he was a big lad and having none of it. I stood no chance. "Come on! Run!" I ordered as I pulled on his shirt and fell over time and time again. I decided after the fourth attempt I was on my own and ran at Mr Fourth and Mr Jamies full pelt. I landed flat on my face about two feet in front of them.

I woke up on a chair with a very straight faced Mr Fourth sat less than a foot in front of me. I was in a small room I didn't know existed downstairs by the entrance. My coat was on the back of my chair and my school bag was beside me. I didn't know if either had been searched so had to play dumb and presume they hadn't. I tried to sit up and look around but kept sliding down and almost falling off before Mr Fourth sat me back up "Fuck off! Don't touch me!" I was screaming half dead from mind to toe. "Drink this" he said handing me a plastic container filled with water. "No, feel sick. Fuck off!" I told him. "I know it will make you feel better" he said gently. Then it happened I didn't decide it to, I didn't want to but it did. "You don't know shit! He killed her, killed my mum!" I shot out. "Murderer, murderer, murderer" I sang. "Dead, dead, dead" I went on "All dead every single one" I added. "What are you talking about?" he asked me with honesty and intrigue sitting me back up again. "I tried eyeballing him and fell off the chair. He picked me up as two ambulance men came in and checked my eyes. "Fuck off! I'm fine! Don't touch me! Fucker! I'll kill you!" I stormed as they grabbed and turned my head to check I was okay. "He'll be fine but have a hell of a headache. He's close but keep him hydrated. His mate's gonna need the pump though" I swung my head back around to the two large figures in the doorway. "You're not my dad?" I asked it was as much surprise as it was a question. "No son, we're not" one of the men said. He had a gentle voice. "Where's Keel?" I asked. "Keel's going to the hospital to be stomach pumped. If you're lucky he'll be alright" He said and left. "Keel's dead?" I asked Mr Fourth "No, not dead but he's drunk a lot. What happened? I need to know everything to be able to help him" I could tell he was serious and I was so drunk I took him literally. So I started with Nan dying and told him everything up to being in care. "So she lay down in front of me, my mums mum who's my nan and now she's dead", "dead,dead,dead, sick everywhere, Onions yuck!" Until I got the the end and he asked "So you're happy where you are now?" He seemed upset but holding it together well. I had a world of respect for him but didn't know how to show it let alone express it. "No!, Won't adopt me. They don't care. Nobody does. Going quiet now" and I refused to speak until George picked me up from the waiting room. "Come on" he said as I walked three steps behind him to the car. "Don't be angry" I said with my head down. "I'm not angry" he said honestly "be Angry" I said getting in the car where he helped me fasten the seat belt. Him not being angry hurt more "Why would you do this to yourself? We thought you were happy" He asked. I was in the back seat trying to lie down but the seat belt prevented it. "I'm sorry. Hit me" I said. "Please" I added. "I'm not going to hit you" George said concentrating on driving. "Please hit me. I've been bad. I'm sorry. You can push me into a wall. He did" I said suddenly back at Gilbert's "Get some rest" George said "We'll talk tomorrow" he added. "I'm sorry, just hit me. No mind games. Not that, not from you" I begged on and off all the way home. Stephanie was in the hall when I returned. She looked worried sick. I felt terrible. I'd caused this. I'd hurt them. I went to bed without a smoke.

I awoke and replayed the previous day in my head. I'd gone to school and got drunk, okay that was dumb then we went on the town and ... oh god I was thieving and then did we nick a smoke off a little old lady? Why did I find this funny? Then I pissed on Keel..why the hell did I do that? What an idiot and Keel got a stomach pump whilst I put all the blame for the car badges onto Lee. It hit me like a tidal wave. I'd told them Lee brought the drink in and asked me to save some car badges he'd nicked because he felt tipsy and didn't want to be caught with them! I couldn't believe the lie I'd told. The rest was not nice and was really dumb but I was upset I'd worried Stephanie and George and more upset that I'd lied. I've done some stupid things but I'd only lied when I'd had to before and always to protect myself or my friends. I wasn't a grass and was totally ashamed of myself.

I came downstairs in the morning ashamed and embarrassed Stephanie and George only asked if I'd had anything other than drink. I'd said no and waited for the roasting I deserved. "Let's forget about it then and remember if you do this again you're only hurting yourself" He said. He was right and I knew it. "Okay, sorry. I really am" I said going to school. Lee wasn't in for days and then eventually there he was in the changing room. Whilst everyone else was getting ready to play rugby he was slumped against the side with jogging bottoms on and a school shirt. His leg was bandaged up from just below the knee all the way up to his thigh "Thirty two stitches" Lee said giving me a fake smile. I was reading his eyes. "Came off my bike and hit a curb" he added with a bigger grin although his eyes looked sad. "I'm sorry" I said knowing I'd told Mr Fourth that everything was Lee's fault. "It's okay, huge payout from the council soon" He lied. "Sure" I said knowing his lie as one I'd just as easily of told myself. His mum must have done him some real damage to give him thirty two stitches. I felt like shit. He showed me the scar weeks later. It was an inch wide.

Chapter 7

Wenzel had agreed Patrick and I could get my stuff when he wasn't there if I gave his keys to Patrick. There was no problem with that other than that Patrick couldn't take my snake because of some social services rule about it being in his car or something so Wenzel would have to drop that off later along with my mirror which was huge as it had two hands coming from the bottom which were oil burners and three wolves protruding from the top. It was beautiful. I went with Patrick and got to work on my stuff as soon as we entered the flat. Clothes, knives, books and paperwork. He could bin the bed and furniture. Then I went around the living room "what's yours?" Patrick asked me "give me a minute" I said thinking "these" I said scooping up his Zippo lighter collection. "All of them?" He asked me suspiciously. I rolled several around in my hands and picked a random one. "Not this one but I bought him the others".

"Pictures?" Patrick asked me looking at the photo's of Jonathon, Jodie, Caroline and I. "No, let him keep them. He'll have to explain to everyone why he sits here every night and doesn't see any of them" I said falling straight into Wenzel's mindset again and noting how easy it was to become him. I opened his display cabinet "mine" I said taking my nan's keyring blade and mum's tape. I left his boxes as obviously moved. Fuck him. I wanted him to know I'd been through his cupboard. I wanted him to know I'd taken what he should never have had. "You want to know what he's like?" I turned to Peter and looked him square in the eyes. I didn't wait for a reply. "He's got a tape here with him explaining everything about mum's death on it. Just so as it can be on full view and people won't know it's there. He's proud of that. Proud that nobody knows but him. I tell you that's how he gets his kicks he's a bastard" I said bending down and grabbing the video case. I opened it up to prove my point to Patrick. It was empty. "I swear it was here" I said shocked. "What else do you need?" Patrick asked me pretending I'd not even spoke. "Nothing, We're good" I said. "Keys?" Patrick asked me when we got outside. "When I get back to Stephanie's" I told him. I unpacked and thanked Patrick and handed him the key to Wenzel's outside storage cabinet. I wasn't giving him the flat keys. They were mine and were stored safely out of anyone's view. I told Patrick it was the only key I was ever given. Then I called Wenzel. "I've took my stuff. I've left my megadrive, Oscar the snake and his gear plus my mirror. When I get those delivered you get your keys back. Turn up and put them outside and then leave. I've told the carers if you approach this house to call the police" I hung up. Apparently Wenzel had a go at Patrick and wrote a letter to social services telling them I threatened him when I lived there. That Brenda was right I am a manipulative liar and I'm not to be trusted. I didn't care.

School was okay but I didn't feel right at home. I was convinced I didn't belong and always brought people pain. It seemed wherever I went shit happened and I blamed myself. Perhaps I was like some sort of crying boy painting. A bad omen. Wenzel knew where I lived and it was only a matter of time until I moved again and then what? Another placement? Supported lodgings like Wenzel had when he came out of prison? No thanks, not for me. I wasn't guilty. I'd not killed anyone. I wasn't going to be made to feel that way. I was low but kept it well hidden. I'd stopped talking to Stephanie and George as much and stopped helping out. My brother and sisters didn't care and I hurt everything I touched. I felt nobody wanted to know me, that I was useless and destined to become like Wenzel whether I liked it or not. I had no friends and sat bored in my room when the door went in the early evening. "Your stuff's here" George told me gently, always as though some calm, gentle father figure ghost that I'd never get to know but came to accept. I came downstairs to two large cardboard boxes. One a little bigger than the other. George was stood beside me. Wenzel drove off without looking back I could see him through the open front door. "I have a message" George said evenly. "Yeah?" I asked. "Tell him I hope they make him happy don't worry about the keys. I've changed the locks" I looked at George who knew instinctively I'd not given him the right keys back.

"Okay, thanks" I said hauling the boxes to my room.

One box was damp it was the smaller one. I opened it first and it contained books and Oscars box of worms and fish that I'd had stored in separate sections of a plastic container. He'd opened the box and then poured the worms and fish all over the books. He'd then poured what I hoped was water over the books. Everything was useless apart from the food containers. I cleaned them out and set them to one side. I then opened the large one. The vivarium was missing it's lid. There were more books, my chess awards and medals for both swimming and chess. My martial arts license was in there along with a few other achievements and my scout book. The trophies had all been snapped, The medals had the circles pulled out of them and the circles were missing, the papers were all soaked as was the scout book and license. More importantly Oscar was nowhere to be seen. I cleaned the vivarium and chucked the rest out and then called him. "Where's my snake?" I asked him. "You think you can play games with me boy? Here's a game for you. Let's play where's my snake? Now it's either in a nice home with a nice family who do as they are fucking told or it's been snapped in half and flushed down the toilet. Do you want to guess or shall I tell you?" I wasn't playing that game. I knew the answer. Oscar was dead. Down the toilet. I went downstairs and chucked the remaining stuff outside and stood looking at the vivarium for a few seconds remembering Oscar running along my shoulders and chest. Remembering buying him and handling all the snakes. I felt nothing but cold. Not the cold as in the opposite of hot but the cold lack of feeling you get for anyone or anything including yourself. The cold that emanates within you when you've seen and experienced too much. The cold that speaks that even your voice doesn't matter, where you are, who you are or what you do doesn't matter any more. Nothing that happens to you matters any more That exact cold. The cold that numbs everything so much it feels like you could be hit with a sledge hammer and you'd just accept it because hey you're used to it. I finished my smoke and was walking upstairs when Stephanie asked me "You okay?" I carried on walking "Yeah" I said and realised that actually I was fine. I was scared senseless of how fine I actually was. Half way up the stairs I realised that feeling that I'd been having for the past few weeks and if I'm honest since I returned to Wenzel now had a meaning.

I was thinking more chess like that ever before and I'd finally turned or been turned into Wenzel. I was at that point where people were just items because attaching meaning to them meant that they could hurt me where as If I didn't I could easily use them for my own gratification. I had no interest in gaining pleasure from them. However I had realised that nobody was going to help me. He'd killed my mum, he'd stopped us all living together, he'd taken my home and now he'd killed my snake. I wasn't even angry. I was accepting in a logical and precise manner and the consequences of that scared me. It was time to make a list.

I sat upstairs and looked around. I don't need this bed, this furniture, this house. I've had it all before and none of it was ever mine. None of it was ever real and nothing here really matters that much. It helps but it's not me and I'm not wanted anywhere. People like Wenzel will keep hurting, killing and abusing people. People like Clive will keep bullying and hurting people. Nobody will do anything because the police are not powerful enough and the social services are not powerful enough. People have families they protect and they have so much to lose that they are not powerful enough. People get killed all of the time and somewhere, somehow this has to stop. I wasn't angry. I was just logically going through things in my mind and something had snapped. Wenzel saw the world as one big game of chess and he could control all of the pieces. People were there to be played with and set up as he pleased. Sacrificed and used until he'd taken all they were worth. What did I have left of worth? I thought about my family. Then Stephanie and George and then answers started to come to me. "Stephanie and George don't have to be involved in this, you don't have to live here", "Your family doesn't care. You don't see them now", "what's the worst that can happen?" I'd answer with obvious statements "I'd end up dead, I'd be in prison. I'd get injured" each one bringing new questions that had little meaning to me. "Is death better than life? Are you happy?" I wasn't. "What's different in prison than living with other people?" I'd still have a bed a wardrobe, food and clothes that weren't mine. I had a point and I didn't fear death. I welcomed it. I looked down at the empty page and my pen and realised as soon as I started writing I'd put this into action then there that there was no going back. I'd made a choice to become Wenzel and I'd have to stick with it no matter what. Until I got the outcome I was looking for.

I couldn't heal the world. I couldn't save myself and I couldn't stop the pain but I could stop Clive bullying people. I could stop Wenzel killing people. I could stop Lesley raping girls and I could stop all the pain I had inside from hurting other people. I could end it all if only I could go through with it and I fought with whether I could become Wenzel or whether I couldn't. I decided I wasn't strong enough to fight him as me but as Wenzel I could. I could hurt anyone and be fine with it. I wanted to join the army part of which may involve having to take a life. I could justify that in the line of duty. In the name of a job but I couldn't justify it for family or physical gratification. I could accept it for self defence but not as a means to an end. I knew the pain it caused. I couldn't accept any of these things but Wenzel could. The police and social services couldn't think like him. Couldn't tap into his mentality at will and understand it because it was so alien to them, but I could. "Who knows him best?" I asked myself. "Bernie" I thought. No, she's dead. Who knows him best now? Inside? In his head? "I do" I answered knowing it. Feeling it pushing its way into my veins. "I am Wenzel" I said to myself. "How would he do it?" I asked myself knowing that like a social services review meeting I had to write out what I wanted. What weaknesses they would find in it and then how to answer those weaknesses. What they wanted and all the answers they could give and then how I'd reply to those. I knew because I'd had to fight for the little contact I'd had already.

I picked up the pen and wrote simply one above the other.

1. Cycle Macclesfield.

2. Find Moss estate.

3. Find Moorhill Road.

4. Kill Clive

5. Kill Leslie.

6. Go into hiding and head to Chester - Woodland only.

7. Kill Wenzel

8. Kill myself.

Writing it scared me and I knew the full stop at the end of myself literally was a full stop. Could it be done? Could I find them? Could I live with it? Could I do it? It worked for Wenzel and he'd keep hurting people. Me, mum, Rachael and the kids. He'd keep on one way or another until he was dead. Why Clive? He'd made us homeless, He'd attacked Alan, He'd hit his wife and he deserved it. Why Lesley? He'd raped a girl. The law had done nothing to stop these people. Lesley hadn't even done time for his crime. They needed to be stopped. Everyone knew about them and nobody cared. Nobody did shit about it and someone had to do something. Someone with nothing to lose, no family, no dreams, no friends. Someone like me. Not out of anger, not because I was mad or upset but because it had to be done right. No dragging it out. No telling them why. Just doing it and moving on. The questions kept coming as I looked at my list and realised I'd have to destroy it quickly. What weapon should I use? What can I get fast that will do the job in one or two hits and leave little mess? The questions got riskier and more scary. I'll admit I scared myself that night as I visualised watching Moorhill road and walking down the road behind my uncle with a hammer jammed down the back of my trousers with my shirt pulled over it. I folded the note and made a mental note to destroy it in the morning on my way to Macclesfield.

Chapter 8

Rule one, no evidence you must destroy everything you write. I cycled around Knutsford in circles for ages. What if someone saw me from Macclesfield? So what? They won't recognise you after all this time and if they do you can just give them a fake name. They couldn't see my thoughts and as long as I destroy the paper before I get there I'm fine. I was just another kid on a bicycle surely? I didn't have to do anything. Just see if I could make the trip to Macclesfield from Knutsford and time it. I started pedalling and took note of places to hide along the route if I was ever followed or needed to vanish. knife? No, too much blood and I'd get dirty plus I mean Clive is huge and he's a lot stronger than me, taller than me and has a bad reputation with a criminal record to back it up. He might beat me. I might die. Too many maybes. A gun? Where would you get a gun genius? No too hard to explain away. Scissors? No too much like a knife. What about a hammer? I'd travelled around a roundabout but which way to go? I lit a smoke and made a mental note to put the fag butt back in my tobacco tin and not on the floor. I didn't know why back then but I knew all the army books I'd read left nothing behind when they were on a job. Even if they did a shit it was bagged and taken with them or buried. It's just a check to see the area I told myself cruising around and hoping straight on was the right way.

It was. I'd recognised a garage from contact visits and swung a left. A hammer? Yeah that would do it. The impact would stun him whilst I whacked him again. I read somewhere once that a rubber mallet rattled the brain. No, it had to be a claw hammer. I could explain that away and didn't know what rubber mallets were used for where as if needed I could just use the claw end. Decision made. I came to a dirt path on my right where the road swung left. I've been here before I thought seeing Alan and me walking down the road in front of me in my minds eye. God how I missed those days. That leads to the tip track I said to myself recalling the cycling trip him and I took together. I followed the road left to where there was a shop. Wenzel used to work here. The memories were getting a bit too much and separating them from my task at hand was becoming difficult. Too many questions in my head time to go home I told myself as the pressure started to build up.

It had become a routine. Happy families in the day, planning where to see in Macclesfield in my head and heading out of an evening. I'd visited the canal where Wenzel and I went fishing one day, the next I went to the road I used to live on and eventually I'd visited every house I'd lived at on the moss estate including my uncle Karl and my old school. Apart from the odd lad knocking around it was always quiet. Not at all like I remembered it. I'd kept the routine up for just over two weeks when I'd stopped outside a house on Belgrave road. I was staring at the first property I could remember mum inside. I remember she was stood by the back door and we could partly see through a plexiglass window as she was drinking something like was clear. The sun was shining inwards and I could see it through her hair as I looked up at her and she stared out through the kitchen window when a guy came out of the house next door "OK lad?" He asked me. "Yeah, used to live here a long time ago" I said elaborating on the word long without thinking. "Yeah, Wenzel's lad. That's right terrible that was. It was in the papers I thought I recognised you" he said. I didn't answer which was enough to let him know who I was. I kicked myself for the fuck up and then my mind started to whirr "Creepy guy next door, buries cars" my father had told me years ago between scaring me with the robot toy and blowing his toes off. "No, never heard of any Wenzel" I replied. "The woman, I knew her. Had a brother didn't she?" I asked. "Aye that's right, ole Clive he still lives around here you know?" He said. "Really?" I answered "wouldn't know where by any chance would you? I was a good friend of his sisters for a while" I added. "If you like lad, he lives down on Moorhill road bottom end. Betty is there too. You know they never left." He said and then his tone changed to one of warning and important information. "Word of advice lad, become a seek. I see your place. Become a seek" He said touching his nose and tilting his head downwards. I didn't know what he meant. Crazy old bastard I thought but I'd heard enough and felt even more. This guy could see straight through me. He knew who I was, why I was there and what my intentions were. What's more is he also seemed to be familiar with those intentions. I feared him and respected him immensely "Wait here" the guy said as I'd not answered for several seconds other than to move my bike four steps backwards so I could take off in a hurry if needed. He re appeared with cakes. "They'd be pleased to see you, you know. It's been a long time" he said. I declined the cakes and took off on the bike.

Why was he wanting me to hang around? Who had he called when he was inside? Why was he offering me cake? Who was on the way? What the fuck is a seek? How did he know me? A hundred and one thoughts jumped through my head but the two that stuck were "become a seek" and "they'd be pleased to see you". I mean, would they? Really? What if everything I'd been told was lies? What if Clive wasn't violent? What if he was just like me and had tried to fight Wenzel but failed? What if everyone was really good on mum's side and I just believed the shitty parts because that's what I'd been told? What if Jack was actually a decent guy and it was someone else who'd scared Caroline into lying about Lesley because it was them that had abused her? My head wanted to shut down and sleep for ten years just to charge up. No they deserved to die, this is one old man who thinks he saw someone he might recognise who was a young lad who rode a bike. So what? Even if he did have feelings that he thought he knew me who cares? They'd be pleased to see me? Fuck off, if that was true they'd have come and seen me in care and they did fuck all like everyone else. Clive kicked Wenzel's back in and we became homeless. He attacked Alan he deserves to die but then.. they are my family? As soon as the word family entered my head I felt tears start to form. Pleased to see me? I repeated. The memories in Macclesfield were starting to haunt me.

Who was I? What about my plan? If I was Wenzel they should all die and so should he. If I was me then I couldn't fulfil my plan without knowing the truth and I couldn't know the truth without letting them know me. I'd decided everything from what to use, what to wear down to how to do it onto finding Wenzel and ending him as well. I'd thought of everything ever day for two weeks apart from how to actually kill myself.

I skipped going to Macclesfield and spent the evening sat on the bench at Stephanie and Georges. I knew I'd miss the bench and knew I'd miss both of them. What if Wenzel deserved the kicking? I couldn't off Clive not knowing but if I met him people would know and I'd be found out obviously. Fuck it how would I ever know if I had family if I didn't give it one last shot? Besides if it didn't work out I could always go back to plan A. What did I have to lose?

I spent ten minutes looking at the houses where I used to live on Moorhill road and thought fuck it do or die. I parked my bike outside the gate ready to leg it if shit went bad. I knocked on a house that looked familiar and not one of the two I'd lived at before. A short round woman answered who I recognised immediately as my aunt Betty. "Yes?" She asked not recognising me at all. "I'm looking for Clive, tall fella used to have a wife called Maggie" A taller slimmer woman opened the door further and stepped out. "Who are you and what do you want with Clive?" She asked she had this way of appearing mad even when she wasn't. Her hair was a yellow blonde colour and looked clean where as Betty looked like she'd just been sat in the washing machine. "Hi Maggie, Betty" I said nodding. "Guess you don't recognise me eh?" I added. "You're Wenzel's brother. What do you want?" Maggie asked. "No, no I'm not. I'm Wenzel's son. Tracie. You don't remember me?" I replied. Betty invited me in and wanted to know everything. Whilst I dodged questions in the living room Maggie made herself busy on the phone. She kept popping her head around the door like I might have a bomb up my sleeve I was ready to detonate at any moment. Less than three minutes later a six foot six form took up one wall in the living room. He was unshaven and smelt of beer and fags. Much more concerning than that was the three foot monkey wrench he was carrying. "Hi Clive" I said staying stock still. Show no fear I thought almost wetting myself. "That's not his brother" Clive said putting the wrench down but leaning it against the wall within easy reach. "Tracie?" He asked. "Clive it's me" I said. "Prove it, when's the last time you saw me?" He asked me. "You approached me at mums funeral. the social workers wouldn't let you near me. you sent a radio controlled car to my foster home and the last time I saw you before that involved Wenzel and an ironing board" Clive laughed "Fuck me! it is him. Pub?" He asked running upstairs and returning with a photo album.

We entered the Golden Lion a pub I'd remembered visiting as a child. Clive had worked there for a while and seemed to know everyone in there. Apparently he was both security and a pint puller but at the moment he was working at a garage down the road. He'd told me all of this before he'd ordered. "Lager?" He asked. "I'm fifteen" I replied "It's okay, I know them all in here" he said putting a pint on a nearby table and taking a long glug from his own. I'd never had lager. It was foul and I sipped it. "So where you been? It's good to see you! I knew you'd come back. You always were loyal to family" He said grinning and putting his huge paws on the table in front of me. His moustache kept rising each side when he spoke. We had a good catch up. I kept looking around the bar for faces I knew. Clive seemed genuinely happy to see me and acted as though all of his fights had never happened. He showed me photo's and gave me some of them. Some were of me, Pat and Alan. Some were of all of us together. It felt good to hold them. His mum was my nan. Did he know how she'd treated Caroline? Bernie? He told me he did. "Pat didn't like girls" he said with a shrug as though it was no big deal. "Any questions?" he asked. Yeah, I had about eight hundred but none I could ask him there or even this soon from meeting him for what felt like the first time but was also like meeting someone I'd known for years. "Phil still around?" I asked just because I remembered he was always a good laugh as a kid. Well until he was there when Wenzel was beaten up anyway. "Yeah, want to meet him. Come on we'll go see him. He'll be chuffed you've come back, remember Roger?" Clive asked me. I didn't although the name rang a bell. "Oh he used to take Caroline out a lot. They went camping together. Roger Mucker silly fucker" He laughed at his own joke and his moustache did a jig. "You done?" he said pointing to the beer as he'd downed his own "Yeah" I said looking at the three quarter full pint. He downed it in one . Nothing changes I thought.

I thought we were going to see Phil but we stopped off to see Roger on the way as he lived around the corner. As soon as I met him I didn't like him. A scrawny white guy with gingery grey hair, small beady eyes and glasses. He acted very pompous but obviously knew very little. He owned his own carpet cleaning business according to the sign on the side of his van outside. He had a ginger ish moustache and seemed like he wanted to appear spooky. It made him look like a twat. He smoked a pipe and when I lit a cigarette he gave me a special pipe lighter to keep. I told him the story of Wenzel's lighters to try and keep him talking. "So, you planning on staying?" He asked me a hint of get lost in his voice. I hadn't thought it and if I did I definitely wasn't staying with him. He was creepy and I was sure he had a thing for kids straight away but I didn't know why. I told Clive later. "I don't like him. There's something about him and I can't put my finger on it". "He's awight" Clive said dismissively. I told him I'd see him again but had to go. I cycled back to Stephanie and Georges. I felt safe there. Macclesfield didn't feel safe now people knew who I was and what I looked like. Moss Rose estate had the highest crime rate in the area during the eighties and nineties.

I didn't tell Stephanie and George straight away. It didn't feel right and I was sure that if they knew social services might have something to say about it. So I kept stum. The following day I cycled back to Macclesfield a little bit lighter. At least I had family even if they were unique. Perhaps they would be loyal and maybe even understand me a little better than other places I'd been because they knew the score. They knew what I'd been through and the people involved. Maybe, or maybe I was kidding myself. Fuck it I still had a plan A it had just changed to being a plan B. If Wenzel could switch people on and off in his head to suit his needs then so could I if need be. There was nothing stopping me learning what I could about my past from them, surely? Hearing their side of mums story? I was told Phil was working in Scope doing something called community service. I thought because of its title it was a good thing he was doing to help out a charity. I had fond memories of him as a child and was looking forwards to seeing him. He used to swing me around the living room at nan's. I stood outside next to my pushbike and watched him serve customers through the big glass window. I turned my bike around and pointed it down hill in case he ran out and wasn't happy to see me after all. He kept looking over his shoulder like he was scared of something it looked like a nervous habit or perhaps he was scared of being seen by someone. Although he seemed happy and friendly when he was speaking to customers when he thought nobody was looking he had a habit of looking very serious like severous Snape from Harry Potter. I went in and made out to be checking out the items on the shelf. He ignored me and went out of the back when he returned I said "Hi Phil!" His thin frame and greasy long brown hair and protruding nose stopped stock still. He eyed me for a few seconds and then his nose darted left and right like a parrot on speed looking for more of me. "Do I know you?" He asked. "You could say that. You're my fucking uncle" I replied expecting a huge "Tracie!" or a hug or some huge reaction. "Oh, erm okay" he replied. "Tracie" I added giving him a name. He looked at me stunned. "Clive said to pop in" I added. "Oh okay, wondered how you knew where I was" he said doing his parrot bit again. No big welcome from Phil then I thought. He made small talk and I left promising to come back another time. "Yeah, yeah okay you do that" he said nervously. I got on the bike with confidence and sped off. I turned left as soon as I was out of sight and counted to ninety and cycled past the other side of the road. He was outside on the other side of the road on the phone to someone just as I thought he would be. What the hell was going on? What was the big secret? Why did my face cause so many people to act weird? Who was he calling? Should I be worried? I went back to Betty's who invited me in "Did you see Phil?" She asked me. Ah that explains the call I thought. We chatted and Betty wobbled when she walked, laughed or moved. She was a sever depressive who'd lost a sister years ago and never recovered. I made a mental note never to turn into her. She went into the kitchen to brew up and I followed. Somehow it felt familiar even though it wasn't one I'd lived in. "Houses are all the same here aren't they?" I asked. "No dear, you lived here with Pat and Alan as a baby" she told me filling in a blank. "All the ones on this side of the road are the same. The ones on the other side are back to front" She said. "When they moved we did a three way exchange and got this place" she explained. "You and Phil are married" I said not knowing how I knew but that somehow they went together. "We were but we split up. Now he's with Willow, we still have fun. He stays sometimes" she added like it was a big secret. I said nothing as far as I knew she was married to Phil and I had no idea who Willow was. "I spoke to Clive he says you can stay here if you like?" I was totally surprised as she hardly knew me but I didn't ask why she'd asked Clive's permission as he doesn't live there. I knew Macc rules as I'd remembered from a kid. Nothing happens in Macclesfield without Pat saying so. Now Pat wasn't around that responsibility fell to Clive. "Really!?" I said shocked.

I wanted to but didn't want to intrude or cause problems and Stephanie and George were amazing but they didn't want me. These guys did want me but something wasn't feeling right. Maybe it was the amount of memories I kept finding all the time. The new information or all the years I'd been told Clive was dangerous. "Thanks" I said noticing a huge wooden spoon over the kitchen door. I took a chair and stood on it and then traced the wooden engraving with my finger. "I've seen this before" I said. "Your nans, Alan bought it for her" It said "World's biggest stirrer" on it. I laughed, "It's been here since she died. You can have it if you want it" Betty said. "No, no it belongs here" I replied knowing that Pat was Macclesfield and Macclesfield in a weird way was also Pat. She was proud to be Clive's mum. Proud to be someone nobody messed with. I remembered Alan having to send Betty home when Pat died because she popped around four times a day telling him "Pat said I could have" this that or the other. Alan hated it and so did I. First lie Betty had told me I noted mentally. "I didn't get much" well you got the house for a start I thought. Betty was comical as long as you took her at face value and never trusted a word she said or left her with anything you didn't want stolen. Otherwise she was totally harmless. She spent her life on chat lines or at Bingo and when she couldn't afford neither she played cards, namely Crash and Rummy. I got to know her quite well over the next three weeks as she always wanted a smoke or a fiver. After the third time I'd learnt to say no. She didn't care as she was used to being told no.

It was hard being on the Moss. I wasn't used to all the rules yet. I was both out of touch and yet a part of the system. It was unlike any place I'd lived before other than as a child and the rules didn't apply to children. I came to understand that all families are different. Dinner at Brenda's was a polite regimented affair with clean food, plates and desert. Yet nobody was comfortable being themselves. They all seemed to put on the show for the parents or foster carers.

At Tony and Pip's it was dirty and careless with no connection to each other or care for the home that they lived in. I say home but to me it was the equivalent of staying at a badly ran bed and breakfast. It didn't feel like a home either but for totally different reasons where as with Stephanie and George it was educational and positive with lots of freedom. Here? Well Betty chucked sausages and chips in the deep fat fryer, wiped her nose on a dishcloth and flicked ash in the sink and then asked me "want a brew?". "I'll make it" I said washing the cups up. There was no washing up liquid or hot water. The door went and a thin woman came in wearing black leggings and a shirt. "Hi" She nodded sitting down and grabbing the cards. She was thirty nine and had long yellow hair. She shuffled the cards and I noticed she had long tapered fingers. "Would you like to play with me?" She asked. I coughed "yeah" I said taking a seat. Betty rattled on about Courtney and how how she'd moved in when I left. Apparently Courtney was the one we'd done an exchange with. I didn't get it at the time I just knew it meant she could give me answers which other people might not be able to. Like me she was both part and no part of the system. Mum's family were all prejudiced because Wenzel had killed my mum. Their relative, Wenzel's side were all protective or dismissive of Wenzel's actions because he was their relative. I needed to know what the family was like before he killed my mum. Maybe he was a decent guy before then and prison changed him? Maybe he was just as much an ass hole then as he is now? I couldn't tell, I didn't know but Courtney did. As Betty rattled on I realised Courtney and I had started playing a game of her own, it seemed invisible to Betty who was happy rattling on about the past from her perspective but every now and then Courtney's leg would knock mine. When I dealt her cards I made sure the ace of hearts was on her bottom pile so it was always her first card seen. It didn't take long for her to realise I wasn't bad at palming cards and what I was up to In between Courtney's leg knocking mine, aces flying and brief eye contact their was a knock at the door.

Chapter 9

It was Lisa, everyone called her Mo but I don't know why. She was my great aunt my nan's sister and Lesley's wife and if she was here that meant he didn't live far away. Plan B suddenly jumped up and took it's place in my head once again. "I understand if you don't want to see me?" Lisa asked in tight blue jeans and a woollen top. "Too soon, he's not ready" Betty said. Then it hit me. Ten years of memories. She was Lesley's wife, She'd had a go at me after nan's death. Lesley hurt Caroline. Lisa was nan's sister. "Brew?" She asked. "Too soon!" Betty said again wobbling side to side in her chair as though trying to get up but without putting any actual effort into it. "No, it's okay" I waved her off. "Sure" I said to Lisa. Purely out of bloody mindedness. I wasn't letting anyone tell me how much I could or couldn't handle and I knew from experience there were some things that If I had the chance to do once then I should have, that chance may never present itself again. Like going to Alan's funeral. I don't remember going because social workers deemed it better for me to miss it. A social worker decided I shouldn't go to my grandfather's funeral. A man I loved and respected. I totally understand their reasoning but it wasn't my choice. "He's been through a lot, we don't want the family to upset him" but let's be fair. I'd seen enough to know whether I wanted to go to my grandfather's funeral or not and I wanted to pay my respects. I owed him at least that much so next time someone's in a position where they have to make a decision for a child. Ask the child what they want first, they might surprise you.

So I knew I might hate what I might experience but I also knew more I'd hate it more if I didn't go through with it. It turned out Lisa lived just next door to Betty. I was immediately on guard as soon as I'd walked through the door. I've been here before, everything's the same I thought. I was getting that a lot and each time it was like unlocking another piece of me but like somehow coming home but that home was hard and spiky and hurt. It was good because it fit but bad because it was hurting. The weight of emotions didn't just wash over me but literally through me. "He's not here" Lisa said misreading my cautiousness. "I don't want to see him. Ever" I said "That's fine, I understand....it was a hard time. We loved Caroline very much. If it helps I don't think he did it. If I did I'd of left him" She told me. I was in the kitchen looking around. Small table to my right, fridge directly in front as I walked in just like mums place all those years ago and now just down the road. My brain thumped with pressure as I spotted a block of kitchen knives on the side. They were wooden with black handles. I touched the wood and then the handles. More memories. Had mum had these? Is this what he killed her with? No it was further back, more distant "Nan's" I said as it hit me. "Yeah you have a good memory, Pat got them as a gift from Alan" I turned around looking for more traces of my past. The kitchen door was half open and something caught my eye. I pushed it back. There was a poster of Mickey Mouse flipping the bird with a poem beneath it. I traced it with my finger. "Also Nan's" I didn't remember at all. I was tuning into my nan but had no idea what I was doing at the time. I just knew the atmosphere had changed and I could feel her again in the picture. The image contained a part of nan. Everything she touched contained a part of her. "Clive bought it for her birthday one year" Lisa told me as she sat at the table. She went on to tell me a lot about Nan and my family. I like Lisa but not Lesley. It was obvious from how she spoke about him that she was scared of him.

They had no television. Lisa told me she'd gone back to using her tarot cards. Did I want to see them? "No" I said not wanting to let her inside my head. I didn't believe her to be like Mark and Anne's mum and if she was I definitely didn't want her poking around inside my mind. I told her before I left "Thanks for telling me about my family, I'll bring you a black and white television I don't use any more If I come back it's not because I accept Lesley. Not for the people, but because in ways Pat, Alan and mum...they're still here in ways....okay?

"We'd love that" she said sounding genuine.

"No, you're okay. You seem honest. I don't see Lesley. Period" I replied stood on her front door step.

"I understand" she said. I knew something they didn't too. Jonathon and Jodie were also in Macclesfield. I couldn't be a part of their lives because of social services but perhaps I'd see them? It hurt more than anything but I just wanted to see them smile, play, happy. I pushed it away as it was too painful and cycled back to George's.

I was playing happy families at Stephanie and George's when I spotted a magazine on the side as I made lunch. I flicked it open at the centre page and there was a story about a man who'd killed his wife. He'd apparently done so out of love because she had a life long condition and wanted to pass. It was written from the perspective of the daughter who agreed with what the father had done. At the bottom of the page in huge text it read "We pay £250 for your story!" I knew Courtney was strap for cash just looking at the property. It had the essentials but the kids often wore the same clothes and there was only one set of bed clothes for the children's rooms. Then a thought hit me. I'd sell Wenzel out. I'd get him back without killing him. That was the smart way and there was nothing social services could do about it. I downed the sandwich in the garden whilst I read the fine print. It could be a great idea, Wenzel would be ruined for life and Courtney and the kids would get some extra bits. If they'd paid £250 quid for that story would they pay more for mine? I wrote them a letter explaining my situation and included my phone number.

I was carrying the portable T.V downstairs when Stephanie saw me. "You okay?" she asked. "Yup, I don't use it. Going to give it to my aunt" I replied. "Erm, okay" she said nodding towards George. "I'll take you" he offered immediately. "It's okay, I'll strap it to my back and cycle it. It's no bother" I told him. He laughed "I'll take you. I don't mind it's no bother" he shot back. I'll admit I kind of wanted the challenge to see if I'd be able to make the trip but also greatly appreciated the lift.

Lisa promised me fifteen pounds for it on payday. I told her I wasn't worried about the money but she insisted. Nobody seemed to work in Macclesfield or at least nobody seemed to have legitimate work. They were mostly on benefits or stole for money.

Courtney and I soon became regular cards buddies, I'd been introduced to her children Marcus and Fawn. Marcus was asthmatic and skinny with freckles, he was around seven years old and very shy. Fawn was thirteen, thin with freckles. She was just two and a half years younger than me. She appeared quite shy like Marcus but soon warmed to me and opened up. She didn't like the constant boyfriends her mum seemed to have around and hated calling everyone uncle who wasn't an uncle. She did a lot for the boys that she didn't have to do and missed her other two brother's Barry and Arron terribly. Arron had always lived with his dad as he'd been taken by him as a baby. I never found out why they split up but Barry had decided to go and live with his dad a few years after Arron had left and both Courtney and Fawn missed him terribly.

I'd done my usual trip and said hi to Betty and then moved on to Courtney's. I'd spent about an hour there when I left to visit Clive. I was back to find my family and he seemed to hold all the cards. Well, all the cards apart from those about Jodie and Jonathon anyway. Clive popped his head up to look in the mirror above the bar as I entered his local pub. I did a quick shirt scratch as I bobbed my eyes left and right to check for faces that might know me as he pulled a stool out for me. "Alright lad?" He said plonking a pint in front of me despite knowing I rarely drink. "You know, a coke is fine?" I said tapping the glass with my finger nail. "Yeah, he wasn't a big drinker either" he replied referring to my father. I downed half a pint which made me feel like I'd swallowed a whale. "Been here long?" I asked. "Next you'll be asking me if I come here often, what are you my wife?" He said downing his pint and standing up, I didn't reply. "Come on, you can come to work with me" he said, pointing to my half empty glass he added "You done with that?"

We were in a garage which looked just like a huge empty warehouse from the outside with no signs or anything on it. However on the inside it was a totally different world. There was a large bench on the right spanning half of the wall and at least two feet wide. To my left were various pieces of metal all stood on end one on top of the other and at the back were hundred's of tools and pieces of wood. There were two cars already in the garage and three more outside. There was also a back office containing a chair, a computer, a filing cabinet and a sink. I made us both a smoke whilst Clive painted black stuff over the edges of some metal and laid them in a line against the desk. He laid down a big board with wheels on and told me to lay on it, then he showed me how to paint this black stuff over the metal beneath the cars. "Make sure you go over it a couple of times. Anything that's shiny needs a good dose of it" he told me. I got to work whilst he tinkered with the other car. After about an hour of me painting underneath these cars we took a break.

I was playing games on the computer with my back to the door, as Clive came in I automatically stood up. "What's up?" He asked me standing straight up. "I don't like people standing behind me" I said as he took my seat at the P.C. I stood behind him, he didn't seem to care that I was there. Could I do it? One swing with something heavy and once more just to make sure, could I? I shook my head and gave myself a telling off. He'd destroy you, he's your uncle. Don't be a dick you don't know enough yet. "Clive, you've done time. What's it like?" I asked from behind him. He turned around to face me so I stepped back and pulled up a crate to sit on. He explained about prison life and I felt kinda sorry for him. He'd told me I could ask him anything and he'd give me a straight answer but that I might not like the answer. "Why did you attack Wenzel?" I asked. "Just gave him a slap" he lied. "I saw it all. I was on the stairs" I said taking a long drag of my roll up. "Oh, you shouldn't have been lad" he replied sounding somehow heavier than before. "Look, your dad accused Lesley through the police right? He shouldn't have done. He should have come to me but I let it go cos he's with my sister right?" I nodded "Well then Alan dies and I know Wenzel was supposed to be making sure he took his pills but he didn't did he? I'd just lost my mum but no, I let it go right?" I nodded again. "Then Phil tells me Wenzel is cheating on Bernie, well I couldn't let that go could I? So I have a word with him and he insists he isn't. Then he asks my advice about Lesley" he added "What did he say?" I asked. "Well he says how would I get out of it if I was Lesley? But it's all like he's asking to counteract Lesley but not like it's actually Lesley that did it, you know?" He said. "So, Wenzel abused Caroline and then had her blame Lesley to cover it up?" I asked. "I don't know do I? But I know I didn't trust him" he said "Then he tells me he's moving out of Macc to get away from Lesley" Clive said shaking his head. "So you beat him up?" I added completing the story. "Well, gave him a slap yeah but then he tells everyone I broke his back so now I'm pissed off and he's done a runner" He informs me. "You found us in Rochdale because Courtney did an exchange" I commented filling in the blanks. "I never went to Rochdale lad, not once. I knew Bernie would call if she needed me. Betty said she called once but next day he'd killed her. Can't believe a thing Betty says mate." He told me. "I know Wenzel thought you wanted him dead" I said. "No lad, If I wanted him dead he'd be dead. There was no hit on him. When he killed Bernie there was. He was in Macc nick for a few days. I went and smashed the nick up hoping they'd put me in with him, but they didn't. Then, well..." He said looking sad and leaning lower down on his arms.

"You had someone throw a brick through his mums window. Phil told me he'd had it arranged but Phil's all mouth. Must have been you that arranged it?" I chose my words carefully and phrased it to sound as though Clive had muscle and Phil had none. Which was both true but had to be phrased properly. I never knew when anyone from Macclesfield would take something personally and explode. As much as I respected Clive's honesty, I also knew he could be explosive. I was on dangerous ground and I knew it. "No lad, I didn't arrange it. I did it" he said pulling two cans from somewhere behind him and tossing me one. I was shocked at his honesty and my words came out without a thought "Do you know the outcome of that?" I asked him. "Yeah, killed his mother. Heart attack, I didn't mean to I was just so angry. She was my sister your mum. It was my job to protect her" There wasn't a shred of arrogance in his voice. He'd said Killed his mother as though he was reciting a time when he was given a rucksack full of bricks to carry for the rest of his life.

"I know how you feel, my turn to be honest. I tripped Alan up" I expected him to explode. I expected him to judge me or ridicule me or something. He just looked at me as I told him everything about that night. "That's a big weight to carry lad" he said. "You're first person I've told and I'll deny it if it gets out" I said. Our eyes met and we clinked cans. "Welcome back, you're not like him you know. You look like him you ugly fucker, so much that it's creepy. Nearly dropped you that first day, but you're not him" he said. "Thanks...I think" I said. We spent a good few minutes in silence with our own personal demons. "Clive?" I said. He looked up "If you knew where he was, could it be done?" I asked him.

"Wenzel?" He asked.

"Yeah" I replied.

"Think long and hard lad. As bitter as he makes me. He's your dad. I know you're angry but trust me you don't want my burdens" He said.

"But could it be done?" I asked.

"Yes lad it could" he said.

I took the keys from my pocket "He goes by the name Gilby these days." I put the keys in his hand and he held my hand with them in his giant paw. He was gentle and firm . I gave him the address. I told him and about Rachael and told him I wouldn't give him her address because of the kids.

"You sure about this?" He asked meeting my eyes.

"Needs to be done" I said. He released my hand and I left.

Chapter 10

Courtney and I were playing cards at her house, nobody at home apart from us. We were in the living room on the sofa with the cards in the middle between us. There was a table which had thick brass legs and a heavy green marble top although it was only a small table. Courtney had some talk show on the T.V and they were talking about a woman with agoraphobia. I'd tried to tune it out for several minutes but I could hear them basically blame this woman for her agoraphobia and it was starting to grate on me. My legs started to shake first "No," I told myself feeling the adrenaline begin to kick in. The guy was getting louder in my head although he was normal volume on T.V I could hear him shouting at her as though he was Wenzel shouting at mum. I turned to Courtney "What the fuck does this prick know?" I said, but she'd not been paying attention to the T.V. "Are you okay?" she asked me having no clue what was going on with me. I felt alone and angry, nobody understood me and nobody would understand that woman on the programme just as nobody had understood my mother. Nobody listened when she cried and nobody came when she needed help. My hands started trembling "Trace, you're scaring me." Courtney said touching my arm as my body started to tremble "Get out, now" I said flatly despite my body shaking violently. "I'm not going anywhere what's the matter?" She tried again patting my arm "Get out" I said scrunching my eyes up trying not to explode and not knowing how to subdue it. I was watching Wenzel beat Bernie in my head as the guy on T.V shouted at the agoraphobic woman. "You're selfish! You don't go out with your own children!" He said "Calm down" Courtney soothed but it was too late. The table was weightless as it rose quickly above my head the round glass ashtray, cards and cigarette butt's going everywhere, the table hit the wall above the fireplace "Bastard! I'll kill you!" I screamed. Courtney was stood in the corner terrified. I paced for a while screaming and trying to calm my breathing down at the same time. I lifted a hand to speak knowing my stutter would be going crazy again and as I did

Courtney flinched. "I'd, I'd,d,d,d not hi, hit, hit you" I told her. "I know, my ex hit me a lot. I'm sorry" she said confiding in me. We had a chat about mum and Courtney's ex. "I'm fifteen. People my age don't get me they are boring. I'm older inside. They haven't seen half of what I have" I said trying to explain. "I know. I was raped when I was twelve" Courtney told me going into detail about a mill she was playing in and a man who abused her. I felt we had a connection, a secret but it still took me nearly an hour to calm down.

Over the next few days I didn't bother with seeing Clive. It hurt when I looked at him as it brought the past back. I didn't bother with Betty much as I knew she lied but also knew I'd beat her at it in an eye blink. I popped in to keep her sweet so if I did move to Macclesfield I'd have somewhere to stay but I wasn't for a minute spending more time there than I had to. I was busy thinking about Courtney. How had she survived what she'd been through? She'd gone on to have a family and four children. I wanted that, I wanted a good life and a family. Okay so she didn't have much money but they had each other and it seemed normal and without violence. Maybe she'd be able to tell me more about my mum? Wenzel? Perhaps I'd be able to help her get Barry and Arron back from her fathers and she'd appreciate me.

Macclesfield was like a wound I couldn't stop picking. I didn't know if I'd ever heal or if my constant pulling at the scab would leave me open to infection but I did know I had to keep doing it. I had to find out what lay beneath each layer of skin even if it meant that I felt more and more pain. It could have been another form of self harm or it could have been a part of my journey I just had to make. Either way I was compelled to continue. Could I get Jodie and Jonathon back? Could I see them playing again? Would Courtney accept me into her family? Perhaps I'd belong there until I got my family back together? Okay so I couldn't grow up with Alan as I'd liked but I could try and fit in with Clive and Phil. The thought hurt, I could easily turn to crime but how would that help with the social services? Fuck it. It was only until I joined the army anyway and I'd know more by then. I'd know enough by then to know what my next move would be but I simply had to move to Betty's. How would I ever know if I didn't? Stephanie and George were amazing and I was sad to leave but they weren't mine. They belonged in the goody goody nobody ever gets hurt world. I belonged in Macclesfield.

Clive had done just one trip in the car to pick up all my stuff from Stephanie's. I didn't have much and was used to much less. George had agreed to drop me off later but neither of us really knew what to say. I had a smoke with him on the bench and smiled my goodbye to Stephanie who I wanted to say so much more to and we got in the car. Less than half an hour later I was outside Betty's. "Are you sure you want to live here?" George asked me honestly. I could tell by his tone he didn't think it was a good idea but I respected him for giving me the option. I matched it with my own honesty, I owed him that much "No, but I have to. It's my family" I told him and shook his hand.

Betty was okay to live with at first, I came and went as I liked but she soon wanted money. I wasn't used to the way of life and didn't have my own room so slept on the sofa a fair bit. I say slept but every time the door went I jumped out of habit. It was a lot different living in Macclesfield to visiting Macclesfield. Living there was somehow like going backwards in time back to when the door went and Wenzel took a beating. Everyone seemed to feel very jumpy all the time though and that bore down onto me as well. I hadn't given social services a seconds thought until Patrick was on my doorstep. "let's talk in the car" he said looking at me and totally ignoring Betty. "What's up?" I asked getting in waiting for him to tell me someone else had died. He wasn't happy I'd gone to Macclesfield without telling him and less happy that I'd left care. He wasn't happy I'd not informed him of my choice before I left and plain pissed off when I told him to find a way to make it work. We went around in circles for about half an hour before I showed him Phil's room and told him it was mine. I had a word with Betty and told her what to say and what not to say and then let Phil chat to her. That subdued him somewhat as we headed back to the car "but what about a background check?" he asked. I knew Betty would fail in a second, she had numerous records for theft and had phone bill's in new names all the time. I had no choice but to front it as he went on with question after question. "Look Phil, less than a year ago I was with a psychopath you signed off on" I told him. It was a low blow but fuck it. "You'll never have contact here, with these people" he warned me I was instantly fuming "because I fucking had it before didn't I? Oh yeah as long as I'm in care, I tow the line I play by your rules I get contact. Fuck off Patrick. They didn't want to know when I was with Wenzel or in Knutsford which was your placement. Why would they want to know if I came back? Whilst I'm at it why didn't I know Clive had tried for custody eh?" I was angry and looking for someone to blame. I stood on the same road I grew up on standing my ground and Phil floored me with two words. "You did" he said. I was too head wrecked to remember, "and for the record Wenzel was your idea. We advised you against it. I told you. Brenda told you but oh no, Tracie knows best" He fired back.

I was in shock and something had happened inside me. I felt like I was just about to lose someone else I could depend on and another piece of foundation was crumbling and I couldn't place where or what to do about it. I did the thing I'd learnt to do the best and took it head on. "I know I'm staying put and if you can't fund it get me a social worker who will. How about I call the newspapers and tell them I'm subject to a care order put in place by the courts and you refuse to fund me?"

Isabel got forty five pounds a week for looking after me rising to sixty five after three months.

I wasn't there for two.

Chapter 11

I turned up at my Uncle Karl's unannounced, In care I'd dreamt of turning up in full Cheshire regiment dress and introducing myself as his nephew. Thanking him for taking me in all those years ago and saluting before I left for a journey abroad but Here I was on his doorstep less than six years after my mother had been killed. I didn't know how he'd take me turning up. I didn't know if or how he had changed. Look what Phil's turned into? I thought. Fuck it, Karl wasn't Phil, I knocked on and he answered within seven seconds. He looked exactly as I'd remembered him and didn't seem too surprised to see me. "Tracie, Wenzel's lad" I said in way of greeting. "Yes?" He asked. "Just came to see you" I shrugged "If that's alright?" I added honestly. He nodded and I went in to find the house exactly as I'd left it before I went into care. I half expected his mum to walk out of the kitchen at any moment. The garden was still beautiful with it's salt stone either side of the path. Nothing inside had been moved. The living room was spacious but had so much stuff lining the walls that it looked a lot smaller and much darker. I felt at home and safe there which is more than I'd felt anywhere else in Macclesfield. I was still on my toes. Karl was still Wenzel's brother after all and I guessed that as soon as I left he'd be on the phone to Wenzel telling him I'd returned to Macclesfield. Did he know already? My brain never stopped asking questions. Questions I didn't have the answer to. "Be right back, take a seat" Karl told me. I ran my hand over the sofa as I sat remembering having lay there with my nan when I dislocated my shoulders. What I'd give to have those days back.

He wasn't gone long but as soon as he returned the thought hit me. Who did he call? Was Wenzel on his way? I remembered the phone was in the hall previously but I hadn't heard him talking. I scanned the room as I made conversation "erm, long time" I said "yes" he answered as he turned the T.V down and plonked four cans of Skol on the floor. He held one up questioningly. "Nah, rarely drink" I answered. "Brew?" he asked getting up. I motioned for him to sit "Nah it's okay, I'll have a can. Thanks" I nodded as he sat back down. I liked Karl and he was the same as he always was. He rarely spoke and I respected that. It must have been hard for him caught between protecting his brother and treating the kids well. On top of that he had to take care of his mum and do all the normal things for his life. "Is it okay to ask about the past?" I asked him. "You can ask" he said with a finality and honesty that told me what he'd tell me would be accurate but that he reserved the right to tell me nothing at all. "Well, what happened?" I asked "We took you and Caroline in but mums health got worse so we had to send you back" he said. "Anything else?" I asked him. "Nothing else I know, you went back to your mum and dad. Next I hear you're in care. The rest you know" He added. I spoke about the last time I was there and remembering what happened with the beret and him coming back drunk. "I want to join the army" I said. Karl snorted "Why?" I told him I have nothing left here. Why wouldn't I? "Just don't tell them anything about me" he said. "Why?" I asked matching his tone. I knew he had served twenty two years in the Cheshire regiment winning numerous awards for boxing. "Just don't" he said. He wasn't threatening and totally at ease. However his eyes met mine when he said that and Karl was the only man who could scare the shit out of me just by looking at me. He never raised his voice, he never played Mr egotistical and he never made out he was better than anyone else. He didn't have to. I stayed a few hours as he watched the news and then a Steven Seagall film and then I left him to go back to whatever he did when I wasn't there. To this day I know nothing about him. I asked him one night about his mum and he told me the same story that Clive had. Clive had told me on another occasion that Karl knew it was Clive. I asked Karl "Do you know who did it?" He looked straight at me "no, do you?" he asked. "No, no idea" I replied as Karl held my gaze for a split moment. I couldn't read him but I was pretty sure he'd seen straight through me. I wanted to tell him there and then and I wanted to know everything he knew. The adventures he'd had with the army, the good and bad things he'd seen. The world through his eyes, I wanted to know all of it but more importantly I wanted him to have closure. I wanted him to know why his mum was killed, who by and how. I wanted to put a family around him and have him cared for and supported. He was totally independent and it seemed to me totally devoid of human interaction. He worked at a local garden centre, came home to four cans of Skol a night and went back to work. He was also totally happy with that lifestyle. I never asked about the lady in the picture frame on top of the television, as much as I wanted to know everything I felt some wounds were too deep to open and I couldn't bring myself to put Clive in danger after what I'd been through. Clive was an idiot who'd made some stupid mistakes out of anger. Some of those mistakes hurt people and all of them were wrong and his responsibility. Yet I couldn't help but feel sorry for him and I didn't want Karl to go to prison.

Lisa, Clive and Betty were in the pub. I'd left Karl's and headed straight there to find Clive and figure out what people did around here of a night time. Clive kept the drinks coming and Betty went home when there was no more free booze left. I was quite drunk in no time and leaned on the bar for support whilst I sat on a stool with Lisa right next to me. She reminded me of a hat stand she was so thin so I stuck my arm on her shoulder and leaned on her as well. "Reckon I should stay at Courtney's?" I asked her tilting my head. "Why, do you like her?" she asked laughing. "Yeah, she's alwight" I said "okay, let's take you around there then" she said walking me to her door which was only across the road and down a bit. "What? Nah she'll be in bed" I said half thinking Lisa was going to walk me back to Betty's which was on the same road. ""Well you'll see her in her jammies then" Lisa laughed meaning her pyjamas, I laughed too. "I think she likes you as well" Lisa whispered. "I won't tell if you don't" she added knocking on Courtney's door. Courtney opened it and pulled a blue dressing gown around her. "Can Trace stay here tonight?" Lisa asked her but it came out more as an order. "Sure"

Courtney said opening the door. We chatted for five minutes and she went up to bed. I stayed on the sofa.

I woke up to Courtney brewing up in the kitchen. Fawn and Marcus were playing upstairs. Marcus didn't want to go to school and Fawn was trying to get him ready and play a game with him at the same time. I stayed at Courtney's for three days, by night I slept on the sofa and by day we played cards and talked about our past. On day three she edged along the sofa right beside me as we played cards. Her leg was touching mine and she ran her hand over my shoulder and down my back. I turned to face her knowing what was coming, being ready but being totally unprepared all at the same time. I hadn't had sex, as a normal if not slightly higher drived hormonal lad I'd wanted to with most girl's I'd met. I just didn't have the confidence to talk to them properly let alone progress the situation. She leaned forwards and kissed me and then moved back against the sofa as I leaned into her. She pulled away and turned her head "I'm sorry, I shouldn't have done that" she said. "Why?" I asked her. "You don't mind?" she said looking back at me. "Haha, no I've fancied you for ages" I replied shyly. "People will talk" she told me. "like who?" I asked oblivious to the rest of the world and caring even less what they thought. "Your family, our friends, everyone" she said. "So? None of their business is it?, It doesn't bother me if it doesn't bother you" I said. We were intimate that evening and it seemed to last for ages. I didn't know fully what to expect but I know it wasn't that. I was nervous and remember thinking "just make her happy, that's all" as well as being hormonal I believe I needed to feel wanted, needed, appreciated. I didn't think about whether what we were doing was right or wrong at all. It was right for me at that time and that's as far as that thought went. Afterwards she got up and put "Will you still love me tomorrow?" on the tape player. I held her and asked what was wrong? She just nodded to the tape recorder. What could I say? "I'll be here tomorrow and the next day" I said leaning back against the sofa with her under my arm. "And the next?" she asked. "Yeah, and the next" I said.

We were soon an item if you can call it that. I was fifteen, she was thirty nine. Courtney wanted Barry back home and spoke about him often. I promised to help in any way I could with the paperwork side of things. I felt I had a good knowledge of how social services works and could be of some assistance. Being with Courtney and talking about the problems in her life were helping distract from everything that was going on with me in Macclesfield. I'd stopped going out unless I had to. I wasn't agoraphobic or anything I just didn't want to see anything or anyone that reminded me of the past. Courtney and I would often go out together and it was then somehow different. I wasn't facing the memories of Macclesfield as much if I was with her because I was concentrating on what she was saying and what direction our lives were heading. She was filled with dreams of getting Barry back and setting up as a complete family. I wasn't sure where I fit into this situation I was caught between feeling great that I was now part of a family situation and terrible that I'd taken on too much. It's not like we'd even tried to keep it a secret. Courtney's kids knew we were together, my family knew we were together and it wasn't long before everyone would know we were together. I was confused in ways but totally self assured in others. Okay so I was totally misguided and a lot of my choices were off the wall as far as normality goes, however I was doing what I wanted or at least what I thought was right for others. Fawn was the same age as my sister and yet I was in effect her father figure. I had more in common with Fawn than I did with Courtney and yet at the same time I wanted to provide, to be a part of the family and to belong.

Courtney was asking me if I knew what love was, It was about a week after I'd moved in. I told her I didn't know and from what I'd read neither did anyone else. I trusted her enough to be close to me, if that was love then I must love her. She seemed to understand but I went on anyway feeling guilty. "If what my parent's had is love....no, I don't love you. Clive and his wife? No, I don't love you but I care about you. I won't hit you. What is love?" I was trying to explain as much as figure it all out for myself.

Patrick was adamant that he was to know nothing of the relationship between Courtney and myself if Courtney was to become a foster placement. I knew Courtney would have a better chance as she wasn't family and had kids. She was accepted as a placement and I was officially with her as my guardian. Betty wasn't happy because she'd lost the income and Clive's wife wasn't happy because of the age difference. Clive didn't give a shit he was fine with it as long as I was doing what I wanted to do, and I was. We decided to try and patch things up with Betty so went around to play some cards and she soon calmed down. Phil was there and kept flirting with Courtney who was having none of it. Betty found it funny and asked us to watch a film with her. We agreed and sat on the sofa as a blue movie came on. I started flicking through Betty's C.D collection to see if she'd stolen any of Courtney's. "That's you and Trace" she said laughing and rocking back and forwards on the sofa with her hands cupped beneath her. "Phil stayed last night, it was goooood!" she said cackling. I didn't know what she expected from us or why she was acting out. I was half thinking she was trying to embarrass us and half thinking she was just crazy anyway and probably acted like this all the time. When she saw me as a child she didn't but now she'd known I had slept with Courtney perhaps she saw that as permission to show her sexual side in front of me. Either way I didn't like it. She was my aunt and I thought she was sick in the head. Courtney didn't seem to mind but didn't join in either. Patrick was right I thought. Courtney and I made a sharp exit and went to see Lisa.

Lisa had taken in two lodgers Timmy and Micky. Timmy had a blonde fanny parting and was a scouser with a really thick accent. It took me a while to get used to how he spoke, he was also a huge Tina Turner fan. Micky was darker skinned but white with brown hair and something about him made me feel like he never wanted to be seen. He rarely spoke but was friends with Timmy. They were both about three years older than me and I knew I'd never be friends with Micky but Timmy seemed alright. We stayed for a couple of hours and then left before Lesley got home. "I'll never push you to meet him you know but I should tell you he'll be back in half an hour" Lisa said around five o'clock. "Time to go" I told Courtney and nodded to Lisa. "What's that about?" Timmy asked and I noted that Micky hadn't despite hearing the whole conversation he seemed totally uninterested. I guessed he already knew, "nothing" I said to Timmy but kept my eyes on Micky.

It was new years eve because Courtney and I were walking home as Maggie approached coming towards us. "Slag" she said to Courtney. "Want to talk to you" she said to me as she stood square on in front of me. I hadn't had chance to answer when she said "just because Clive gets it doesn't mean I have to like it. Your nan would be ashamed that you're with her. Now I've said my piece, you'll do what you want to do but if it was up to me I'd kick the shit out of her but it's not." She was calm by the time she'd reached the end of her speech and then turned on a big smile "now," she said exhaling. "Will you babysit for me tonight?" She added cocking her head. I kind of admired her, she was trying to protect me and was totally honest about everything which was pretty rare how I grew up. I didn't like her poking her nose in, I didn't like the threats nor the mention of my nan being ashamed, but I can't deny she was probably right and hell I had a lot of respect for Maggie for saying it as she saw it. "Sure" I said shrugging my shoulders. That's just how Macc was and although I respected Maggie it did grate on me. Clive and Maggie seemed to believe they ran the estate as Pat had once thought she had? Although Maggie was family I'd reached that point where I'd had enough of people telling me what to do. I'd lost too much and seen too much. My family was Jodie, Caroline and Jonathon. Even though my responsibilities had become Courtney and the kids, I got on great with the kids not far from being one of them myself and promised Courtney that when my compensation money for mum being killed came through I'd treat the kids, but they weren't my family.

Patrick Benson visited Courtney and me to talk about contact. He seemed visibly uncomfortable in his brown shoes, jeans and suede jacket. His jacket reminded me of Wenzel's but I had to remember I might need Patrick's help. I made a real effort to be nice, after all he had turned a blind eye to the situation with Courtney and me. I knew the drill by now "What have you guys been up to?" He asked wanting something to put down on his review form. I smiled and Patrick put his head down sharing the joke but not being a part of it. I don't think it made him feel any the more comfortable "We went to the local museum where the kids and I had a great time. We learnt a lot about animal's and the kids seem to be accepting me just fine. I really enjoyed it and I'm looking forwards to going again" I said. Patrick looked at Courtney and I nodded "That's right, as he said Trace really liked it". We'd been nowhere near a museum but we needed crap to add to the form. "How have you found meal times? Trace have you lost weight?" Courtney turned red. "I serve myself although Courtney is always on hand to cook whatever we have in if I need it" I replied. Patrick turned back to me "Courtney does all my washing and ironing and the house is as you see perfectly clean and tidy for a home with two children in as well as me and I have my own room as the kids are still sharing a room. Would you like to see it?" I hadn't even taken Fawn's duvet cover off the bed and it was bright pink. I knew Patrick would say no and he knew I'd be prepared with another bullshit answer if he said yes. It was like one big game of chess and as much as I hated it, I'd come to understand it was part of my life. Patrick was being too nice for someone who didn't approve of Courtney and I. Something was wrong and I couldn't place it "Well I have good news! Even you'll appreciate this Trace" I let it go that he'd said even. I just smiled and waited for him to continue. "We've arranged contact for Macclesfield bowling alley." I asked straight away if it was supervised without thinking. "Yes, Brenda and one of the adoptive parents will be there" the word "parents" vibrated around in my head for a few seconds. Parents my ass I thought. I was so excited but immediately terrified as well. I knew Clive, Phil and Lesley frequented the bar in Macclesfield bowling alley and if they turned up at the same time it could be disastrous for the kids and for me. What if social services thought I'd told everyone where the kids were? It could really harm Caroline and confuse Jodie and Jonathon. What if I was followed because I made a shitty excuse and they then found them at contact? I was fucked either way. I wanted contact so much I couldn't turn it down but at the same time I couldn't put the kids in any form of contact with the Macclesfield lot. "It can't happen" I told him. "What? I thought you wanted contact" he said concerned. "I do, listen. This isn't about this bullshit tiff we've got going on. This isn't about whether you think I'm okay with Courtney or not" I said at which point he cut me off "I don't know anything about you and Courtney other than she's" I cut him off "Yeah alright, I get it. Just listen" he sat back. "Lesley, Clive and Phil go to the bar there. A lot, what if they turn up? It would terrify Caroline and the carers would blame me when I don't want them there. I don't want the Macc lot around Jodie, Caroline and Jonathon. Can't we move it somewhere else? Somewhere safer?" I asked.

"The adoptive parents and Brenda have agreed it's at Macclesfield bowling alley because it's closer for you and they both drive, they've used it before and it's been fine so why is now so different?" he asked me. Although I understood he was genuine I was flapping big time. "Because last time I wasn't living in fucking Macclesfield was I? As soon as I go out that door I'll have twenty questions about why you were here and these aren't people you bullshit. I'll make something up but trust me they will know I'm lying and keep a close eye on me" Patrick nodded. "Are you saying you want out of here?" He said. "No, I want to see the kids. I want contact. I really do. I just can't have it at Macclesfield bowling alley. It's not safe Patrick, please" I said. "Last time I was here you didn't want to do anything but move in with Betty without telling us. Then you moved in with

Courtney. You've had three confirmed placements inside one year Trace. I turn up with contact and you throw it back at me. I think you just want to disagree with everything I say don't you?" He told me flatly. I sat shaking my head and trying to find the right words "Brenda and the adoptive carers have the best interests of the children at mind. They wouldn't let anything happen to the kids. You need to stop blaming people for what's going on with you" he said. I presumed he meant Wenzel killing my mother. "This isn't about fucking blame I just said that! Listen to me!" I said standing up. "No Trace, I'm going now" he said standing up and walking to the door. I caught up with him before he got in the car "I've tried Patrick. I'm serious I explained honestly but I have no choice here. If you can't change contact placement. I won't go and you can get me another social worker. I'll flat out refuse to work with you" I told him with as much calm, flat honesty as I could muster. My insides were doing somersault's and I hated it. Moorhill road was spinning around in my head as I saw Patrick looked down at me "have it your way" he said as he got in the car.

Chapter 12

I was nervous for the two weeks leading up to contact day. I knew I couldn't go if I did I'd never forgive myself if I was followed and if I did Patrick would believe what I'd said was lies. He knew how much contact meant to me, surely? I'd asked him about Jodie, Jonathon and Caroline every time I'd seen him. I missed them terribly and it was something I always carried as much as blamed myself for. I hated myself but I kept my word to myself and spoke to Alan in my head. "I'm doing this for them. I can't have them hurt again. They've seen too much. I want to see them granddad I love them, love them more than anything but I can't see them. If I do and I'm followed I'll always be an outsider and I can't have that either. I'm sorry I told Brenda about mum sleeping with your brother. I'll keep my word, I'm sorry you're dead too." I'd imagine him reading a western book with his hat pulled forwards and my words would magically appear on his page. I didn't get to thinking about how he'd feel. I trusted he'd hate me but I had to tell him anyway.

I spent less time with Courtney and more time walking the streets. I visited the allotments and my old school both of which held no answers. I visited the church my nan went to and the hundred and eight steps of Macclesfield which are quite popular, they held even less answers.

It was contact day and I'd already found out Phil was working at Scope so I knew he would be busy all day. I got some money off Courtney and headed around to Lesley's "Lesley in?" I asked. "Well, no actually. He's at work until five. Are you okay?" She asked. I smiled "Yeah, going to find Clive now I've got some money and take him to the pub. Was going to invite Lesley too. The past is the past and all that" I said walking out of the front gate and heading towards the bowling alley. If Clive had already left for work then he might cross paths with them as it was on the same road. He hadn't and I caught up with him at his house. We went to the local pub and

Clive talked about the past whilst we both got drunk. I can't tell you what he spoke about. I was ten minutes walk away mentally watching Caroline, Jonathon and Jodie have a great time and wondering why their older brother hadn't shown up. I was pushing more pain on top of pain and was starting to feel as heavy as I was over loaded.

Patrick called me several times and I didn't answer. Something was wrong with me but I couldn't place it. I didn't know what it was I just knew I was numb. So numb. I cared about nothing and it wasn't the pretending not to care about anything any more because it sounded like I was angry. It wasn't even the pretending not to care because then I might get someone to listen. It was the genuine not giving a toss about anyone or anything at all any more, including myself. The phone went and Courtney answered it. "It's Patrick" she said holding the phone out. "Tell him to fuck off" I replied loud enough for him to hear me. "He is a little busy at the moment can I help?" She asked him. "He wants to see you" She told me. I shrugged. "He says that's fine" she told him as they arranged for him to turn up later in the day. I didn't ask what he wanted. I didn't care.

Patrick had brought a social worker with him. His name was Mick Sharpe I kid you not. He was a big fella with broad shoulders and jet black hair. He had an ear ring in his left ear and a tight white shirt and black leather jacket on. I always wore either leather or denim when I went out and liked him straight away. "Patrick tells me not to ask you what your favourite team is" he said without humour. I turned to Patrick "I like him. He's making an effort" I shot elaborating on the he's. "Mick is a good social worker." Patrick told me. "Anything else?" I asked Patrick. "Not if you're happy Mark stays to chat with you for a while. Get to know one another" he said. "Okay, Cya" I said turning to Mark and not getting up to open the door for Patrick. Mark's jaw closed when he saw me looking at him. "So, how long you been with social services if you don't mind me asking?" Mark seemed honest and I liked him. He'd had a few other kids in care but not many. He liked motorbikes and wasn't gay. I was under the assumption a man with an ear ring meant he was gay. I think I'd learnt it off Wenzel somewhere so I made an idiot of myself and actually asked him. He assured me he wasn't gay and then asked if it would matter if he was gay? I thought about it for a minute and then told him "No, not at all. As long as you don't hit on me." He promised he wasn't gay and even if he was he wouldn't hit on me. We both laughed. I never saw Patrick again.

It would be three months before my next contact and it was eating me up. Mark had told me he could help me write a letter explaining to the adoptive parents why I wasn't at the contact but that it had to be done properly and Patrick was his boss so everything had to go through him. Where were they? What were they doing? I wrote the letter and four times it was ran by Patrick and four times I adapted it, changed it and had it turned down because Patrick said I sounded and wrote like Wenzel or because I'd refereed to them as my brother and sister. Mark gave me a message from Patrick, "Contact is arranged so the letter won't be required" I didn't exist. My input wasn't needed, required or wanted. A cab would pick me up all paid for by social services and drop me at Tatton Park for contact and then pick me up again. I was over the moon! I was so excited I ironed my clothes and had them ready to go the same day. I was also terrified at the same time. What do I say? I love you? I miss you? How are you? Would they know me? I had Courtney wash another pair of clothes two days before and I ironed them as well and placed them side by side on the bed so I could pick the best set. "Clive called he's at the pub if you want to go" Courtney told me when I went downstairs. "Nah, I get to see my brother and sisters. I don't care about the pub" I said close to tears. The day before I had a long bath, did my nails and made sure I'd shaved. I hung the clothes on the back of the chair ready for morning and polished my shoes for half an hour. Everything was perfect. Nothing could go wrong.

I looked good in my grey trousers and crisp white shirt. I kept spraying deodorant because I'd smoked at least ten before the cab arrived. The got in the cab and waved to Courtney. It was a silver vehicle with a mid forties male inside with white hair. I was talking away "I missed one contact you see and haven't seen them in....oh it must be a year and a half now! Today is good though, social services paid for everything so I can see them." Suddenly the car stopped. "I don't take credit mate" He told me. I half thought he was joking. "No, no you don't understand. Call the office I promise you've been paid" I said hurriedly "No, I've told my base before. No credit cases. Out" He said.

I stood there on the side of the road like an idiot for five minutes after he pulled away. I was a good distance from home and my patients had well and truly vanished. I called Patrick "What the fuck's going on!?" I'd shouted before he'd even said hello. "Why hasn't my cab been paid?" I stormed. "They have, you weren't in it" he told me. "Bollocks! Here's his reg" I said reciting it from memory. I'd recalled it as he left because I thought "I'm gonna fucking have you". I described the driver to Patrick and gave a description of the driver. Patrick told me he'd sort it. Half an hour later he got back to me by which time I was almost home. "Is another cab on the way?" I'd said as soon as I heard the ring tone. "No, no I'm sorry. Seems there was a mix up at base and it wasn't funded. I'm sorry you'll have to sit this one out. I'll explain to the carers. It will be okay" He said. "What!? It's okay? No it's not fucking okay book me another cab!" I replied.

"No Trace. I can't do that. Call me when you've cooled off" He said and hung up. I walked home not knowing what else to do. I reached the top of Moorhill road and stood there looking down the street like it was a bomb I just wanted to explode and destroy the lot. I wanted that road dug up and turned upside down so as the houses and people in them were buried forever. I wanted to do the same to the social services. "I hate this place" I said out loud. "Sorry mum, nan, Alan. I hate this. I can't be here. I can't hold Jonathon, Jodie or Caroline. I can't. It's not fair." and then I screamed. "It's not fucking fair!" A couple were walking down the road in the distance hand in hand with two children in front of them. They were so lucky to have that, all of them.

I went to meet Clive at the pub by Macclesfield bowling alley. "I was supposed to have contact today. Cab messed me around. Can't go. Sorry to tell you because I know you'd love to go and see them but I need to talk. I'm sick of it. I've had enough man" I said leaning my elbow on the bar and barely holding my head up. I wasn't sure if Clive was going to smack me in the mouth or whether he'd just sound off about social services and at that moment I didn't care. I had no energy and wanted out of everything. "You need a drink" he replied. I told Clive about my other visit with Patrick. "So I couldn't tell anyone mate. As I know you think the world of them but It'd scare them, right next door man" I said pointing to the bowling alley. "It's okay lad, social services are all full of shit. Half of them don't know what rough life is. The other half are trying to escape it themselves" He told me. Phil joined us and we changed conversation to happier times. I didn't trust Phil. He'd changed since I knew him as a kid and I wasn't telling him shit. I had to tell Clive, I felt he genuinely cared in his own way and knew if I didn't tell someone then I'd crack. I could feel it. I'd felt it for weeks, something big was brewing and I knew I didn't want to gulp down whatever it was.

I was lower than I'd ever been when I walked back to Courtney's house, Roger was there, he wanted to take Fawn away with his daughter. It wasn't my call, I didn't trust Roger but Fawn wasn't my daughter either. Courtney was fine with it as Roger had taken her out previously and all had been fine. I called Patrick Benson to set up another contact, after all it wasn't my fault I'd missed it. I got a flat out "no contact" from him. I tried to explain, I complained that a cab wasn't provided sufficiently to begin with and another wouldn't take me. It was no use Patrick wasn't listening and the adoptive parent's had the perfect opportunity to say I'd missed so many contact's it was causing distress for my brother and sister. I hung up and sat numb for a while before calling every local social services I could find to explain. Each said the best they could do was talk to Patrick Benson. Patrick called me back before five o'clock "I'm sorry Trace, I meant no contact until Jonathon and Jodie's parents will let us know when" he said flatly. Fuck it. I couldn't win.

A week passed at the most and with each day I was getting more and more irritable. I saw families everywhere and hated them. My old plan had gone out of the window and I wasn't thinking at all straight. I had no plan but I knew if I'd had one it would have been where I jumped straight to killing myself. I fought with the idea a lot and kept not doing it several times because I was too damn stubborn. Fuck them? Let them beat me? Let social services win? Wenzel wanted me dead at one point I'm certain of it. Let him have that satisfaction? Besides, everyone kept telling me how one day Jonathon, Jodie and Caroline would come back. After all, I did. How would it look if I had killed myself? What future would they see in themselves? Then the pain of just thinking about them would kick in again and I'd shake or feel sick or sometimes just plain numb. I'd have to hold my head down when walking so as I didn't see anything that remotely reminded me of them for fear of busting into rage or tears. Looking back now I was in a pretty shit state but nobody noticed and social services certainly didn't give a toss. As long as I towed the line or they could find an excuse why I was acting out then they weren't bothered. Only when it became their responsibility to assist or they thought I was going to make a lot of noise did I become important to them.

I had gone to Betty's, she was weird but she was family and there was something about listening to her rattle on about how much the world owed her something and how depressed she was that somehow took my mind away from my problems. If I was drowning out her moaning about not having bingo money whilst she smoked one roll up after another and drank Bailey's then I wasn't drowning out my own inner voice repeatedly telling me how useless I was. "Let's go out" I said from the opposite end of the kitchen table. "Yeah, I'll borrow some money off May, she owes me and we'll go bingo" she said. "No, just a walk. let's just go for a fucking walk" I said standing up and heading to the door. Betty grabbed her coat and followed and we headed towards the town centre. Betty left her keys hanging out of her pocket slightly as we walked. I knew it was intentional, she was waiting to see if I'd take them and give them back to her as I had as a child, she was trying to cheer me up. I didn't have the enthusiasm "keys" I told her as we walked side by side. "Huh, what?" she asked. "you're an idiot Betty, keys!" I said pointing to her pocket. She slid them back inside and nudged me with her shoulder "You're an idiot too" she said laughing. I smiled but my heart wasn't in it. I was an idiot, yet as I'd lifted my head to make eye contact in that moment I'd caught sight of a silver range over on the other side of the road. What made me turn back I don't know but I'm glad I did. "Carry on I'll catch up" I said turning back and noting the registration down 8008LS. I recognised it from somewhere, I searched my memory looking for flickers of matching pictures. Things from care flashed passed. It wasn't a social services vehicle. Wenzel's cars flashed passed my eyes, it wasn't his. Where the hell had I seen it before? I watched me stood in the middle of the bowling alley car park at a previous contact as a big black vehicle parked up. It had blacked out windows and I was certain it was Jonathon and Jodie. It wasn't and my heart sank as another silver range rover pulled in behind it and parked up the registration was 8008LS and out stepped Jonathon first. Like being slapped in the face with a canoe paddle I was back on the road towards the town centre in Macclesfield and looking at Jonathon and Jodie's adoptive parent's vehicle.

I was scared and looked around but I was also feeling something. I felt fear and anxiety and shame and love all at the same time. I wanted to see them so much but I wasn't allowed and they could be right here in any one of these houses having dinner right now. Maybe they are playing in a yard somewhere and I'll get to see them? Or maybe they are visiting friends they see once a year and will never come back again and this is the last chance you'll have of seeing them? The thought scared me more than my fear of seeing them and getting in trouble. The more I was feeling all these combined emotions the more my mind whizzed. I stepped slowly backwards along the wall and found a hedgerow to push myself into as far as I could. I couldn't tell which house they were in but I could wait for them to come to the vehicle. I waited for over half an hour, there had been no movement that looked like Jonathon and Jodie or their adoptive parents. I crossed the road and walked past the range rover glancing in for signs of anything I could use. Anything that would tell me something. What if I was wrong? What if I had the wrong reg? As I passed there was a school photograph of Jonathon and Jodie in uniform attached to the dash board. I couldn't even make it look natural by carrying on walking and glancing through as I passed, I just stopped dead in my tracks and stared at my brother and sister. A little older than I remember them and gorgeous. I felt the tears start in my stomach and gave myself a mental slapping "Take a mind shot! Remember this! Remember this!" I told myself knowing I was missing something important. I looked around as though I was Wenzel. "What can I use? What is useful to me?" Car clean and tidy, picture on dashboard of two in school uniform. Anything in background to tell me location? Anything in car I can reach? Nope and might be alarmed. Must be the picture.. and then I realised the uniform had the name of their school printed on it! I memorised it "I love you, I'm sorry" I said walking off as the tears began to fall. I crossed back over the road and edged backwards into my hedge never letting the vehicle out of my blurred sight.

Chapter 13

Bastards! I thought over and over each time getting louder in my head. I knew what was coming. I'd felt this before when I was angry at everyone. Last time I'd turned a marble table over. The time before that I'd bust up a lad that came at me with a pair of scissors. I knew I had to control it. "No everything happens for a reason. I was meant to see this" I don't know where I'd heard that snippet of advice, probably Louise and I didn't believe it for a moment but it somehow helped me think a little clearer. What now? I'll need to follow the vehicle if they are visiting friends. I can't do that without my bike. I can't get my bike in case I miss them leaving. Shit, that's a problem. Okay why have the picture right there on the dashboard if they are local and know the Daily family are around Macclesfield? That's plain asking for trouble. They wouldn't chance it...in which case this must be a one off and they are visiting friends and this is a one time opportunity. They probably won't visit Macclesfield again and I need to be able to follow them. A picture of a fence and some fields slammed into my vision and I recalled from somewhere that they live on a farm. There's no farm's around here. I told myself knowing there were hundreds but none that I knew of in Macclesfield. Make a choice! I screamed at myself and imagined them coming out of the house and driving away...what would I do? What could I say? I'd see them and it would be great but they would drive away and I would have no idea where or when I'd see them again. I watched Jonathon get into the car and it take off without them even knowing I was watching them from my own self created vision and I felt them leave again without knowing I existed and I was off at a full run towards Courtney's house. I need that bike.

My key was out before I was in the pathway. I slung the door open grabbed my bike from the hall and shouted "explain later!" I was on the bike and pedalling as it hit the pavement outside. "Please be there, please be there" I told myself over and over as my legs whizzed in rapid circles. The vehicle was still there, now what? I made a smoke. "Be Prepared" my old scout leader had told me. I saw myself from his position from a split second as I stood there with a bike in plain view of the entire street smoking a roll up and covered in sweat with no waterproofs, no bin bags, no first aid kit nor knife. Just me, a paper and pen, some smokes and my bike and I felt stupid for about a second. "What do you have?" I asked myself. I recited what I'd read in every military book and heard at every camp site. I have the ability to make fire and shelter. Good, what else? I have a chance to see Jonathon and Jodie if this is done right. Good, how? Well if... I ran through at least eight scenarios in my head and they all boiled down to the same thing. Follow that fucking car, don't be seen and don't lose it.

I don't know how long I'd stood there with my foot on the peddle positioned at four o'clock exactly as Alan had taught me years before on a road not five minutes away, but it was a while. I never took my eyes off that car and felt like I'd somehow extended myself to take in any movement from all surrounding properties. A man walked out of the garage as it started to turn dark. He was a big man but I took no notice of him. I was waiting for someone with children and it wasn't him. He walked as if to pass by the car and then opened the door and got in. I was moving before he was seated and he took off before I was behind him. He took the first left and I followed up a winding hill, just my luck. I gave it hell with my legs and managed to catch up before he flew down a straight and turned into a dot in the distance. I followed the road to a cross roads and he was long gone, which way? left? He'd done a left before but that didn't mean anything, right? It was all country and although I knew they had a farm it gave me no help in these parts as I was surrounded by woodland, it could have been anywhere. Straight on? Fuck it! Time to go home "what do you have?" I asked myself and visualised the situation again as it had played out before me. "He came out of a garage and seeing his car means he's local. If he was at garage he wasn't visiting friends. You'd only go to a garage that's local to you. People are creatures of habit. They walk the same side of the road to work or school" I remembered it from a book I'd read but couldn't remember which one. Did Sampson work? wasn't his farm his work? What type of farm would I have if I thought like Sampson? The biggest! I answered. I have a private reg with my initials on it. I have a big car that stands out. I have a family photo on my dashboard. I wanted to scream "I am important! I've made it! Look at me!" So yes, I'd have the biggest damn farm I could afford. One problem I told myself. They are all big. So start again he came from the garage....let's check that out.

The garage was closed but I could see through the bars in the metal fencing. It was just a closed up garage that gave me no information at all. I nicknamed it Sampson Motors so I'd remember it. I didn't know if he worked there, owned it or was just visiting. My money was on him getting a one off repair and me never seeing the vehicle again and yet every day I'd head to the same road. Sometimes the car was there and sometimes it wasn't. When it was there Sampson would come out of the garage at the same time and I'd follow the car. It took me a while to figure out he always went the same way and I'd always lose him before the cross roads. I figured if I saw his car in the afternoon I could wait at the cross roads and see which way he went. Then I realised he's a guy with kids now. He'd understand surely. I missed my brother and sister and wanted to see them. Maybe it wasn't them blocking contact, maybe it was social services lying to me like they'd lied about the cab. How would he react if I just took Jonathon and Jodie? He'd be heartbroken surely. He want to see them and he'd do everything he could to visit and so he'd understand if I just spoke to him. Maybe we could get along?

I had a smoke as I cycled back down the hill and pulled up outside. I left the bike around the corner so it couldn't be seen but was worried in case I needed to make a quick exit. I went straight in as I knew if I thought about it too much I'd never do it. "Hi Sampson" I said. "One moment" he replied "not here for work, it's about

Jonathon and Jodie" I said as he looked up. "What?" he asked standing straight up and crossing his arms. "My name's..." I began. "I know who you are, why are you here? You're not to come here. Don't come here again" He said smugly. "I want to see Jonathon and Jodie mate. I don't want any trouble" I replied honestly. "Call your social worker, the answer's no. You can't just turn up you know" he added. I stood there trying to think of something smart to say to get him on side. "You can go" he said pointing to the door. I raised an eyebrow and left. I replayed the conversation in my head over and over. Three things stuck out, firstly he wasn't scared of others, he didn't look around once, secondly he was concerned about me. Not scared but definitely worried. What had he been told about me? Finally He wouldn't be swayed. He seriously thought he was God of his world and nobody else had a right to an opinion. I was missing something...like when you've had a stone in your shoe and it's gone yet the feeling is still there. I had the feeling but something was missing. "The answer is always in the question" I felt the words falling into me from somewhere and I didn't know where. I was pushing the bike towards Courtney's when from somewhere in my subconscious it returned "You can't just turn up you know". It started off as Sampson's words. Something I cannot do and then repeated itself until it was an echo and the end of the sentence was missing. "Just turn up you know" that's what Sampson had said. Well...why not? I knew where he worked. I knew his registration and I knew some of the route he took home. I even knew when he was at work so what's stopping me? I thought. "Yes! Do it!" and my head lifted as I looked at my surroundings and judged the distance from London road to the crossroads his car turns down. I can't see my brother and sister? Really Patrick? Really Sampson? What would Alan do? I was getting angry but not in the physical sense. In the cold hard logical truth sense. The same part of me that had decided I was going to see Wenzel, the part that had decided I was going it alone when I was homeless and the part of me that had decided I was moving back to Macclesfield. Hell if I had told half of the family in Macclesfield where Sampson worked he'd be dead by now.

I considered it for half a second and then decided against it. That would destroy Jonathon and Jodie. My anger returned at them potentially losing two sets of parents and yet I was just trying to see them because I wanted the best for them and I missed them. What if I told Wenzel? That would scare the living shit out of Sampson having him turn up at his work place. Perhaps I could scare Sampson into giving me contact? Yeah you'd look like a right gent then wouldn't you eh? nob head. I told myself. No, not a good idea. Just tell nobody and go visit Jonathon and Jodie Tomorrow when Sampson is at work. I told myself but my body wasn't listening. "Go tomorrow, it's fine" I told myself as I watched myself hold my head up and climb onto my bike. I made a roll up slowly and relaxed and looked back towards the garage without caring if he saw me. "Go tomorrow, it's fine" I repeated smiling as I cycled towards the crossroads.

I reached the crossroads and went straight across and then stopped. I checked my phone, he was due out of work in twenty minutes. If he went straight across I had a head start. If he didn't then at least I had a direction I looked back beneath my arm at the road behind me. I jumped with each car that came down the road until his did. He had to slow at the cross roads and I couldn't see an indicator on so started pedalling He rounded two bends at the top and disappeared into the distance. I reached where I'd last seen the little silver dot in the distance and was at a junction. Fuck! I turned right, there was no logic behind my decision "Stay on the right path" I told myself and so I turned right. I couldn't see him anywhere. I stopped and asked various people by making random excuses. "I used to work for Sampson but I've lost his number. Do you remember where he lives?", "I haven't seen Sampson in years. He used to babysit me when my mum died and now I can't remember which farm it is. Do you know?" People were really helpful. A couple asked me a few questions so I just acted as though I was really shy, fuck them.

It wasn't long until an elderly gentleman gave me the answer I needed "Sampson, Sure I know him. He lives there" He said pointing to a corner surrounded by fields with a huge house behind it. "Thank you sir, thank you so much" I said pedalling in the general direction and stopping out of his line of sight but a good distance away from the farm. I'd already checked behind me to see if the old guy was watching. I wondered momentarily if he was good friends with him and would call him. I shook off the feeling telling myself there wasn't time for those thoughts. However this raised more questions. Was there C.C.T.V? Should I tell family I know where they live? No that wouldn't help. Should I knock on? No not with Sampson there. Maybe I should just wait here until I could see them. They would never see me but I'd get to know that they are okay. Yeah then I'd have to say Hi because it would kill me not to. "Go home!" I told myself as I saw a shadow me walking across the field and up to their front door. "Go home!" I repeated to myself but not moving a muscle.

One circle of the property couldn't hurt? It was too big to circle or even get anywhere near without being seen. I realised I couldn't see Sampson's car anywhere though. No car meant no Sampson Fuck it, he could be back in five minutes but if I do go in when he was at work he was still only ten minutes away by car. "It's now or never" I told myself walking towards the door. I'd left my bike well out of sight. I didn't want it to be seen because they would look for it next time.

Chapter 14

Lynne answered, tall and thin. She looked me in the eye for two whole seconds and then looked around outside for others. "It's just me. I want to see Jonathon and Jodie" I asked. "You shouldn't be here" she said half order half pleading. "I want to see Jonathon and Jodie" I repeated looking up and holding her eyes. They were in the room to my right. I could feel them, inches away. I never took my eyes off Lynne. "Sampson's just nipped out, he'll be back home very soon" she began "I want to see Jonathon and Jodie" I repeated again flatly although Lynne looked up the road to see if Sampson's car was coming down I took it as a positive as now I knew which direction his local shops were in. I caught myself thinking like Wenzel and kicked myself for it. Time was seeming to stand still with her holding the door open and leaning out and me just stood there holding her eyes. As soon as that thought had occurred she'd said "Okay, five minutes. You see them, you say hi and see they are fine and then leave. Ok?" The question wasn't an invitation she was telling me those were my only options. We were never going to be friends. I was however still gob smacked. I just stood there looking at her with my Jaw down by my ankles "yeah" I uttered in disbelief.

I walked through a large kitchen with two of the biggest cookers I'd ever seen in my life before or since, they were green and cast iron with extremely thick wooden sideboards. I moved through to the right into the dining room. Jonathon was sat opposite where I was stood in the doorway on the other side of the dining table. Jodie was beside him eating dinner. "Hi" I said sighing. I hadn't thought this far ahead. I didn't know what to say. Jonathon just looked at me with a "Who are you?" Expression and I felt a knife turn deep inside me. "Hi" he said giving me a wave. I looked at Jodie simultaneously taking in every line of both their faces. I wanted to capture this forever. I might never see them again. I might hurt like I'd never hurt before but I wanted to capture their faces in my mind for eternity in that moment. I was in big trouble with social services and probably everyone else too but I didn't care. I smiled at Jodie. Jonathon looked at her and his expression asked again "who's he?"

"Ok seen enough. Times up" Lynne said blowing my dream into a million pieces. Jonathon put his fork down which had been suspended in mid air through my entire visit and I left. They were alive, healthy and had no clue who I was. I saw my bike and got on out of habit. "They are safe" I thought and said aloud. I needed the company. Even if the company was my own voice. I was so tense and so angry, "It's time" I thought "Fuck Wenzel, Fuck Lesley don't care any more!" They were gone and happy and didn't know me. I didn't exist. I was rolling down a hill fast and began pedalling until I felt the burn in my legs and then I pedalled some more. I wasn't stopping for corners or cars. Then I pedalled harder and my chest hurt. "Aaaargh!!" I screamed the tears running down my face, burning into my wind drawn cheeks. I didn't care. "See my pain!" I screamed. I cried hard and every part of my body was pumping as I flew down the next hill which was winding. "No lad" I heard Alan clearly within the wind. "Don't lad, it's not time. You can handle this". He was calm and controlled. "Fuck you!" I screamed "Arrgh!!" I pedalled harder. I could see traffic criss crossing in colours beyond my tears and in front of me maybe three hundred yards ahead. I pushed harder and looked beyond the traffic "I don't exist" I told myself with two hundred yards to go. "They don't know me" another knife in my chest. I bent over the handle bars. Fuck it I was dead anyway. I stood up giving it all I had left with my legs and arms to go faster when I heard "No, please!" It was Pat. "Fuck you! I'm coming" I shouted back through gritted teeth and zipped across the road and straight through to the other side.

I didn't have time to think how I'd made it, I didn't have time to slow down nor the inclination to care. I was heading down a very steep hill, fast. Too fast. The wind whistled noisily and all I could do was hold on. I could turn the handle bar sharply, one twist and I'd go straight into concrete or a tree. It would hurt but it wouldn't kill me.

I realised I didn't want to die. Not really. I just didn't want to hurt any more I don't want to hurt any more I told myself sobbing as I reached the bottom of both the hill and myself.

I turned past Samspons garage "One day they'll come back you bastard. One day" I said not believing a word of it. I got off the bike picked it up and threw it over my head into the nearest wall. It didn't break which angered me even more so I kicked the shit out of it. I looked down at the two buckled wheels. "That was dumb" I thought exhausted & referring only to the bike. I sat there for ten minutes chain smoking and crying before I carried my bike the half an hours walk home. When I got in I threw it in the hall "Bike's fucked, don't ask" I shouted out before sitting down on the sofa.

Some guy was sat on the armchair beside the door, big fella. "Courtney's new man I presume?" he said sitting forwards and eyeballing me. "Who's this?" I asked Courtney as I nodded towards the fella. "Dave, he's aight. Popped in to say hi didn't you Dave?" she said. I'd caught a lie in her voice and didn't like it. "How long you plan on staying Dave?" I asked him as he was still trying to stare me out. "Trace!" Courtney piped up. "What?" I said daring either to start with me. "I'll just have a brew I think" Dave said leaning back on the chair and folding one leg over the other as he faked acting comfortable. "Fawn" Courtney spoke up. Fawn made the brews she was thirteen and in school uniform, long brown hair, pale features and freckles. Me and my new best friend just sat eyeballing one another whist he made small talk with Courtney. "We met on chat line didn't we eh babe?" He asked. "Had some good times you and me" he added "Can see you're settled now though" He hadn't taken his eyes off me the entire time. I'd said nothing just smiled and leaned forwards enough that if need be I could be standing instantly. Fawn was coming through with the drinks on a tray when Dave pushed the door closed knocking into her and laughed. I got up and took the tray from her. "Upstairs babe, now" I told Fawn quietly and she vanished to dry off. Courtney was laughing. "You think that's funny?" I said as I stood by the coffee table in front of Dave with my back turned to him. I turned around "That's hot fucking water" I said pointing to the cup and taking a step towards him. "Ok mate, chill, chill" he said laughing. I didn't move. "You get rid of this dickhead or I will" I told Courtney as I started taking the cups into the kitchen. Dickhead left within moments and Fawn came downstairs all apologetic. I gave Fawn a hug and and told her she'd done nothing wrong. Apparently Dave had dated Courtney and he'd always bullied Fawn. Courtney was pissed because Fawn was telling tales on her. Courtney was trying to explain whilst Fawn was filling in the gaps with accuracy. By now I'd calmed down and Fawn was settled Courtney however was still visibly tense."No guys over that I don't know or we're done. Pick one?" I told her. "It's not like that it's..." she began. "Fucking pick one or I leave now?" I told her. By this time we were stood in the kitchen and Fawn was stood beside me explaining what her and the boys had been up to all day whist her mum and I were having this conversation. Courtney was boiling a pan of water on the stove, I can't remember why. "Will you.." Courtney said with anger in her voice and I saw her arm twitch as she began to turn. She was going to throw the whole thing over us. I stepped forwards and chopped her hand knocking the lot into the sink. Fawn stood frozen "What the fuck are you doing!?", "Do you want her scarred for life? That's your daughter!" I slammed my keys down on the side and walked out.

I came back a couple of hours later after sitting in the church. I wasn't religious my reasons were simple. It was free, it was warm, dry and nobody would disturb me. I decided it was time I needed to set a rule. I got home and told Courtney I was sorry for chopping her wrist but I wasn't going to have her throw anything over anyone. She insisted she wasn't going to throw it over me so I asked Fawn to come downstairs and give her side of what happened with no prompting from anyone. Fawn confirmed she thought her mum was going to throw the water over me or her but definitely at least me. I told both Courtney and Fawn from here on in there's no bullying of anyone from anyone whether inside or outside of the house. Courtney agreed. "Right I'm going for a bath. I don't want to hear about this shit again. It's forgotten let's get back to normal" Upstairs I ran a bath and got undressed. The steam was everywhere. My body wanted to shut down I could feel it but I fought it off. "I'll just lay here for five minutes" I thought as I lay down on the floor. I tried to keep my eyes open but couldn't even though I could still hear the water running.

My uncle Clive was sat at the end of the bed. It was Courtney's bed and oddly I was in it. I was sat up and Clive was sat looking at me from a chair beside the bed. I was naked but covered with a duvet. I was also very groggy "The fuck you doing here?" I said. "Welcome back" Clive replied smiling. "The fuck I get here?" I asked trying to look around but feeling dizzy so not bothering. "Clive carried you. you passed out. You've been out for days" Courtney said appearing in the doorway where I could hear her but not see her. "Meh fuck off" I replied. Clive laughed "What's the last thing you remember?" He said. "Found Jodie and Jonathon" I said without thinking and instantly blacked out. My body couldn't handle it. Apparently the doctor said it was exhaustion. I'd been on pills for three or four days and slept right through. I don't remember any of it. It felt like I'd simply gone to sleep and woke up again. Year later I'd realise this was a physical breakdown.

Chapter 15

I soon realised that whenever I started feeling things from the past my body started to shut down. This was problem enough in itself however made much worse by the fact that there were reminders everywhere and initially I couldn't pinpoint which parts of the past would cause me to shut down. I would be with it one minute and then feel myself going dark and withdrawing and then bang. I'd be out. Thankfully I didn't have any major repercussions in that I didn't lose days after those first few, only hours.

Courtney was busy at the front door trying to explain to a debt collector why we didn't have any money. It was news to me, I didn't even realise we had a debt. It wasn't much I spoke to the guy and he agreed he'd pick up money weekly and it would be resolved. As soon as the debt was paid off Courtney took out another with the same company on the same day. She tried to explain it to me as though having this extra money was a good thing. After a big argument it was time to introduce rule two. No loans - ever. She didn't like it but she stuck by it. She liked it even less when I asked her to cancel her puzzle book subscriptions and the chat line.

I couldn't face social services at all and told Mick Sharpe that he could check on me but not to talk to me about Jonathon or Jodie, I simply wasn't up to it. A reporter came to chat to me about the article to be produced. I even managed to talk her up on her offer. I'd get two hundred and fifty pounds for the story and another two hundred and fifty if I let them write that I was having a relationship with Courtney. Why did they care that I was having a relationship with an older woman? I didn't know but I did know that five hundred pounds no questions asked would really come in handy.

Phil turned up on my doorstep a few days later. I'd liked Phil as a kid however this was strange not only because Phil never asked me to go with him before but because he was almost begging me to go. I didn't want trouble on my doorstep and it appeared as though he would start shouting and acting like an idiot if I didn't go, so of course I went. I felt a set up coming on but I couldn't figure out how. Something wasn't right and Phil was immediately on edge as we walked side by side to the pub near Macclesfield bowling alley. Phil chugged one thick ale after another whilst telling me stories about how hard he is and so called fights that he'd been in. He was so full of shit. I sipped my drink, whatever was wrong, it was brewing and I needed to be sober to react to it. The door burst open and Clive stood in the doorway like he could just push the sides in and the whole building would collapse. "You, outside" he said pointing to me. A couple of punters shrank into their drinks. "This isn't good" Phil said totally failing at covering himself. "What's up?" I asked walking out the front door just behind Clive. There was no point prolonging it. Besides whatever was going to happen was going to happen whether I sat there or not. "What's up!?" He screamed leaning forwards so he was half an inch from my face. "What's fucking up!" My bike was with him and he was pacing towards it and back to me. I'd sidestepped to the left and inadvertently put myself between a wall and a cast iron fence with spikes on the top. Not the smartest thing I'd ever done and I couldn't move to my right because Phil was there, nor forwards because Clive was there. I managed to distract myself enough even though I knew Clive would turn violent if he decided by noticing that my Bike had actually been repaired. He came forwards with his head down as though just walking towards me to pace backwards again but instead of turning and walking backwards he simply lifted his arm and pushed me backwards into the wall. "Hey, what's going on?" I said pushing his arm away. He'd hit me before I'd even seen it coming, my head flipped and I turned against the railing with the impact. Spikes! Big metal black spikes right next to my face, this wasn't good. My mind yelled "Run!" I was physically shaking and Clive was still pacing like a lion waiting to take down his prey. Images flashed through my head of Wenzel taking the beating with the ironing board. "No" I said audibly to myself and then turned away from the railing. "What's wrong?" I asked Clive calmly. He came at me again. I stood no chance and I wasn't going to try, but I wasn't going to be Wenzel either, I wasn't running. He slapped me hard and it hurt like a punch. "Newspapers! Fucking newspapers, really?" He stormed. I hadn't moved nor let it be seen that the slap hurt. "Oh, it's that. Yeah, what's up?" I asked totally not realising I should have ran it by Clive first. "Bernie in the paper, disgracing her name! Don't you get it?" He said his face next to mine. "Obviously not, think of how it will hurt Wenzel" I said knowing he had the keys and had done nothing. He turned around and kicked my bike. "My Bike?" I said getting a little bit of confidence back. "You should have told me. At least fucking warned me!" he said lifting his arm slowly this time as though considering hitting me. I just looked at him. No attempt to run or move. Phil was silent and kept stepping backwards. He was worried. He'd expected me to cover, to curl up like Wenzel had so then Phil could put the boot in and be a hero. So they could both call me as bad as him. Fuck that I'm not my dad. "Yeah, I should. I didn't think of that you're right. Now, my bike?" I said as he still had his arm in mid air and I couldn't think of anything sensible to say. Clive laughed he actually stopped and just laughed a big full on belly laugh."You may look like him but you're not him. I really want to smack you right now but you're not him." He said. "That my bike?" I asked pretending I'd ignored the comment. I didn't care what he thought of Wenzel and if he couldn't see I wasn't him because of looks I didn't care about that either. I knew if I thought too much about anything to do with Wenzel I'd pass out again and I couldn't do that right now.

"He cowered like a pussy you know that? That night" He said referring to the night he'd given Wenzel a kicking and not realising I'd seen it. "I know, I was there. I'm not my dad" I replied. "Got it from Courtney's to come find you. Take it" he said gesturing towards the bike. "You could have asked me" I said without being cocky, we both know I'd not of said no. "Fair one, come on" he said heading towards Moorhill road. "No more talk of papers though eh?" he said. I could feel Phil calming down as he walked behind us. "I'll do it, but no pictures of Bernie and I'll show you before it goes out" I replied without looking up. Phil seemed a lot less comfortable all of a sudden as I listened to his footsteps and waited for him or Clive to start swinging. "Okay lad, okay" Clive said and took off on my bike to replace it where he'd took it.

Phil fell in step beside me but said nothing for several paces. "I didn't know, honest I didn't" he said. "I knew Clive was the muscle Phil. I had you down as the brains. I guess I was wrong there though" I said not bothering to look at him. "I didn't know, you scared me there though" He said. "Why?" I asked. "Nobody stands up to Clive" said Phil his voice faltering slightly. "I didn't" I replied this time turning to look at him as we walked. We made eye contact. Any trust I thought I had in Clive or Phil was gone. Clive didn't cause me any problems and was always polite after that but word gets around fast. When everyone knew I'd been to the papers I got the name of a grass. Even though Wenzel was the killer and I'd not technically grassed on anyone a rumour still gets around. Kids who would usually be playing football further down the street started throwing mud and stones at the house. The washing line was cut twice before we got an indoor airer and because they were kids I couldn't do a damn thing about it.

Courtney the kids and I were at the park. By now Arron, Courtney's eldest boy was also living with us. He was a good lad, quiet, well built and strong for his age. We were having a picnic on the grass with a blanket minding our own business when I saw Fawn's eyes flash. I turned around quickly to see a group of lads heading our way six, maybe seven of them. Varying ages, the oldest I'd later find out was called Peter and he was nineteen. "You're not from round ere are ya?" The tallest asked as he approached. "Wait here" I said to the kids as I walked over. "Actually I was born around here. I've probably got more right to be here than you so if you don't want anything I suggest you fuck off" I answered. I figured get in there first and either they will all disperse or....well. "Oh big words" one said "Just wanted to know if it was true?" The tall guy asked. "What?" I asked. "Mummy got herself killed did she? Ran to the papers I heard" he taunted. I took one step back and threw myself forwards just as Peter pulled this guy to one side "Don't!" He said to his mate. "Clive's his uncle" he added. What just happened? I thought as I stood dumbfounded literally within the group of people I was trying to avoid. "You are a Macc lad then?" He asked looking over Pete's shoulder. "Clive's sister was my mother, you know. The one you just took the piss out of?" I replied. "Now now mate, Clive doesn't need to know now does he eh? Give him a whack and it's done or just leave it yeah?" Pete said all Macclesfield like. He was smart and I liked him. "Hey Courtney!" He said waving to the kids. Nice touch I thought "Nah, it's done" I said walking away. I heard him giving his mate a bollocking as I left.

"We're leaving" I told Courtney as I reached the picnic blanket "What?" she asked. "Well, I'm leaving. If you want me, you and the kids can come too. Otherwise I'm leaving Macc. I'm not a fucking pawn. I'm nobody's chess piece and if I live here I'll be forever looking over my shoulder. Besides I can't be this close to Jonathon and Jodie and not see them." It was the first time I'd been able to speak their names without my body shutting down. Progress.

Chapter 16

It wasn't long and a property became available in Bury, Manchester. The road was Goldfinch drive and it sounded perfect. A Scottish fella we knew called Craig said he would happily take Courtney and her stuff up to the house for sixty quid. I gave him thirty and told him I'd give him the other thirty when he arrived on site. He wasn't happy and wanted the payment up front. I got it and gave it to his missus. I travelled up there a couple of days before they were due to arrive. It needed decorating and carpeting but otherwise it was a nice place. It had a big garden at the rear and the area seemed quiet enough. I got most of the unpacking done which I'd managed to take with me via a standard removal company.

I don't know if it was because I didn't have the electric on for two nights or if it was just being alone for the first time in a while but something didn't feel quite right. I slept on the sofa and got the feeling I was being watched the entire time. Unfortunately the feeling didn't disappear when I wasn't trying to sleep. I'd found one of my lock knives during unpacking and decided to keep it on me. It looked like a beautiful summers day outside and yet it was freezing indoors. I chucked an extra sheet on the sofa for later and headed out.

It was lovely and warm. I envisioned red and white roses in the front garden. Yeah I could get used to this. It would be okay here. Two woman were walking down the footpath towards me "Excuse me, nearest call box?" I asked making it obvious I was completely new to the area. "Oh go and see Andy. He lives there. He'll let you use his phone" She said pointing next door but one to my house. "Thanks" I said slightly more cautious than I was before. They are just being friendly I told myself. I knocked on this fella's door and explained about the two girls. I could smell weed coming from the living room. "Phone" Andy said pointing to it on top of the television beside a set of Brass scales. Two lads were chonging away on the sofa. Great I thought not wanting to owe this guy anything. I knew Macc rules if he did me a favour today I'd owe him a favour tomorrow. "It's okay mate, just point me towards the nearest call box yeah?" I asked. "Use that" he replied nodding at the phone. I didn't argue I bunged a quid on the side once I'd done. Alan was busy and it would be two days before he could bring her and he wanted more money. I told Courtney to get here and I'd pay him. I had no intention of paying him I'd unpack and drop him if I had to.

The night was very windy. I had a lie in though and was surprised because I'd slept until gone ten am but I could still hear that whistling noise, perhaps the property had a hole? I checked everything it was definitely outside There was no damp, no chimney as we had a gas fire and no holes in any of the walls or window frames. They were single pane windows though, perhaps one had warped? I checked everything making a mental note to get some locks for the windows as I knew from experience a butter knife could get those things open easily. The front door had a chubb and Yale lock so I was happy with that yet I'd still add a bolt out of habit. The back door led into a coat room and then had the rear door behind that so it was plenty secure. I went through that door checking the locks and stood outside in the large garden making a note to repair a piece of fence. Strange, no wind at all. Another gorgeous day.

I went to the chippy and returned home just as a van pulled up behind me. Courtney got out and ran up the drive "Say nothing to Craig I've sorted it" she said quietly. I presume she'd paid him thirty quid that he wasn't owed but hey my stuff was here and I wasn't going to kick off in front of the kids. I unpacked and sent him on his way without a brew. Courtney told me that night she'd spoke to Maureen, Craig's wife and she'd spent the money on a night out. She couldn't tell Craig because he'd beat her. Courtney felt sorry for her and gave her some jewellery I'd bought her as payment for Craig. I was not amused but there was nothing I could do about it and I didn't need the aggravation

The problems started almost immediately. First Courtney felt cold for no reason. So cold that she'd shake. I felt nothing. She wasn't sneezing or anything and she'd be totally fine a half hour later. We put it down to the stress of moving. I was used to it. She wasn't. We got the kids into a school and a doctors and got to settling in. Away from Macclesfield where everything would be relaxed and easy, with no memories. I was watching T.V with Courtney when I heard a bang in the kitchen "Stay" I said pointing as I ran towards the noise. It was stone cold in there but nothing had moved and it was completely empty. I checked the door and looked out of the window. Nothing apart from a pool of water in the corner of the room that had started to build up. "We've got a leak" I told Courtney. She mopped it whilst I checked the nearest radiator which was a good several feet away and bone dry. I checked the pipes behind the washing machine and sink but again, nothing. We called the council the following day and they came out to check for a leak and found none. This would repeat itself several times over the next three months sometimes the water would be over half covering the kitchen floor and yet bone dry the next morning. In the end I pulled the lino floor up to see if there was some kind of piping beneath the flooring. I could find no causes and nor could the council. The floor was solid and bone dry. There was not even water damage left to any of the wooden units where the water had touched several times. I told Courtney it wasn't right and I started to feel edgy. Courtney told me she'd had a couple of bad dreams and also felt watched within the property. I'd just come off what years later I'd find out was a breakdown and could be related. However at this time seemed totally unconnected.

I was fifteen, trying to provide for a family on the money social services were providing for Courtney to Care for me which was less than forty pounds per week, plus Carols benefits and trying to find a job. I'd handed C.V's out all around Bury and eventually a sandwich shop took me on cash in hand. The lady had just taken over from the previous people who'd moved on to a more profitable area. I was there four days mainly preparing sandwiches and cleaning the store when she asked me to serve a customer. "I can't" I replied as I was stood at the bottom of the stairs keeping an eye on the shop floor. "Why not?" She shouted down. "I can't use the till?" I replied. "Why not?" she challenged. "Because you haven't shown me?" I replied looking apologetically at the customer. That was the end of that job. Back at Courtney's money was tight. We couldn't afford cigarettes and Fawn's shoes were the wrong colour for dance lessons. We couldn't afford new ones and it was eating me up. Wenzel had a job? Clive had a job? Why can't I have a job? Who will hire a fifteen year old? I thought of the fruit and veg shop and felt very sad. I went to the library and spoke to everyone I could until I discovered the army. I told Courtney I was signing up and that they'd take me as soon as I was sixteen. I'd send her money for the kids, she'd never see me but I'd be helping her family and she'd not have to live like this.

I'd just got home and Fawn was crying in her mums arms. What's up? I asked as Fawn pushed passed me and ran upstairs. "Huh?" I asked Courtney who went on to explain Fawn was getting bullied at School for not having the right colour shoes and so wasn't allowed to do dance lessons. Hers were brown and had to be black. I was gutted for Fawn and felt really bad because in my mind it was my responsibility to be taking care of her. I could only think of one thing under the circumstances. "Get me her shoes" I said. I'd had some spray paint left over from when I'd re done my bike. I spent hours that night going over and over Fawn's shoes so as they were perfectly black. At the time I was quite impressed. Unfortunately Fawn was doing dance lessons when some paint came off her shoe's and showed the true colour beneath. She got bullied for having shoes which had been painted black. I couldn't win and felt totally incompetent.

We'd had some money through from the council which would allow us to decorate. I was decorating the living room when Courtney returned home with a pit bull terrier. "What the fuck?" I asked. "I thought you liked dogs" She replied. "You said we could have one when we moved" She added. I failed to respond that what I'd actually said was "when the place is all set up and we have enough money then you can have the rough collie's you want". So instead replied with "We can barely feed ourselves. Take it back". "He was free. I can't, he was being given away. I couldn't just leave him" she added. We had an argument about how he could be vicious, how she knew nothing about his medical history and how she's going to pay for his upkeep. Which somehow turned into "who's going to look after us whilst you're in the army?" I told her she did alright before I turned up and she'd do alright after. It was around then that I knew things were never going to work out.

The newspaper reporter turned up. Cute girl with red hair who kept flirting with me in front of Courtney. I tried not to let on I'd noticed and answered the questions. I gave her a picture of Wenzel after I'd cut Rachael and the kids out of it. This wasn't their fault and there was no need to include them. I was told when the article was complete I'd get a copy of it to check before It went to press, then I could make alterations if it needed any. I received the article very shortly after and I had no issues with it. I signed it and Courtney signed it. We got paid five hundred pounds and I blew it on kids clothes and shopping inside two days and I was chuffed. I'd got back at Wenzel and helped the family out. Fuck him, it was finally over. I had my own personal closure. I could join the army, find a bird and settle down.

Who was I kidding. It had only just begun.

Chapter 17

It was early evening and Courtney had brought home another dog. This time a golden Labrador, he was cute but still, we couldn't afford him. We had another argument "He was £50 that's a bargain!" She'd offered as explanation. He wasn't house trained "That's not the point, we need electric, food, what do we have left until Friday?" I asked "£16 but we'll be okay" she said having no clue about forwards thinking and it was only Tuesday We sat in silence and waited for the kids bedtime to arrive as the curtain blew out into the room and it became very cold. I looked at Courtney as the curtain moved along it's rail and Fawn let out a "Muuuuuum" as she pointed towards the window and turned white. "Time for bed guys, school tomorrow" I said opening the curtain all the way. The windows were closed. There was no draft and even if their had of been it couldn't have moved those curtains in that way. "What was that?" Fawn asked on the way up the stairs, "Just the wind" I replied. Fawn ran down the stairs ten minutes later as Courtney and I were trying to figure out how the curtains had moved. "There's smoke in my room" I flew up the stairs, there was no smoke but I could smell cigars clearly and only in her room. I checked all the windows and again they were closed. I called Fawn and Courtney upstairs and explained how our neighbour may be smoking a pipe or cigar and it could be that she's smelling. I stayed with her until she fell asleep. Downstairs Courtney said she'd felt as though someone was in Fawn's room. "Brew?" I asked changing the subject and heading to the kitchen. The floor was piss wet through. "I've had enough of this" I told Courtney. "Something's here" she said. "Well something can fuck off" I told it and her. I was shaken but otherwise okay. We spoke about getting the housing association back to check everything and went to bed around eleven, after ten minutes I fell asleep. Upon waking I found I couldn't move. It was dark out and I was stuck to the bed. It felt like something was smothering me. I tried to fight but couldn't move. After several seconds which felt like an eternity I broke free. I was gasping for breath and sweating heavily. Courtney was awake staring at me. "You have fits?" she asked. "No" I replied explaining. "I could see you moving, struggling but didn't want to touch you in case it scared you" she said. We sat up all night. In all honesty I was too scared to sleep.

My mums compensation money had come through and both Courtney and I decided we weren't staying there and put in a bid for an exchange. I'd got two thousand five hundred and fifty six pounds for my mothers' death. They worked it out in a really strange way it was either that I'd known her the least amount of time and so I'd got the least because the other siblings would have theoretically had chance to know her longer or that I'd got the most because I'd known her longer and their fore had more of a loss. It was a strange system and one I found totally ridiculous. My mother was dead, no amount of money was going to change that and even though I was flat broke, young and often naive, I knew that I didn't want anything to do with that money. That money symbolised my mother and I couldn't keep her and so I didn't want the money that signified her death. I bought a 0.22 Webley Vulcan with a hurricane spring just in case It was someone messing with us and the property and not what Courtney and I were presuming was a spook. Courtney got a new jacket and I got a five disk multiplay C.D player because I remember my granddad loving the three disk one he'd got years earlier. I got the food in and the rest was for when we moved.

I made a mistake here and wish I'd never done so but I did. I took Courtney out to a pub and a couple of games of pool and let Fawn babysit. We'd told Andy our neighbour that Fawn was babysitting as she's thirteen and she had our phone number and his if there was any problems. He said he'd keep an eye out for us and we had no reason to doubt him. Fawn didn't call at all when we were out and when we returned everyone was in bed apart from Fawn who was sat crossed legged in the living room. The T.V was off and she'd been crying. "You alright? What's up?" I asked. "Water in kitchen, I didn't do it I swear, curtains, lights! I sent them to bed" She said panicking and looking around the room frantically. After calming her down she told me the curtains had blown out on her and scared the kids who she sent to bed. Then she'd found water in the kitchen and thought we'd blame her for it so tried cleaning it up when the lights went on and off. She didn't call because she thought she'd be in trouble so sat watching T.V and trying to forget about the water when the T.V turned itself off. She'd been sat there alone since just waiting for us to come back. I promised her I'd never leave her alone again and then I did something which to this day I don't know if I was right or wrong to do. I told her the truth, I explained that we had no idea what it was either and that we were sorry everyone was going through this but we thought it was better to keep it from them than to tell them. That when I was ten I just wanted answers from everyone and she was thirteen so we thought it right to tell her the truth rather than make up stories. We told her when we moved she could choose her own room. She took it well and the following day I went to see Andy. After listening to my story intently and giving me several funny looks I came to the conclusion that Andy simply thought I was mad however did say "There's a church over the back there, ask them" We spoke to several people at the local library about the church and our property to see if anything had ever been recorded. They listened and came up with several theories but nothing in concrete. It was feasible that the churchyard had moved over time downhill and somehow that it was now beneath our garden and through putting fencing in we'd disturbed something was one of the wilder ones. If this was true however we were still left with the same two questions. What was it and how do we stop it? We also discovered our next door neighbour's brother had killed himself a couple of years back. Could that be related? Wouldn't any of these disturbances be in his property and not ours?

A few days later and after another dream where I was a woman trying to protect my child which was in a cot in front of my window as a man was walking towards me and I woke up just as he reached me. I was sweating buckets but also angry, I was so angry because I felt the person in the dream had been killed and the baby had at least been hurt. I was so upset. Had this happened here? Was this something to do with mum? Was I losing my mind because of mums death and this in some way was about protecting her or not being able to protect her? I was over thinking everything. I kept telling Courtney over and over that if I was wrong then I wasn't well but if I was right there would be some kind of sign knocking around somewhere which would confirm what happened... but why hadn't Andy said anything if someone had been killed here? We decided to go over every single part of the house to find out about this leak and the wind whether it was likely or not and eventually got to checking the loft.

I'd had to stand on the balcony bannister and then onto a chair back as we had no ladders. I was halfway through pulling myself up when I heard several sharp thuds coming straight towards me. I dropped down and pushed Courtney backwards into the bedroom and shouted for Arron to step back at the same time as I thought whoever it was would jump down. There was no further sound but Courtney said she'd heard it whilst Darren just looked concerned. I took it all in whilst not taking my eyes off the open ceiling hatch. "I pointed to the bedroom corner" and Courtney walked around the chair to grab my rifle and a torch. I took the torch and she held the rifle. I was petrified but looked around and there was absolutely nothing there at all apart from two bin bags beside the water tank. There was no places for anyone to hide and no rats or creatures that I could see. I grabbed the bin bags and threw them down and made a quick exit. I was convinced more than ever that I was either losing my mind or there was something paranormal going on. We waited until the kids were in bed before opening the bags.

They were full of baby clothes.

Chapter 18

The reporter had been out and taken my story down a few weeks
previously. I had given the okay for the article to be done however I
was told the title would be decided later. I didn't query it. The lady
seemed sound, very friendly, a little flirty and sat smoking with us.
How bad could a title be? Well I don't think anyone was more gob
smacked than me when it came out. In big writing it was written
"She's my lover not my mother." I immediately called the news of
the world and told them I wasn't happy about it. They informed me
I'd given the go ahead and so their was nothing they could do about
it now. Fuck it, I consoled myself, who reads these things anyway?
Centre page of a magazine in the news of the world. Well as it turns
out, pretty much everyone actually.

We had chat shows ringing up wanting us on their programme. They
wanted to put us up in a hotel and could pay our travel. I asked
what we get for our story and our time to be told they could give us
fifty or sixty pounds. Embarrass ourselves again for next to nothing?
No thanks, not good enough. I'd rather just limit the damage
already done. I'd gone from being a lad in care paying social workers
wages with my silence to paying wages of someone else to make
fun of my life whilst I talk about it? No thanks. I have an unorthodox
life, I took a shot. I was trying to help my family. I fucked up, it didn't
work but I'd be damned if I'd let it continue.

Over the next two months we had calls daily. I was polite every time
apart from once. I'd opened the door and a redhead asked. "How do
you think your love life effects her children?" I'd played dad for
nearly two years and thought the world of those kids. I was wrong
in a lot of ways but I'd done my best. "Where did you come from?" I
asked innocently. "I'm Jane with x news" She said with a big fake
smile. I didn't even listen to which place she'd come from, inside
was fuming. "Then I suggest you fuck off back there then!" I replied
slamming the door on her. Not fun times, I was scared too. What

had I brought to Courtney's door? The kids?

It didn't take long, I was in the bathroom when I got that dread feeling coming over me. It was instant. Same feeling as Alan, Same feeling as Pat's death. I was being warned. "Don't answer it!" I shouted just as I heard the door start banging downstairs. I ran out of the bathroom and grabbed my sheath knife on the way slipping it up my back and into my trousers. I had two choices end up like Wenzel had when he took a serious beating or worse or I could scare the shit out of them. I wasn't a fan of option one and there's no way I wanted her kids seeing the shit I saw as a kid. "In the kitchen! Stay there until I come back" I shouted. I leaned on the window to see outside It was Timmy and Betty. "What do you want?" I said opening the door a notch and looking around for trouble. "It's just us" Timmy said. "That's no way to great your aunt Betty!" she said pushing past me. "Upstairs" I told Timmy as I closed the door and locked it in several places. I pointed to Courtney's bedroom and we went in. I walked past him and motioned for him to close the door, as he did I walked up behind him. "What do you want?" I told him as I leant on the wall invading his personal space intentionally. I needed to appear not afraid. "Saw the paper man, Clive's pissed, I thought we'd come see you".

"Fuck off!, Clive will be around the corner with Phil the second you leave. They'll take the door down. Why are you here?" I said spitting on his trainer and eyeballing him. I'm not sure why I spat on his trainer. I didn't want to hurt him but wanted to get my point across that I would if I had to. I also wanted facts and wanted him to know never to turn up again. A shame because I really liked Timmy but after the newspaper stuff and Clive with Wenzel, I couldn't just let up. "Hey dude chill" he said lifting his arm an inch. I don't know what he'd planned on doing with that arm but by the time he'd moved it I'd jabbed his chin and grabbed his shirt with my left and pushed him backwards against the door "chill dude, fucking chill!" I screamed grabbing him with both hands and pulling him towards me fast then pushing him back into the door. "See that rifle?" I said not waiting for an answer "It's loaded, see this knife?" I said reaching around behind me and pulling the knife out. "Chill?" I asked calmly holding the blade up. He went to speak so I stabbed the door as hard as I could about an inch away from his side. "If anyone comes through that door I'll kill them, tell Clive, Phil, Wenzel and any fucker else who wants to have a go I'm both armed and ready to die" I was pushing my forehead into his mouth with each word purely because he was taller than me. "OK man, OK" he said softly. "You go downstairs, you get Betty, you fuck off. Clear?" I said. "Sorry man, sorry, I didn't know you were upset like" he said either genuinely concerned or just wanting to get the crazy lad from care to calm the fuck down. Unfortunately my brain was going in another direction "How did you get here?" I asked.

"Roger brought us, he's around the corner" he said visibly shaking. "Which corner?" I asked holding the knife up. "He's alone man I swear, it's just us" I put the knife under his chin and used it to push his head backwards. "If you're lying I'll do them and then I'll come for you" I told him. "I'm not, you'll see, trust me" He'd gone remarkably calm. I didn't like it. He was telling the truth but that meant he could be dangerous if he thought I had decided to hurt him he could flip. "Get out, I always liked you Timmy but I told you if you visit, you come alone, nobody else." He walked downstairs and Betty followed quickly behind. I never saw them again.

It was around a week later, I was repairing a fence when I heard "What you up to then?" I'd know that voice anywhere. "Inside boys" I said to Arron and Marcus who'd been playing in the garden as I turned around to face Wenzel. He was wearing blue jeans white trainers and his customary suede jacket with his trade mark sunglasses clipped to his normal glasses. "Time for a chat?" He said nodding to my hand which conveniently held a claw head hammer. "Sure" I said using it to point to the chairs by the back door. He still had his hand in his pocket. "So, how you doing? I heard you settled now?" He asked cocking his head and smiling at me. I needed his hands free. "Want a brew?" I asked ignoring the question. "Yeah, can't stop long though" he replied. He was worried I'd call Clive, that's how Wenzel's mind worked. "Wait here, I'll bring it out" I said heading to the kitchen. "Sure, whatever" he said in a carefree tone whilst standing up to see directly into the kitchen. I put the hammer down beside the kettle "Saw what you did with the paper, interesting read" he said "Get much off it?" He added as though he wasn't bothered. "Five hundred quid" I replied putting his cup in reach of him but not to him. I picked up my brew and the hammer. His eyes flinched "Five hundred quid for stabbing me in the back, nicely done" he took his left hand out of his pocket and took the brew. Definitely armed my mind warned me. "We needed food, carpet etc. How's work?" I asked him trying not to let on that I knew he wanted to drop me when I was in the kitchen. I could see it in his eyes but he hadn't tried. I didn't know why but took it as a sign he was waiting for a better opportunity. "I quit, some guy tried grabbing a woman's bag so I dropped him" he said. "Can't work there now as it looks bad me dropping the little shit so I quit." He'd glanced at me when he'd said "Dropping the little shit." I knew he was lying, his eyes always said more than he could ever mean. He'd been fired for being in the newspaper and he'd come to take it out on me. "Not because of the newspaper then?" I asked eyeing him over my coffee. "Nobody cares about your shit lad, I did my time. I'm here nice today but if you ever pull that shit again" he said shaking his head and getting mad. "We've had loads of offers of T.V and newspapers. Right now we're not doing anything, neither of us want it, okay?" He understood but was holding it together "You do what you want but you keep me the fuck out of it, there's Rachael and her kids to think of, did you think of that?" I put my cup down and stood up straight. "I never had a problem with Rachael, don't make this about Rachael. You got involved with her, that's your problem" I walked to the garden and he followed two steps behind me. He didn't like that I wasn't the terrified ten year old any more I was fifteen and I would lamp him if I needed to. I was surprised he was quiet and waited for him to move quickly to hurt me. He didn't, at the front garden I sidestepped and he walked past and got in the car. "I won't come again, you don't exist, keep me out of it!" He said pointing through his red Honda Civic's window. A different vehicle from last time. "Somebody's working" I said ignoring his comment. "Yeah, with some bad people but it pays well, now remember what I said!" He drove off calmly enough but was also full of shit. If he'd worked with people who genuinely were that bad he wouldn't turn up by himself. He'd have brought them with him. "I'm sick of this shit" I told Courtney later that night. "If its not newspapers or family or Wenzel or care or money then it's fucking social workers. I just want a quiet life. No hassle, no needing to be a big head, no bullshit. The sooner I get in the army the better". I still hadn't applied. Courtney was spending money before it was received, I couldn't find a job and we were looking after three kids, additionally the place was spooky as hell and I was not impressed. "Let's go see Dean" I said.

Dean was Courtney's uncle the only family that kept in touch with her, A dirty old man who had his own home with three bedrooms and worked five days a week, I presumed him a dirty old man because Courtney told me a few years ago he'd hit on her. I didn't ask for all the details and didn't relish the idea of accepting his help. However we were in a corner and shit needed to change. I told Dean about the place and situation and Courtney backed it up. Dean said if it got worse then we could stay with him until an exchange became available. He was actually quite decent about it.

We'd all been out for the day, I'd unlocked the front door and Arron shot past me to try on his new trainers. He'd entered the kitchen to put some shopping down first. I was closing the front door when I heard him voice "errrrm Trace?" I went in and he was frozen to the spot. He'd been in the room maybe fifteen seconds before me and was staring straight at the back door glass window, and for good reason. Looking back at him was a face in pure white. We both stood routed for several seconds. It looked like some kind of chalk and had been done on the other side of the door which meant the person had been in the back door but not the kitchen where me and Arron were. My five disc CD player was untouched as was everything else, I checked the doors and windows to find them all locked. It was a male's face and it was smiling at me, taunting. I'm ashamed to say I flipped out. We'd cleaned the windows a couple of days before and it had not been there then. Nobody had been in bar us. I couldn't figure it out and now it was laughing at me. I grabbed the broom and kicked the head off from it and then used the end to put the window through. "You want us out you bastard! You win! Fuck you! Fuck you!" I went off as I put hole after hole into the mesh enforced window. When I finally calmed down I turned to Courtney "Dean's" I nodded and we were packed and gone inside an hour. I promised I'd come back to feed and walk the dogs daily.

Dean was sound and gave us free reign. I slept in between two chairs whilst Courtney took the sofa and the kids had their own room, it was year 2000 and I remember the T.V being full of fireworks. I'd secured a job in Manchester selling stuff out of a bag until I could get in the army. I'd signed up and was awaiting my medical. The pay was commission and so some days was better than others depending on how well I could sell. I worked the pubs, clubs, shops and shopping centre's. I met a fair few unsavories. I remember it was roasting hot and I'd bought a can of coke in the garage and started to head to the mechanic's across the way. A guy came out of the building and I put Mr Smiley on "Hi I'm from Tuscon Marketing, I've got some great stuff if you're interested?" "I asked. "No thanks mate" He said. "No squidgy purple things today? OK mate" I said heading towards the building he'd just left. "Oi, don't go in there. He's not in the mood" He called after me. "It's OK mate. I'll cheer him up" I said all smiles. I should have listened. I pushed open the door maybe two inches before it was flung open. Next minute this guy about a foot taller than me has a spanner around my neck and is half marching half lifting me and choking me off site. He was gobbing off the whole time but I couldn't make out what he was saying through my attempts to breath. "Alright, fuck me relax" I managed to let out as he spun me around and took two swings with the spanner. The first hit my bag and pulled me down onto the wall. I moved as the second swing landed with a grating chink on the wall where my head was previously. Fuck that time to go, I grabbed the bag and did a runner as I heard his mate shout "I did warn him." as guy with spanner started gobbing off at his mate.

Another time I was in a pub and was making alot of good sales when I got called over by a group of lads. "What you got then?" I made a point of always showing one item at a time. They started grabbing at stuff and so I put it back in the bag. "Enough to go around lads, one at a time yeah? Plenty here, photo album just £6 mate you want two for "11?" He looked at me not answering, medium build dark skinned, brown eyes, his mate wasn't looking for trouble but I could feel the tension coming off him. "What if I just keep it?" He said holding it out but not letting go. "You wouldn't do that you're a nice guy, want it for £6?" I asked smiling and not letting go either. "Or" He said snatching it away. "I keep it, what you got to say about that?" He said moving it down to the table as he stood up and pushed his face into mine. He was now eye to eye. I had two choices and I'd been on my feet half the day. Fuck it, I chose the second one "Well, you can give me that back now or I can put you across this table in front of all your friends?" I said calmly. He took two seconds and stepped back slightly as he went to speak I cut him short "Pick one before I do" I added tilting my head slightly. All of a sudden we were best friends "I like you" he said to me "This guy's funny" he told his friends "Here man, only fucking with you" he said handing me the album. My shit was away before anyone could blink. "Have a nice night lads" I said leaving them to it.

In another section of the same pub I saw a skinny white lad chatting away to his mates sat at a table. He kept looking up so had caught my eye. He wasn't watching me but he was wondering who was watching him which I found a little suspicious. Naturally I headed over. "Mind if I show you what I've got guys?" intentionally implying other things and getting a laugh then trying to cover my "Mistake." "Go ahead" the pale lad's mate said. They weren't interested but were very polite and I left thinking I knew him somehow. It wasn't until a few nights later the penny dropped. I'd tried to sell Rodney Trotter some shit out of a bag! I so wish I'd got his autograph!!!

I was due some care leavers money and Tuscan Marketing had promised me my own team if I fronted them two thousand five hundred pounds for the start up and stock. I said I'd think about it. Pay as it stood depended on what I sold as everything was commission based however as a team leader it depended on what my team sold. It sounded good to me but I had little perception of a bigger picture and no idea about business. Their was a blonde girl put with me to train me up for two weeks She laughed at every word I said to the point I actually started saying things that were not funny just to see if she'd laugh, and she did! As much as I realised she was fake as hell I was actually loving the attention. She seemed genuinely interested in anything I had to say. She was quite pretty and only a year older than me. When I told the boss I wasn't sure about putting this money forwards because it seemed his right hand man couldn't count properly the commission she suddenly found another guy just as funny and interesting as she had me. I wasn't going to let it show that it stung after all I was technically with Courtney. Although I had told her as soon as I joined the army I was off. I'd been short changed by the accounts guy several times already and always had it resolved with the boss until one day, He was only out by three pounds but still... The fourth day this happened I took my bag to the boss and asked him to count it up which he did. I told him not to pay me just to do the maths and I took the exact same money and items to his assistant who paid me short. I took my pay and paper confirming amount to the boss and told him "I do his job or I'm out" He tried talking me down. I ignored him, left his bag in the middle of the room and walked out.

Chapter 19

Staff sergeant Mike Paye was his name. I remember walking to the Armed forces careers information office in Manchester for the first time. They had a little quiz for people interested in signing up. I remembered what Karl had said about not telling them about him. I wondered why not? After twenty questions and the quiz I was asked if I had anything against various cultures and how I'd feel if I was sent to an active zone. "I have no family. It's part of the job" I replied as I dreamt about row after row of women watching me master an assault course with an M16 slung over my back. Mike ran through my answers on the quiz. I knew every weapons question but had failed a maths question. "We'll work on that" he told me handing me his card. I wanted the uniform. It was where I belonged. Putting my life on the line for others and knowing that they would do the same for me. I wanted the comrade, I wanted the morale, I wanted the family. I loved the idea and I hit training hard. "Oh and get a hair cut" MIke told me tugging my long brown hair gently and laughing. I visited every week just to see how my application was coming along. Mark took me to lunch one day. I was dead impressed that he had a CD player in his car. "Why do you really want in?" He asked me. "I've wanted in since I stood in front of my uncle's beret. He severed 22 years in the Cheshire regiment and boxed for his country. My father killed my mother. When I lost my mother I knew it was the life for me. I promised my friend I'd return one day in full military uniform and I will." He seemed to understand. I liked Mike.

My basic training forms had just come through. I was to go to Lichfield for my medical. Then I was to take the physical directly afterwards. I wasn't worried about the physical I knew I'd fly through that. "Don't mention your shoulder" Karl's words echoed through me. I was two days away from sitting the Medical and I'd just got home from a run. "Babe?" Said Courtney as soon as I'd closed the door. "What?" I asked not really looking at her and chucking water on my face from the kitchen tap. "I'm pregnant" she said "What!?" I asked. "I'm pregnant" she repeated. I was in total shock. My world shook. This couldn't be? This wasn't planned. I wanted to be a dad but not now, not with her.. "I'm joining the army" I said feeling like a bastard. "I know. I'm sorry" She said... "are you sure?" I asked. We had a big long chat over two days about how sure she was that she was pregnant and the best course of action to take from here. I couldn't abort, she could but I couldn't. I didn't want kids with her but now I felt I had one I couldn't not have one. I couldn't kill a child. If she was pregnant it was probably mine and so I'd take responsibility for it. I'd do whatever was needed but I had to see if I could get in the army too. Was I good enough? I sat upstairs wide awake the whole night before Lichfield looking at my piles of military books, leaflets and paperwork. I sat there just staring at them for over an hour. Then I picked the lot up and carried them downstairs I opened the front door, opened the big black bin and dropped the lot inside. Courtney was downstairs on the sofa "I'm going to see if I can get in. Whatever happens we'll have that child. We don't get on now like we did but we'll work on that for the kid, okay?" She agreed, her eyes were full of tears of relief. It was as though she'd got what she wanted. Whether this was natural behaviour, me reading too much into things because of a feeling of low self worth or just me being overly analytical and distrusting because of the past and wanting to join the army I didn't know.

I went to Lichfield where I sat patiently for hours before taking a sight and hearing test then filling in some more forms and then the medical. Pass, pass, pass and I felt great! Yet feelings of being a dad kept cropping up and I couldn't seem to shake them. I could be here surrounded by military personnel, friends and a secure environment learning a trade and here I was thinking about how that child would survive without me. I certainly couldn't leave it with Courtney alone. Look how she treats her own children? "Is there anything else we need to know or you think we should know before your physical?" Asked the very polite young man at the end of the hall. I knew the wrong answer and I gave it to him. "I can dislocate my shoulder at will. It doesn't affect me physically but watch" I said popping my shoulder out and then in again. "I'm sorry lad, you can't get in" he said. "Don't mention your shoulder" I heard Karl say in my head. Fuck it, I'd done right by my kid but I wasn't giving up "other options?" I asked. "Well you can sit another medical we'll send you to a doctor but the result will be the same" he answered. "Can you set it up?" I asked. He agreed he would. I returned home and started applying for jobs. "Why do you want to work for McDonald's?" A guy in Manchester asked me. I had no work, no interview skills and no qualifications. I also had no idea what to say "I've worked warehouses before mate it's not much different is it? I've got kids they need to be fed it's that simple mate" I said leaning forwards and opening my arms because I'd read somewhere body language was important and opening my arms apparently made me look like I had nothing to hide. He was a thin weasley looking man with black hair and eyes. I didn't like him but figured I could work for him if it meant my kid was happy besides, people respect honesty right? Wrong. I was turned down for every job I applied for including that one.

After spending the day handing leaflets out I walked into an undertakers. "My name's Tracie, call me Trace. I've tried everywhere, I know it's a long shot but got any work for me?" Looking back the guy was really decent about it considering he could have just laughed at me. "Got any qualifications?" He asked behind a large oak desk all suited. "No sir but I learn fast and well...I saw both my grandparents die, my mum was murdered so I can handle death you see and I tried to join the army so I don't mind dirty jobs. You could always train me up?" I said full of hope and enthusiasm. He informed me I'd have to go to college and then university for a long, long time to do his job. At home I was ranting out loud "turned down by fucking McDonald's!?" Wenzel was right I am useless I thought. I did the only thing I could think of that might give me some idea of advice, I called him.

I was going to be a dad I needed dad advice. What was I supposed to do? "Hi listen, I need advice" I said. "What you done this time?" He said. I didn't argue "Courtney's pregnant" I said just as he started laughing. "I told you to use your head with a bird, but then if you'd used your head you wouldn't be in this mess would you?" He started cackling at his own joke. He didn't mean protection it was an oral sex joke. "Oh that's brilliant! Best laugh yet" he said as I hung up. Yeah I was a joke but I was a joke who'd die before he'd not take care of his kid.

I went to see Mike again, maybe I was looking for guidance, maybe I wanted out. I wasn't sure "What other ways in?" I asked him "well, you could do six months in the T.A then get a transfer" he told me. "T.A? Toy soldiers?" I asked him. Apparently they weren't like that any more...and if it could get me into the real army... what's six months in the grand scheme of things? I signed up. The guy who signed me up was more interested in showing me his screen saver where the girls bikini fell off. He was a big fat fella who thought he had a sense of humour. "Look mate, I've got my missus's kid with me I'd rather not do the tits out bit at the minute....could you tell me what else you do here?" He nodded to his pc "Here look at this...." he said loading a game up.. I walked out with her lad. Six months of that I could not handle. My old scout leader would be ashamed. I was an hour from heading away for my second medical when Courtney stopped me "I need to talk to you, it's about the baby" she said. "Okay, what's up?" I asked her. "No, no nothing, you've got a big day ahead. You go I'll be fine" she said. "Look if there's a problem I'm here. What's the matter?" I asked. "You sure on the name?" She asked. "That it?" I replied. "Yeah" she said. I told her we'd talk tonight and I left. When I finally reached Lichfield both hungry and thirsty it was a private doctors. The receptionist asked if I'd had a good journey? I'd never been to a private doctors before or since and was cautious "erm, yeah" I replied. "Would you like anything to drink?" she asked me. I was gob smacked. I grew up on a council estate and wasn't used to the etiquette. A doctors offering me a drink? They must think I'm fucking royalty. I declined but made a mental note that these military guys were made of money. The doc saw me and asked me to lift my arms up. I did that just fine and then he said we were done. That was my entire physical. "You have a subluxive shoulder displacement" he informed me. "What?" I asked. "You have a recurrent dislocative shoulder" he said "yeah I know that" I replied "but it only does it when I want it to." I said. "Sorry son, you can't get in. Let's say you're on active service with four mates in the field and the enemy is all around. Your shoulder pops and gives away your position, what happens next?" He asked. I hate to admit it but he had a point. Fuck. "Look if you want to contest it you need a civilian doctor to say your shoulder's fine. Then we could look at it again but the truth is the answer would be the same" He said sincerely. I thanked him and left. A civilian doctor to say I'm fine? No problem. I'd once told a lady doctor I'd had about my mum and she'd fallen apart in front of me. I was pretty sure I could swing it so she'd say anything I wanted her to. She had a soft spot for me and hell I was Wenzel's son if need be I'd turn the charm on. I'd got home late the doctors was closed and Courtney was asleep.

I left early after getting the kids up for school. "There's a bit of a wait I'm afraid" the cute receptionist told me. I Smiled and clutched my head "Tell her I've got terrible head pains and I feel like I'm dying" I said winking at her. She eyed me with a smile "one moment." When she returned I was ushered straight in. I gave her a wink "Thanks." I said. "I believe you're dying Mr Daily" She asked looking up over her glasses. "Yup, dying to see you doc" I replied. I got a telling off which I totally expected and then somehow managed to talk her around... She'd be happy to sign that I was fit for civilian work but she couldn't sign to say I was fit for military service which was fine for me. The military doc didn't say which service he just said to get someone to say I was fit for service. "Fair play thanks doc and just out of curiosity what is the truth exactly?" I asked. She sighed like she was about to give me bad news. "The truth is over time your shoulder has got worn cartilage and that will get worse. We'll be able to operate with a metal pin but you'll only be able to move it up and down or side to side not both" "Can I be honest doc?" I asked. "Sure, " She motioned palms up and shrugging. "We'll fuck that off then eh? Whilst I can still use it fine then I will. When I can't then you can pin it. Deal?" She laughed and I realised she was super cute when she laughed.

When I got home to update Courtney Dean was at work and she was watching T.V all smiles until she saw me. "I lost it" she said straight away. "What? Erm, what happened?" I asked not sure whether to hold her or not, she started crying. "I was on the loo and it just sort of fell out" she said. I questioned everything. I had no reason to doubt her. She'd had four children but something didn't feel right. "Was it formed?" She was only about a month in and I knew nothing at all about pregnancy. "Yeah, it was tiny. Little blood" She replied. Something wasn't adding up and I was putting it down to my brain not working correctly, shock? "Why didn't you call me?" I asked blaming myself. We'd chosen names. I was ready or at least part ready. "You shouldn't have to deal with this on your own" I added. "I didn't, Dean was with me. Don't tell him I told you he's really embarrassed" She said. I didn't know what to say so I just held her until she slept. Dean was on night shift and Courtney was out like a light. Perhaps if I'd not tried to join the army? Maybe if we'd of had our own place? Maybe if I'd of stayed home? The stress I caused could have done it, I believed that. I believed whole heartedly the stress I caused had meant a baby passed all because of my selfishness" I sat in silence for a few days whilst Dean and Courtney watched T.V and chatted. I did nothing but sit in that chair and when Dean went to work I tried comforting Courtney. She didn't want to talk about it in front of Dean because apparently he'd once lost a child. Courtney didn't appear to need comforting as though she'd somehow dealt with it. She kept telling me what's done was done and I shouldn't keep going on about it. I presumed she was in shock and didn't realise that she wasn't ready to deal with it yet. I offered to make food for all of us but Dean was getting ready for work.

Dean was washing his hands I approached him. "She asked me not to say anything and I'm sorry it's taken me a while but I just want to say thanks man. I should have been here" I held my hand out to shake his and his reply lingers to this day "What you on about?" he said genuinely bemused, his curly grey hair covering one eye "It's okay, she's told me about the..." I started crying "baby" I added. He shook his head "I'm sorry, I don't know what you're on about. You need to talk to Courtney" I nodded. "Okay, I understand if it's hard for you" I said walking away with my head down. "No lad, I don't know what you mean" he said nodding to me and closing the door behind him.

I told Courtney I was going for a work and walked out about five minutes later. I didn't tell her I'd spoke to Dean. Who could give me answers? Why would she lie? She wouldn't, surely? She's had four kids. How well do you know anyone I asked myself. Fuck it, I needed to see her doctor, it was the only answer. I had to argue with the receptionists until he finally agreed to see me. "Okay doc, I don't know how to say this but - How can I help her now she's lost a child?" He looked at me blankly and told me he couldn't discuss Courtney. I told him my story and explained I needed to know for sure. He told me he couldn't discuss Courtney but could help me with information about pregnancy. He told me about morning sickness, she'd had none. Mood swings - none, Pregnancy test-none, Check ups - none. He was a good doctor and to get him to even explain I'd had to be quite persuasive and I'd hated myself for it because he was a good man. I'd come away with the truth, a clear conclusion and although I didn't know the why I did know the conclusion. I walked in looked through her and said with no feeling "we are done, we are civil for the sake of your kids but the first chance I get, I'm off. No questions" She asked, begged, pleaded, threw a strop. I wouldn't budge. I either replied "No questions" or

"Not interested" I hated her but hated myself for hating a woman too. I felt it made me just like Wenzel and I still felt like I'd lost a child. Like the baby had been real, I had a name! I had shock, emptiness and pain. What the doctor and Dean said didn't take that away. My knowledge didn't change my pain, another hit to a growing list. I was heartbroken.

Chapter 20

A girl with dark red hair knocked on our door breaking me out of the repetitive silence. It was 1999 because I remember the lead up to the millennium celebrations was on T.V. Still She was about seventeen and I was letting her run through what was obviously a sales pitch before I'd close the door on her. Except I heard the word "Karate" and my ears pricked up. I'd had an idea, I asked her to come in and I spoke to Courtney. Inside half an hour I was working for a club which went door to door getting people to sign up to their form of Karate. In return I got a poor pay by commission package however included in that was free Karate training. Anything I made I gave to Courtney out of either habit or guilt. I still blamed myself for the baby. Getting anything for myself was simply out of the question. Not because of Courtney but because I wouldn't have deemed myself important enough, for anything apart from my smokes. Some days I made eighty and other days I just came home with a five pound note. We had free training weekly though. free use of sauna and swimming pool and then a sales hour where we concentrated on different sales techniques. Sensei Wayne ran our group and I was soon asking for more and more information every time their was a lesson. Apparently there were our style clubs all over the country. However whenever I asked for written material, background history or something showing me the Kata's I got very little feedback every time. We had a grading system however it was exactly the same as a local Karate club's of a different style. I really enjoyed both the work and the training for a while"You work here now, you're one of us." Wayne would tell me often. Soon Courtney and I got a new place in Whitefield and I simply stopped going.

I thanked Dean and told him he was welcome anytime. Home still wasn't home, I always had the mentality that home was in my mind. I had seen more than most at an early age and thought I knew it all. It could only stay the same level of shit I'd always had, right? So why worry, home's just a building. I was a confidant survivor but an unconfident person. It took about a week before Arron was truanting school due to bullies and Courtney was keeping Marcus from school because she was lonely again as I was refusing to talk to her still. We had plenty of arguments about his education. "Don't tell me how to bring my kids up!" She'd yell with Marcus stood behind her. "I'm telling you how not to you stupid cow!" I'd retaliate. It was all pointless, my social worker knew nothing other than I'd failed the army and I wanted away from Courtney. To be fair he'd offered me another foster placement and I'd told him to shove it. I wasn't going back into care. I wanted my own place. He came back a week later and offered me a halfway house. A place where I'd have my own room, be with other children from care who have some kind of requirement and who have someone on site to help them with cooking, cleaning and paying the bills but I was adamant "Do I look like I need help cleaning? Paying the bills? I look after her and her children as well as myself. I need my own place. If I start hanging around with kids with issues I'll either end up joining them or hurting them. I ain't interested get me a flat of my own" I'd tell him. and he'd explain that it wasn't possible and he was right. He was a decent guy and I knew he was doing the right thing and I even knew the halfway house was a good call it was just that I was sick of running, sick of moving and Courtney had become regular.... stupid, argumentative, pointless, bad for me and down right wrong but at least she was stationary. She wasn't going anywhere and that I hated as much as I liked. I'd got what I can only describe as comfortable with the routine. Even if that routine was hating being there at least I could come and go as I pleased and nobody was trying to kick my ass daily. Besides, Wenzel was in a halfway house when he came out of prison and I associated them with him. I'd not killed anyone. I wasn't a criminal. I didn't have plans as such I just knew once my care leavers money came in I'd buy a PC. With that I could advertise for people and make money, how hard could it be? In the mean time I signed up for two catalogues which allowed me to make money on a commission basis, both of which flunked as soon as they'd started. I signed up for a private investigation course paid for by social services and dropped out at the first hurdle. Who did I have to impress? Nobody gave a damn, why should I? Nobody cared about me and neither did I. This wasn't teenage bravado this was just plain fact. I wasn't upset, it wasn't my attitude, it was just life and I was used to it. I was also getting to the point that there was no point in trying if all that was going to happen was that I'd fail.

Chapter 21

The care leavers money had come through and I treated myself to a first edition X Files magazine. It was my prize possession I'd been watching it for years and had a big thing for Gillian Anderson, I was officially off the care system and an adult. No ties and no review meetings. I could do as I pleased and I got myself a thick brown heavy leather jacket from a second hand shop. It was ugly as hell and twice as comfortable. The rest I spent on poor choices considering we had no carpets or curtains but I spent on the kids. They got a playstation, a pool table, space crusade board game and the house got a new dining room table. I gave Courtney money for rent and nothing else. I'd been sleeping on the sofa since we moved in. I liked my own space and didn't like being touched much unless it was simply sex. I wasn't good generally in an intimate sense. When Courtney ran her fingers through my hair before it had felt like she was mothering me and I hated that. I couldn't relax but wasn't aware I'd actually never really relaxed around anyone apart from with Anne or being alone at Pettypool. I was definitely my happiest when I was in the woods in the middle of nowhere.

I couldn't sleep so fired up the PC. It wasn't long before I'd encountered chat rooms on AOL. I could be anyone, from anywhere and talk about anything. I'd been talking to several different people all of them female and concocting different stories for each. I was enjoying the thrill of not being me and seeing how people reacted differently to each situation. It was brilliant that I didn't have to be me. I was talking to a lass on there for about two weeks. She thought I was twenty one when I was actually nearly eighteen. She also thought I owned the house I was living in and that I taught Karate to kids in care for a living. She promised to call and help me set the speakers up to my pc. I told her Courtney and her kids were staying with me for the time being as they had nowhere to go due to an abusive ex husband. The house was actually Council and in Courtney's name and so I gave her my number. I told Courtney she was calling later and to make herself scarce or at least leave me alone whilst I sorted these speakers out. Courtney was not impressed and ranted the rest of the day. I told her again and again that we were done. "What do you want from me?" I asked her repeatedly. To which the answer was the same "You used to love me, I want us back" I told her there was no us and never would be. To be fair it can't have been easy for her but hey, she'd lied to me and despite my lies I hated any kind of lie being told to me and believed whole heartedly that I'd fight fire with with. If she hurt me, I'd hurt her more. Although I was never physical with her I was cruel during our arguments. I could see myself turning into Wenzel when she started. "You can't mother your own children what makes you think I'd let you mother mine?" I wanted her to slip up, I wanted her to admit she'd lied about the baby. I wanted her to grieve like I was grieving but she never did. I told her Dean had no idea and that I'd seen her doctor. She told me Dean had lost a child and wouldn't discuss anything with anyone due to his bad memories. I told her she was talking shit and I knew it. The woman online was called Megan and I arranged for her to call another night. I was drained by the time Courtney had done talking and I still didn't believe her.

A couple of days of weird silences passed with me just speaking to Megan via text or the internet and ignoring Courtney. I knew the day would come when I'd be moving out so I started decreasing the amount of time I spent with the children. I stopped playing Hogs of war with the kids on the playstation. I stopped playing Space Crusade and I stopped helping Arron with his homework. Marcus never had any on account of Courtney not sending him to school and to be fair if It was anything mathematical I was horrendous at anyway.

I was sat on the sofa staring through the T.V and thinking about how to make a clean break when I realised I'd only ever met Dean from Courtney's family and only every spoken to her once about my family and her ex's which all turned out to be violent affairs and so I knew very little about her. She had no photograph's and never spoke about her parents. I was sat on the edge of the sofa turned to the T.V with my back to Courtney. I didn't want to give her any reason to speak to me but she was still rattling on and had been for hours. There was only us in the house and I was completely blanking her despite her being on the same sofa but at the other end. It was then I started to feel a vibration, what I can only describe as an internal humming. What I didn't know then is this could well have been the start of an entirely different kind of breakdown.

I wasn't paying any attention to the T.V despite looking straight through it and I wasn't paying any attention to Courtney. I looked at Courtney and back at the T.V, she gave me a strange look as it was the only time I'd vaguely acknowledged her. It got more faint when I wasn't concentrating on something but when I concentrated on it then it vanished altogether. I stared back to the T.V and tuned both Courtney and the T.V out again and it returned. The more I tuned them out the more it increased. I looked back at Courtney and saw a mist on the chair "You're seeing things" I told myself turning back to the T.V when I immediately felt "No, you're not" then an "It's okay" it added. I looked back knowing that the feeling was coming from the chair to see a male with blue jeans a white open shirt and trainers sat on the chair in the living room. "What's up with you?" Courtney asked me. "Shut up for a minute and listen" I replied calmly. There was no malice, no danger and nothing negative in this entire situation. It felt perfectly calm and perfectly normal. As though what I was experiencing should be what we all experience at all times however I knew with my rational self that what I was experiencing definitely wasn't usual. The male smiled. He was wearing no jewellery apart from a watch. His hair was fair and quiffed but short. Both hands rested on the arms of the chairs and it was as though he knew I'd be looking for signs of danger from him. He showed none what so ever. I spoke to Courtney but didn't take my eyes off the man in the chair. His eyes were light and calm, almost welcoming as though he wanted me to know more. "What

I'm going to say now sounds crazy. If you think I'm nuts I want you to just call an ambulance, the funny farm or whoever straight away, okay?" I was worried my past had started to catch up with me and that perhaps being in care & losing my family had sent me over the edge. Again I wasn't panicking, I was merely very intrigued but at this point I was willing to take Courtney's opinion as better judgement than my own. Which should confirm I definitely wasn't in the correct state of mind. "What you talking about? You're acting weird" she said. "Promise me?" I said firmly pointing at her briefly but looking at the man still. "Okay..." she said standing to get her drink from the table and then sitting back on the cream sofa just a hairs width further away from me than she was previously. I explained what I could see and asked her if she could see anything. She couldn't. She wanted to know more. "Am I crazy?" I asked her genuinely concerned. "It's possible with my past you know, I don't feel crazy. He seems calm and happy enough." I added. "What else?" Courtney asked. "I don't know, I am saying what I see. He's not here for me. He never lived here." I added. "What else?" she said "I don't know, I don't know anything...there's a guy sat in the chair that's all I know" "Okay, how do you know he's not lived here before?" She asked. "I don't know. I just do" I said with certainty. The man gestured at Courtney with his hand but kept smiling at me. I shook my head. What I felt he was indicating was too hard to do and even if it was right would I want it? Would I want someone telling me some spirit had appeared and wanted to talk to them but couldn't so was talking through me? Nonsense I'd laugh them into next year. There's no way on this planet I was accepting that. "Nothing" I said to Courtney. "I'll describe him again" I added and did. "What's his name?" She asked me which was a fair question. If he's here he must know his name, right? "I don't know, I can't hear him and I don't want to, that would be too real" I said. "Okay, ask him?" She said. "What's your name?" I asked in my head. I knew he could hear my thoughts but I also knew he could only pick up thoughts I wanted him to hear. Again I have no idea how I knew this but I felt it to be true. I immediately confused myself by wondering what If what I knew was exactly what he wanted me to know and he was knowing all of my thoughts and creating himself through my mind and he wasn't real at all. I justified asking his name by the fact I could see him sat on the chair and if I'd created him or he was using me then neither of us would have gone to the trouble of creating an image of a person. I saw an empty lemonade bottle in my head as though I'd visualised it but I hadn't. He'd put it there as though on a screen but without the actual screen just there in my head. I started telling Courtney what he was showing me "I see bottles, loads of bottles, I'm joking with a guy whilst a wagon is packed full of bottles" the entire scene had changed I was now this man and seeing what he had seen. I was both in the house on the sofa and somewhere else entirely seeing what this man was showing me as though it was his life. "I's 8:52am it's on my dashboard. I'm taking a corner and there's a car coming" I explained as the scene played out in front of me like a movie I could feel. "I wanted to say I'm fine. I never got a chance to say bye" I said turning from the man to Courtney and I was humming with the same vibration I'd had initially. I could feel it like a motor was implanted in every area of my body. Courtney was in tears and I immediately thought I'd said something awful and mean and that I was totally insane and should be in the loony bin before I became a danger to myself or others. "I'm crazy aren't I? I'll call them. I'll tell the social workers first" I said pulling out my old Nokia with the twist off antenna. "No, no" Courtney said sniffing. "His name's Graham, he's my brother" she said sobbing. "So...he's real?" I asked her. "I mean....I see him and whatever he sends me but he's erm...actually alive? Erm was alive?" I asked her tripping over all my words and trying to ignore Graham was still sat there but had crossed his legs. I nodded to Graham apologetically like I was sorry I mistook that he was dead and for some reason I should show that some respect even though he seemed as alive as Courtney and I. Ironic considering he seemed more worried about whether I was okay or not than if he was alive or not. I was comfortable, normal even but knowing I was experiencing something abnormal.

Courtney asked me more questions. I kept tell her to just ask them out loud as he could hear her and then he could tell me and so it was a bit awkward. It was even stranger when I tried explaining that he could feel her thoughts too so technically she didn't have to ask me anything she could just ask in her head and he'd tell me and then I'd tell her. I answered questions for hours and then he left. Most seemed to comfort or upset her which both appeared to be kind of the same thing. Graham let me know he'd be back through a feeling he sent me. Courtney and I spent the rest of the night talking about Graham Courtney routinely asking "Is he here?" and me replying with similar things to "No, well I can't see or feel him so I don't think so?" I felt a right idiot saying to an empty room "Graham, are you here? Graham?" Nothing.

Over the next few weeks things were happening daily. Things I couldn't explaining and even bordered on pointless but that happened none the less. My mobile rang as I was lay on the sofa facing the ceiling with the phone on the floor. Patrick's face had jumped in front of my line of sight. "Your phone" Courtney said from the pc behind me "No point, it's Patrick It's contact" I said seeing Jonathon and Jodie in my head "I'm not invited" I said and sat up to watch T.V and take my mind of it. Courtney passed me the phone "Patrick" Flashed on screen. "Answer it" she said and I did. He told me what I already knew. "As you're not in a care placement and visited Wenzel and other family we don't feel it's suitable you see Jonathon and Jodie" He said. "Fuck off Patrick, Lynne and Sampson don't feel it's suitable. You'd lose your job if you stopped a court appointed contact" I replied."Yeah well, okay they don't think it's good for you or them" he said. "Thanks" I replied and hung up. He called back and I ignored it.

Maybe it was the baby stuff, maybe it was the lack of family or maybe I was just having a breakdown. I didn't know all I knew was that despite missing Jonathon & Jodie like they were organs I wasn't actually lonely. I loved my own company I just missed Jonathon and Jodie. I wanted Caroline around and family as a whole that I felt I'd never have but I wasn't lonely. I was however pissed off that I couldn't see them and sad that their was nothing I could do about it. I'd chose to move away from Macclesfield so I wouldn't keep going to visit them. The closer I was the more I'd just up sticks and go to them. I went for a bath. "Graham, Graham?" I said over and over in my mind. Nothing, I tried the visualising thing. I figured if I could see him then perhaps he'd turn up. Nothing. Then I started getting angry. "Well fuck you then Graham, perhaps I'm just nuts and if I am then fuck you! Who are you to turn up randomly in my head? Fuck off!" Nothing. I couldn't conjure him up at will or perhaps I just couldn't communicate sometimes and could at others. It wasn't like I just had a magic switch just like I couldn't just go and see Jonathon and Jodie.

I was talking to Courtney about Graham and why he would turn up one minute and not the next? What could he possibly have to do that's so important? How does time work over there? Why can I see him but not the millions upon millions of other spooks that must be dotted around? Courtney told me she felt sad for me that I could see Graham but not my mum. I told her it would be too weird if I saw my family and I'd never believe it even if I did. I felt sad that I could see Graham and she couldn't or at least that I'd had that one experience We were chatting away like friends when the door bell went. "I'll go, it's the debt man" I told her knowing I was right before I reached the hall. I opened the door and he was suited and booted which I'll admit was a bit unusual. He always looked smart but not that smart. "I won't be a minute mate" I said grabbing his card and cash out of the tin in the kitchen. As I passed him the card to stamp his fingers accidentally touched mine and as they did a bolt of grief went up my arm and into the back of my head and before I knew it I was talking "Fuck me mate, who died?" I said without thinking. "My mother in law" He said jaw dropping. "Erm, sorry to hear that." I said making sure not to touch him again as I took the card. I could feel Graham immediately behind me and wondered if debt man could sense him. Graham had appeared instantly and without warning. No vibration, no massive light, no sirens nothing just one minute a standard life as routine as normality and then Zap bolt of grief up the arm and wham Graham stood behind me.

I walked into the living room through the doorway after leaving a bewildered debt man on the front door step where I'd simply closed the door on him as Graham walked through the wall and sat on his chair in the living room. "He's here" I said realising Graham did everything for a reason. Including walking through the wall. He was answering my questions. "Why sit on a chair?" I asked him without explaining. I knew he could read my thoughts. "Would you rather I stand?" He replied meeting the sarcasm. "I mean, why sit at all? Do you even feel relaxed?" He was starting to answer with something about fields of existence like sometimes I'm awake and sometimes asleep and it's the same for them but different although the long and the short of it is without a body they don't get tired and so no don't need to rest he did it out of technicality because it makes me feel better. I asked him if his usual existence was just floating around then and he went on to explain that I wouldn't understand and it's more just about varying degree's of vibrating light and that we can and do exist in all of it to varying levels. He didn't answer any of my questions whilst actually answering them. I was irritated with him. "Brew?" I said to Courtney as I got up and headed to the kitchen. Graham's in the hall I told Courtney as she came into the kitchen to talk to me whilst I brewed up. It was still light out but early evening the neighbours Koi Carp were being attacked by the cats again and I banged on the window. "How does this work?" I asked Graham. He showed me no pictures and I heard nothing but I felt the words "I can feel you instantly with your thoughts. I can choose to come or not but you can't always see me. We have to think the same to be in touch" I knew he was right but I was human.

"I need an off switch, how?" I asked him trying to keep my questions short and monotone. "Same as before, vibration the same" he said and I felt. "Before I'd been ignoring Courtney and this time you appeared instantly with the debt guy, why?" I asked him. "Want me to go?" I felt him ask and I knew then that he already knew the answer and knew I didn't want him to leave but I wanted to know more. It was polite of him to ask and it was genuine but it was starting to confuse and annoy me. "No," I said mentally presuming he was actually meaning did I want the experiences to stop. I looked at Courtney "I want to test this" I told her. She looked at me quizzically "I need to know it's real" I added. Graham was in the kitchen no idea what he was doing but I explained to Courtney he'd come into the kitchen from the hall. "Why?" She asked. "No idea, he's stood slightly behind you looks like he's spinning two small balls around in his hand" She gasped but less shocked than she was initially, by now I wasn't surprised I just didn't know if Courtney was going along with everything I said or if Graham was real "Worry balls, he used to keep them in his truck" she told me. "He's moved again he's sat on the sideboard kicking his feet against the wood." I said. She laughed "He was always like that" she replied "Why can't I see him?" she asked and I knew she was asking him, not me. I was about to say "I'm sorry, I don't know" when it hit me from Graham "Because you're too close, it's too hard. Emotions make us question everything and if you can't be clear you can't communicate" I told Courtney what I felt but felt like an ass. "So I can't talk to my family?" I asked him. I immediately felt warm all over as though he'd hugged me but he hadn't moved. "No, but you might see them if they are around" he said. "Okay, thanks... I'm fine with that" I replied and realised I actually was fine with that...how could I possibly live my life if I was forever in the pockets of dead relatives? It hit me again this time like a book slamming closed "If you question me and so you should, how much would you question Alan or your Mum?" He didn't need an answer. I followed Courtney into the living room after she'd asked if it was OK to go through or would he find it rude we just walked off. I explained it didn't work like that but we went through anyway. Graham walked back through the wall and I realised how limited we were as humans. "He doesn't need to eat or sit. He walked through the wall. He sits out of choice to fit in, to show the true him to us as we or in this case you knew him when in actual fact yes he's Graham but he's so much more. He's like a very real, very solid memory. It's Graham in whole independent thought but there's more to him. More we can't see or understand yet" Graham seemed pleased with my explanation but I wasn't done. I was scratching just the surface of my questions and with each answer a hundred more questions appeared. Each question brought answers I didn't understand or open ended. Emotions were our biggest flaw as humans and needed the most for lessons as humans. Emotions were what could be used to communicate if tuned properly. Love was hugely important to them as though it gave them something like to us would be electricity to them is love and as much as I said them I also meant us for we are them just encased in a human form. "We are all connected" he finally sent me. I accepted it but didn't understand it "I question everything" I sent him back. He smiled. He was friendly and I was cautious. I liked having him around. I turned to Courtney.

"Is there anything you know about Graham that I don't? If there is concentrate on that I'll try and get Graham to tell me it" I said. "He had a pet, what was it?" Courtney said audibly for both of us to hear. "Okay..." I replied relaxing and looking through Graham. I saw Graham by his truck. I walked around it in my head but saw no pets. The scene changed and I started to speak to Courtney "I'm walking in a field I don't see any pets. I'm visiting a lady, she's young. Brown hair, eyes are light but brown...it's you...there's a field outside to the right...a blue car to the field entrance.. another man...no, that's all I get" I said opening my eyes to see Courtney and Graham again.

"That happened Yes, I was with Tony at the time" She said as thought recalling a memory "Wait" I cut her off Graham in the chair bent down as the atmosphere in the room changed again he put his hand down and a medium sized white dog appeared beneath his hand. It's fur was really thick and white I spoke quickly taking it all in without thinking about what I was saying at all. "Thick fur, white dog, male, light eyes, thick fur Sammy? Sam? He's playful Silver chain not worn now had silver chain" Courtney was crying again she ran upstairs and I just sat dumbfounded looking at Graham and this big white dog which again was strangely human. Courtney returned with a tag with "Sammy" Etched into it. "We gave him away when he died. He wasn't in the truck. He died soon after and I took the tag" She told me. I was trying to understand how she got the tag if she'd given the dog away and then understand who I'd said the name Sammy and had her provide me with a dog tag with "Sammy" written on it that I'd never seen before...had she hinted at her brother owning a dog? I didn't think so when I felt "How you finding this?" in a deep male vibration that wasn't coming from Graham.

Chapter 22

"Too soon" Graham said. Why let me feel or understand "Too soon?" If it was too soon? Why not just pretend nobody had heard "How you finding this?" Apart from me? "You can understand me?" I asked the white dog "no language, all feelings" He replied as way of explanation and turned away and walked straight through the wall. "You won't believe this" I told Courtney. I went on to explain about the dog which I kept calling a husky type dog but wasn't a husky and it really annoyed me for ages that I didn't know there was a dog called a Samoyed. Which is what Sammy was. Graham was a regular occurrence for around three weeks maybe longer. I didn't tell Megan at first, we'd become a regular "online couple" which was a weird thing to say the least but worked for both of us. No attachment and no physical expectations. Neither of us had seen pictures of the other. I'd literally got to the point where I could turn on and off the spiritual side almost at will. Sometimes were worse than others but mostly got clear connections. So I presumed Graham would be around forever. However I wanted to progress personally with whatever this situation was. I wanted to know more about it. How to use it. What it could be good for and what ways it worked. Megan said she knew about birth charts, tarot and horoscopes. She'd later tell me she collected crystals. I knew very little about any of these things. She lived in Kent which was a long way away from me and she had an over powering mother. He ex had abused her sexually and physically and again I believed her. It wasn't until a couple of weeks down the line that the stories started to take a more sinister turn. "I worked for m16" She told me on the phone one day. I presumed it was some kind of role play thing and turned it into a joke. Later on she'd approach the subject again. "I worked for mi6" she said simply and not usually in context to anything. "Don't you mean mi5?" I asked having never heard of Mi6. "Nope, I was a secret agent... " she went on to tell me a story about her being an assassin hired by the government however none of her stories added up and she tripped up several times explaining the weapon's she'd had to use incorrectly. I cared enough to know something wasn't right and that she was a bit weird but not enough to actually think anything serious could come of her lies. After all she was listening to me rattling on about my past and I'd told her some huge lies and she'd accepted me when I'd told her the truth. Perhaps It was time I broke down some of her barriers. Who knows? Perhaps it would work out. I told her that her story fell apart but that I didn't care that she'd lied. She insisted she hadn't and that she'd been having panic attacks due to the agoraphobia and depression and so took too many tranquillizers which apparently made her act funny and say silly things. Having no experience of tranquillizers I took this at face value. I confided in her about me wanting to join the army and Courtney saying about the baby. I spent half that night in tears. Most of our conversations were online. Megan could read just fine but her spelling was poor due to a form of dyslexia she said.

I was talking to Courtney about Megan when she asked if I'd told her about Graham yet. I said no as an idea hit me "Pass me a book" I said pointing to the book shelf. She grabbed a history book and I flicked through it until it fell on a picture of an Egyptian death mask. "Perfect" I said. It wasn't real because it was a clay copy of the mask. I intended to "tune in" to that and see what I could pick up. I gave the book back to Courtney having taken a mental picture. For the next ten minutes I relaxed my breathing and found the vibration and then increased it whilst concentrating on the image in my head. The image became fully formed and turned golden with green and orange around the neck area. Then when I got nothing more I'd finally had enough and tried closing down.. I couldn't. "Won't go away?" I told Courtney "Oh" She replied helpfully. "Suggestions?" I asked her panicking slightly but trying to keep a lid on things. "It's in my head, perhaps a quarter to the right covering over a quarter of my sight and it won't go away. It's not a spirit, it's doesn't communicate but it won't leave either" I told her. I was worried after five minutes and after ten I'd tried drinking, eating, having a wash and jumping up and down but nothing was working. I put the T. V on and told it to leave. I swore at it. I visualised it vanishing. No luck. Eventually after a couple of hours it just ceased to be there. I threw the book away and vowed to learn to control it. I called the first Psychic medium I could find with all the extras in a magazine for £1:50 a minute. The medium was intent on giving me a reading that I wasn't interested in. I had two questions "How can I learn more about this?" and "How can I turn it off?" after giving me all the options for every amazing reading under the sun the lady asked if I wanted her to use the cards for my question. By now I was a little aggravated "Listen luv, I just want you to tell me how you learnt spirit stuff and how to turn it off?" She told me I needed to find a spirit circle which would be found at a spiritualist church. I told her I wasn't religious and she explained it wasn't that kind of church.

I headed to my nearest spiritualist church which was filled with elderly couples and me at eighteen. I stuck out like a sore thumb. I got several questions from thinking I was waiting for my nan to "Do you work for the newspaper?" I gave bland answers to all. I didn't want anyone knowing anything about me and then telling me things about me they'd "heard from a ghost." I was very sceptical of everyone, including myself. I felt sorry for them though. They were looking for someone to tell them their wife, child, parent or other loved one existed. They hoped they did and it kept them going for comfort. I guess many were worried about when they would pass and I was in a strange position I didn't usually find myself in, because for once I was lucky. I knew we lived on. Not knew as in having faith or knew as though I know tomorrow is Wednesday, I can't see or feel Wednesday and I'd seen and felt Graham. Wednesday was made up, it wasn't tangible. Time was made up by us, Graham was made by? My inner questions were endless. As soon as I answered one another ten appeared. We all went from the corridor which smelt like an old second hand shop's clothing department to the main hall with a stage. Donations were taken at the door and woman after woman got up and gave messages. I sat straight faced, I saw no spirits and felt no presences. "I have a woman who passed in her fifties here of chest pains, I feel tight in my chest can anyone claim this woman?" A lady asked from the stage. She was talking to a room of at least forty by this stage. Several hands shot up and I was not impressed. A name? Why doesn't the spirit know where their relative is? Why aren't they gesturing like Graham had? The night continued in this fashion and only one woman came close to giving near clear messages. I caught up with her after the presentation. "How do you turn it off?" I asked her as she sat at a table with several others. "What an odd question child, why would you want to do that?" She asked. I didn't answer she was surrounded by sheep and had a holier than thou attitude. I could feel her getting a kick out of being the centre of attention. "Never mind" I said walking away. "Buy a lucky heather dear and all your worries will be gone by the time you leave" She said producing a basket from nowhere. "No thanks, you need it more than me" I said as I left. I could almost feel the scorn staring me in the back. I returned every week for a couple of months and then gave up. Graham was regular and I'd just have to accept that stuff I didn't want to happen would happen.

I told Courtney I need to talk to Graham because as amazing as this was it couldn't just keep happening. I need a warning or to be able to turn it off or something. What if I'm eating and then zap I'm out of body? I choke to death, no thanks or I'm in the bath and a spook walks in just to chat? Graham explained we have personal space that cannot be invaded unless we choose it. He went on to say that they are all around all the time yet want no part to intrude any more than we do to them. He did make two very good points. "If I didn't want to be here. I wouldn't come and if your mind wasn't level with mine, you wouldn't see me even if I did come" It actually made perfect sense. It made me realise more about my life than I'd thought about previously. I chose to be at Courtney's although I didn't want to be there. Yes other paths were hard but I was here to learn and experience not to dick around. As an adult I had a choice over everything. They might be shitty choices sometimes but they were choices. I called Megan "Want a visitor? I'll probably not be going home too" I added.

"What? When? Really?" She sounded so excited.

"Tomorrow Okay?" I asked her.

"Sure, I love you!" She shouted down the phone.

"Tomorrow then!" I replied hanging up. I never said I love you unless I meant it. I didn't like it. Nan said it all the time and then she hurt Caroline. Alan loved me and he let it happen. Wenzel loved me and he killed mum. Fuck love, when I love I'll do it properly.

I got the train to London from Manchester just me, a good book and my mobile phone. Although I'd figured out chat rooms I was now twenty and had no clue how a pc worked. I followed the directions given to me by staff at each station. I enjoyed watching the farmland whiz past me. I called Megan. "Won't be long now... I see horses....sheep..." I went on in a similar vein about the beauty of the countryside. I'd never thought about it much before as it was always just there. My security blanked. If shit turned bad anywhere and I couldn't find a secure place to stay I always had my northern countryside. I could build a bivouac anywhere and I was home. The country soon started to change to towns which were much bigger than those up north and then even bigger buildings. I had to change to the underground, I'd been on trams many times and enjoyed them so thought this wouldn't be much different. I hit a London station and headed for the big underground sign where I put my ticket through a turnstile noting we had these up north to segregate cattle. I walked through a large dome and onto an escalator, the only way being downwards and their were hundreds of people.

Everyone was in a hurry. I presumed it was the time of day. no "morning" no chat. Just a simple one directed mindset. "I'm heading this way - now!" Their body language was horribly distorted into robot drones, their minds presumedly left at home. I felt so many scrambled energies coming off at once. "I'm late!", "It's always packed", "Only five more days", I started to feel their anxiety underneath their cloak of robotic compliance. I wasn't a quarter of the way down the escalator when I got a glance ahead of me through the crowds and by ahead I mean straight down almost vertical a very, very long way. My rucksack and I didn't think things through we did a complete three sixty and took off like a shot running through people back up the escalator. My voice polite but uncaring "scuse me, coming through scuse me." We didn't have stupid amount of heights up north, we herded cattle not each other and people were losing their damn minds down there. I felt trapped and terrified of falling at the same time. I wasn't turning into a drone for anyone! I had no idea why I felt this way. My legs were still pumping when I saw the top of the turnstile I ran at it as a hand hit my shoulder in an attempt to stop me. I sidestepped flipped a one eighty and carried on running I got to the turnstile and dropped to my knee's with the ticket held in the air as the ticket guard reached me. I was panting heavily "Too fucking high" I said gasping for breath. The ticket guy was giving me a rollicking "You can't come this way, you can't do that, I check bag" Yadda yadda, I stood up. "Here's my ticket, I need to go down there. Bit high that's all mate didn't expect it. Is it flat down there?" He checked my ticket and said I could get a bus or a cab to other London station. "Which is fastest?" I asked him He pointed down the escalator. "Which is cheapest?" I asked knowing I'd already paid for the tube. He pointed again to the tube station, fuck it. I had no choice. I got back on the escalator and down through a tunnel into a maze of other tunnels each leading to a dead end they liked to call platforms. I was reminded of Arnie my Gerbil who I used to put in a ball so he could run around and not go anywhere. I now understood why he ran so fast.

Standing there waiting for what I presumed to be an underground train I felt stuck. People were reading papers or listening to Walkmans I asked two people if this one went to my stop. They both gave me a yes grunt of acknowledgement and looked at me as though I was a moron. The higher IQ'd of the two drones even pointed to the tiled tube like an extension that counted as a wall here and I'd missed it. I saw no map, I saw a line with dots and names and my dot wasn't on it. Give me a real map any day. I did my best Mr Happy impersonation "Thanks! really appreciate it, first time here no Idea where I am" Mr businessman turned back to his financial times just as my silver bullet shaped thing appeared a foot in front of me. I got on and nobody made eye contact. I'd been told often growing up that southerners were rude but this was another world and again I was on my guard. I tuned out after a couple of minutes of darkness and not actually certain if I was going anywhere. If it wasn't for the people randomly leaning into each other due to the bullets movement then I wouldn't have known. Train wasn't an accurate description, A train viewed the countryside and was an enjoyable ride. This spectacle was not enjoyable and I felt like it could explode at any minute. When I finally got off I had to climb two escalators to get to the exit. I intuitively knew people had been trapped down here as I felt the urge to run through the crowds despite everyone moving at a reasonable pace. I felt stuck like I couldn't escape the entanglement, I fixed my eyes on a decent pair of legs in the distance and just concentrated on them until I was out of the mass of bodies. Small heels and a white skirt kept me sane for the three minutes it took to get out of the tube area and into the station where I fought with the ticket machine until a guy snapped the ticket out of my hand and jammed it into the machine "Thanks" I shouted as he continued walking. I was just starting to feel better when I realised I was on a ledge up in the air and their were trains beneath me, fuck! I ran to the only area that seemed open which was to my right and discovered I was somehow on ground level outside. I had to wait for my hands to stop shaking before I could make a roll up.

I looked around for a forest, a bit of country, something I could relate to. I was on a short road with huge buildings either end and either side, in between these buildings were more buildings, in fact any space that was at one point a space was now a building. So, this was London. I looked upwards pleased I could see the sky but upset that it made me feel like I was falling. I had two choices, I could go home or I could get the next train to my destination. Something I'd read came back to me "When in doubt, do nothing" I was definitely in doubt. I rolled another smoke and headed to a stall which sold magazines and pop, it was basically a news agents inside a train station. I'd never seen that before, as far as I knew we didn't have them up north. I pulled out a pound and grabbed a mineral water. "That's one eighty five please" The cashier said smiling. I felt the weight of my jaw hitting my hiking boots and sink through to the trains below the balcony and run all the way back to Manchester, what the hell? The parts of me that remained on autopilot however paid the extortion and left. The same bottle was less than a pound up north. I drank my two mouthfuls and headed to the information point. This bird better be worth it. The man on information was full of anything but love and told me the huge sign gave me all the information that I'd need and so I stood there scrutinising it. When I'd done I returned and informed Mr Smiley that unless I was wrong the sign told me my train, the time and platform but doesn't tell me where the train or the platform actually are? This question was lost on the guy who simply grunted into the speaker piece. Luckily for me a semi drone was also in the queue and pointed me in the right direction. I was not a happy bunny.

I remember going over a river on this train and having buildings either side of me larger than I'd ever seen. Then we seemed to be up high whilst the buildings got lower and lower. What was wrong with these people? Stop building things! These monstrosities finally evened out as we hit a place called Bromley South. I was on the phone by then and not impressed "Right, I'm here. How do I get out of this one? Is there a maze? A river to walk through or am I on another fucking ledge?" Megan laughed down the phone "Go up the stairs and you're out" she said. Finally a bit of space... I still had a bus to catch but first I wanted food. I couldn't find a chip shop anywhere that sold Meat pies or sausage, chips and gravy. I settled for a chip bap from a place I affectionately nicknamed Mario's because he was Italian He however didn't know what a chip bap was, I had to point and discover that apparently what I wanted was a chip roll and not a chip bap. The fourth time that I'd tried explaining what I wanted he asked me if I was foreign. The irony was killing me.

There was a lot less people in Bromley than their were in London however still a good two hundred or so more than I was used to up north. Nobody said "afternoon", I stopped after my fourth attempt. When I got on the bus I asked the driver "How much mate?" His eyes were facing the road not towards me. "Depends, where you going?" he asked. Up north I could pay a flat fare and stay on that thing all day if I wanted. "Erm, Bromley Common bus garage" I recited from a text message I had saved. "One pound ten pence" he said which was a result. Up north it was two pounds forty. I called Megan once I'd got there and she said she'd walk down and meet me. It was nicer here and there were less people. Still no country but at least a small amount of land. I was content that I'd meet her and see what happens. I'd be going home tonight or tomorrow though for sure. I couldn't live around here for long but thoughts of going back to stay with Courtney weren't helping either.

Chapter 23

A large woman walked around the corner, blonde and not Megan as she's a red head I remembered her telling me that. Then a larger woman behind her on the phone "Nearly there! I see you!" She said into my phone. "Great! Well done for coming out! I'm so pleased!" I said immediately wondering how she managed to get around as she was so over weight her thighs brushed together. Later she would inform me she was nineteen stone and five foot two inches in height. "Fancy a walk?" She said taking my hand. "Yeah, long trip" I replied thinking no, but I could use a brew? Megan told me her parents thought I was twenty five and that I should go with that as she is thirty. "Fair enough" I replied. We walked around the field near her home a couple of times that she kept referring to as a farm. There's no way it was a farm. It wasn't big enough to be a farm. It was a field with a shed in it. After a brief walk and a chip shop stop she introduced me to her parents.

They immediately reminded me of Tony and Pip from Care. They sat glued to the T.V and didn't make any eye contact. I immediately got the feeling something was wrong. The house was dark and smelt of dogs. Mum was very over weight and dad was the total opposite whilst both were in their seventies. I said my hello's and was ushered into the living room by Megan. The curtains in the living room were closed and I could feel the tension coming from the other room. To give them credit they had replied with a "hi" each but kept staring at the T'V and didn't make eye contact with me once. It was surreal. When I asked "How are you guys? Thanks for inviting me over" They totally ignored me apart from her mum who grunted. Megan found an electric candle and pushed the button so it lit up and then placed it on the table in front of me. As she leaned forwards her leg touched mine. Whether intentional or not it was hard to tell. I moved to the sofa "OK to sit here?" I asked her trying to avoid the candle situation. "Sure" she said nipping off to make a brew. When she returned she sat back on the well worn sofa and leaned her head onto me. I should have bolted for the door. Every instinct in my body was telling me to get out but I was tired and didn't care that much anyway. I rested my arm on her "You did well today going out, you tired?" I asked her. "I can go if you want to sleep" I added gently. "You don't like me! Course I don't want you to go! You just got here!" She snapped sitting bolt upright and staring into my face. "No, no I didn't say that did I? I said if you're tired I can get to know the area and come back later. I'm not going anywhere" Christ frying pan and fire I thought.

She had surprised me with coming across so aggressive and I wanted to leave but I'll be honest I was a little concerned about her. She didn't seem quite right and I figured it was a temporary thing. Megan spoke to me mostly about her agoraphobia and didn't want to talk about much else unless it included an us component. I ducked and dived as much as I could but when push came to shove it boiled down to two things. I wasn't strong enough to stand up for myself and I wasn't going back to Courtney's lies. I cared for Megan but I didn't love her. I knew I'd never love her. She however was head over heels for me or so it seemed. I didn't even particularly like her if I'm brutally honest it was more a sense of responsibility. It felt like I had to be doing something to make sure she was okay and it didn't help that she seemed to have an abusive background which I wanted desperately to rescue her from. Whether it was because I couldn't rescue my mother or a genuine concern I can't tell. Either way, I wasn't going to walk away like Wenzel had and I'd never had anyone to teach me that simply put, some people are just ass holes and so I didn't know the signs. I put the negative feelings from her parents being down to being southerners and supped on my brew. The water was harsher here and I didn't like it. "Ready for dinner?" She asked me. She hadn't moved in two hours and was content to sit beside me and answer any question that kept her talking and preferably not progressing with the hand that kept raking my leg every so often. "I had dinner on the train, tea perhaps?" I answered. Which prompted another north south divide issue. Up north we had breakfast, dinner and tea where as down south the meals are divided into breakfast, lunch and dinner. Medusa returned from the kitchen "Dad's making dinner for them, shall we eat out?" She asked. I agreed and as I was leaving I overheard her dad "I'm not cooking for him, who is he? I didn't even know he was coming" he said. wonderful, Megan knew I'd heard but I said nothing. We had more chips at another shop locally this one was ran by Indians All our northern places where I was from were English or Chinese so this was totally new to me. Megan told me her dad had been cold about me and I explained he was probably just worried about his baby girl. She had met a random guy off the internet after all, She insisted she'd told him about me and he was playing up. I said I'd try and talk to him when we got back. I bought some strawberry's from the shop on the way back and handed it to Toby her dad. "Thanks for having me, I'm sorry it was short notice. I only decided last night. Your daughter seems a bit upset so thought I'd say hello so you know I'm not a loony" I said smiling. Neither of them replied, mum looked at me and then back to the T.V and dad just looked at me blankly like he'd never seen a real person before. "Well if it's okay with you I'll stay an hour then I'll be off, nice to meet you" I added. "You do what you want!" Toby shouted. I was taken back but that was just rude. "I can leave now if it's a problem?" I asked him. He snorted and turned away. "Megan I should go duck, I think I upset your dad." I said grabbing my bag and feeling a split second of relief before she grabbed my arm. "No, no please don't go!" she said almost dragging me towards the living room. "The neighbours! My parents are terrified of them. That's why they are so weird it's because I stay up at night talking to you so they can sleep properly, they are just scared. That's all...I need a pill" she said through sobbing, "What's the matter?" I asked her. "I need a pill" she said physically shaking and walking out of the living room and back into the dining room. I should have walked out but I could taste the abuse in the air. She was controlled but it wasn't by any neighbour. I wasn't angry, this wasn't my fight but I did feel bad for her. "Toby

I'm off listen mate I get it. You didn't know I was coming and you don't know me so I'll be off but before I do look, she's obviously terrified and I saw no problems on the street, no cars on bricks, no graffiti, no broken windows and her reaction...well it's just not right. Is there something I should know about her?" I asked him. "Like what?" He asked. "Well, mental conditions and such. I know she's agoraphobic but there's more to it than that, isn't there? She came to the shop with me just fine" I said. "That's first time she's been out of this house in three years. You think you can help her? Nobody can. We've tried, she'll be fine later" He said. "Ok, thanks for your honesty" I told him offering my hand. He shook it and I left.

I'd been stood at the bus stop less than two minutes when my phone rang. I ignored it. I sent her a text "Try and relax, I have to go. I'll call you when home" Megan was at the bus stop about two minutes after I'd hit send. "Dad says come back, he's sorry, you can stay!" she said. "What? I have no intention of staying. I came to see you. I've done that" I replied. "Just a night? You'll see. They like you.....trust me... please?" She added.

"Okay, I'll come back but I'm not staying, okay?" I answered.

"Okay whatever you like but come back don't leave it like this" she said and prize melon head here returned Megan to her cave. The second the door closed behind us all hell broke loose. Mother was shouting at Toby "You trapped my arm in the door you little bitch! Who do you think you are! I'll.." She wobbled forwards arm lifted to slap Megan. Megan ran into the living room and slammed the door behind her. She must have been leaning against it because mum was leaning on it and it wouldn't move. "I didn't!! You locked me in my room!" Megan shouted back "I got out and you hurt yourself!" She added through the door. I looked at Toby who was cowering behind his wife, he looked scared that she might turn on him next. "What you doing here?" She asked but before I could reply she turned to Toby "This is your fault, what's he doing here Toby? Tell him, tell him to get out now" My mind has a habit during violence and shouting of slowing everything right down so during this mad chaotic scene I was actually stone cold calm. I also take in everything from what was said to what was meant cutting through all the bullshit. It was a survival mechanism that turned up due to Wenzel's crap. A number of things became obvious. One mummy was a bully, two either Megan or her mother were lying. Three they both had some serious issues that I wasn't familiar with. Four her mother wanted to hit me I could see it in her eyes but she didn't know if I'd whack her so she refrained. She wanted total control and she'd got that in Toby but not in Megan. Her usual slave was not doing as she was told and she hated it. Five Toby had no intention of fronting me. Whatever he did next his wife would see as wrong. If he did nothing she'd have a go at him. If he fronted me she'd have a go at him if he won or lost. Finally after several seconds silence and nobody talking or moving I spoke. "Let me calm her down, when I know she's both calm and safe I'll leave. That okay?" I didn't wait for an answer I tapped on the living room door. "It's me, open it" I said calmly. "No, she'll hit me and lock me in my room" She replied. Her mother started gobbing off about her lying. I didn't care I was talking to a door. "Do you really think I'm going to let that happen?" I asked the door, it opened and I went inside. We chatted for an hour and played pontoon. She told me she'd taken Valium and shortly after her actions became weak and her mind unclear. "What you got?" I asked her "red one" she said putting three cards down. "Cool! You win!" I replied trying to cheer her up. Courtney called me "are you coming home tonight?" It was gone ten o'clock. I went to see Toby who was still in the dining room but this time mum had vanished. "When's last train mate?" I asked. "Dunno, she alright?" He asked half hearted. "Yeah, she's passed out on sofa, those pills always do that?" I asked. "Good" He said, not Mr sociable then. "I'm off mate, cya" I said and he told me to "wait a minute." I was intrigued so stood in the garden waiting for him, he returned inside five minutes. "You stayed and calmed her down. You stay tonight, go tomorrow" he half told me. "No, it's okay. Thanks though I do appreciate it. just point me in the direction of Manchester and I'm good" I said trying to get my route in reverse order. "Stay tonight, go tomorrow" he said walking back into the house and leaving me in the garden with the door open. I made a call outside and explained to Courtney what a pigs ear this had all been and that I'd be back tomorrow. She laughed, alot and I can't say I blame her. I fell asleep on the dirty old sofa as Megan fell asleep in the armchair.

Chapter 24

I awoke to Toby stood over me holding a coffee out at arms length. How long he'd been there I didn't know. It was 6:45am according to the little gold plastic clock above the fire place. I took it and thanked him. Then I turfed it into a plant pot the second he'd left the room. I had trust issues at the best of times, even more so with people who I knew didn't like me. I saw how those pills had effected Megan and there was no way I was trusting anything I hadn't seen made.

Megan was all smiles when she woke up despite sleeping in the chair her only concern was that her parents wouldn't have slept because they'd be scared of the neighbours attacking them, and so she thought she'd be in trouble for sleeping. I told her they'd gone to bed early and were fine when they got up. She insisted it was because I was there and that they felt safer that way. I got talking to Megan about Courtney, Megan insisted I call her M.J instead of her full first name because she didn't like it. I told her about the baby and the army and before I knew it I was quite upset. I hadn't realised how much I'd needed to talk, it didn't matter who to. Just that I had the opportunity to speak. I had no idea how much I'd actually locked away. M.J started to teach me how to use the internet and we looked up facts online about childbirth and the whole process. Through what I knew about Courtney and the situation with the baby and what I'd read online I knew there was no way Courtney was ever pregnant. I already knew of course from what the good doctor had said but still. The pain and self doubt was a struggle. I told M.J the name of my child, it was the first time I'd spoken it to anyone bar Courtney and burst into another bout of tears. I cried for over an hour about a child which never existed. I was surprised I'd let go. It still hurt but not as much "you can't go back" Meghan told me. "I can't stay" I replied.

We talked all day about getting our own place. She had some savings and she wanted us together no matter what her parents thought. I raised issue about the neighbours and she blew up again. This time about her parents never standing up for themselves and expecting her to do everything. I didn't understand how she could go from wanting to protect her parents at all costs against these vile neighbours one moment and the next hating her parents because they wouldn't stand up to the neighbours. She couldn't have it both ways. Her parents couldn't be aggressors and victims, it just didn't work and yet I put it down to her being controlled and angry. Then I ran with the options that worked out in my favour "Well...only if you're sure? Otherwise I have to leave tonight." I said.

"Tell me you love me and I'll believe you" she said. I looked her dead in the eye "I've been through so much it wouldn't be fair to say that to you but lets see how we go yeah?" She agreed and prided my honesty.

How could I know what love was? Any love I'd known involved pain and I knew they didn't belong together. I knew M.J and I didn't either but I felt I had little choice at the time. I felt totally useless and simply reacted best as I could to what situations were around me at the time and I'll admit I convinced myself on some level that I may actually be helping M.J and that made me feel useful. I felt if I actually had any control in my life then I was like Wenzel, a control freak. I felt if I did anything for myself like buying a new jacket that I wouldn't be worth it. I felt if someone bought me something it wasn't because I was a nice guy. It was because they wanted something. I am not alleviating myself of responsibility, I'm explaining I hadn't been taught the simple process of loving myself and so, I didn't. That aside I knew exactly the choices I was making.

I had zero self worth. If someone asked me if I wanted a brew? I would hear "Make me a brew" It was my job, I had to. That stood for everything and if someone needed a cooker connected and I didn't know how then I felt bad because it was my job to take care of people and I couldn't, just like I couldn't take care of Alan or mum. This was mostly due to Wenzel's mental training but the world of negative self talk hadn't helped much either. I just didn't realise at that time that's what I'd been doing.

It was late when Toby asked what time I had to go. M.J took the tickets from out of my hand and looked at me over the plastic candle. I nodded and she ripped them in half. I'd had no decision to make, she'd taken all the responsibility from me and made it easy. I was grateful "I want him to stay, if not we'll get a hotel until we get our own place" she said to Toby. Toby didn't say a word he simply shuffled off into the living room presumedly to talk to his wife. I didn't see them all night. I slept on the sofa with M.J. She tried to be intimate but I told her I couldn't because it would be disrespectful to her parents. It wasn't true. The facts were simply that I wasn't into her physically and intimacy meant babies and I wasn't going down that road, not now and not ever and that thought alone hurt me. I blamed myself for the death of a child which hadn't lived.

I was living at M.J's parents for about a week. Toby was actually okay once you got through his strange quietness nor mention how obvious it was that he was absolutely terrified of his wife. I looked at that nice house one day with the beautiful garden and what could have been a perfect family. I took it all in like a video camera saving a minute worth of clip as Toby pointed to a bird and told me it's name. I noted how pale and frail he was stood beside his little apple tree and I told myself in the sternest voice ever "Whatever happens, don't turn out like him" and I felt truly sorry for him. The things he must have seen and felt powerless to do anything about it showed physically, and I could feel the energy coming off him like those little bobbles you just can't get out of old shirts and it itched me thinking about it. Who would believe him? Beaten by his wife? Man enough never to hit her back but scared and ashamed enough never to tell anyone. I took another mental snapshot and named it "don't be him." just to be certain it would remain in my head forever. "How's it going?" Toby asked me as he looked for plane lines in the sky and telling me stories about when he was a postman who used to deliver to Bob Monkhouse, the only good memories he had. "She's packing now mate" I said "You won't lose her, I'll make sure we visit" I added. "You're okay" he said tapping my arm gently. "But she won't let her" his eyes turned steely grey and I felt all emotion leave him and then he relaxed. "Ah it will be bad" he said turning to his tree again. "The neighbours?" I asked standing beside him but out of hitting distance. He looked at me and held my gaze a moment like I knew nothing and then looked back. I'd caught the meaning "Not bad for us...bad for me, she'll have me doing everything again" He didn't need to say it. My sympathy was immediately gone. No man worth his salt would put his daughter in place of an abusive position he'd once been in no matter how scared he was.

M.J and I were packing the car, I'd told her to give them a hug and tell them she loves them before she left. She explained they don't do that and never have. "It'll make a change then" I said insisting they left on good terms. M.J was in there nearly twenty minutes before the front door opened and then closed again. Something wasn't right I headed towards the front door as her neighbours came out, a young couple both clean cut and medium build. He was fair haired and confident, she less so with black her but still confidant just not as much as him. He saw me "Morning" I said out of habit, he nodded and got into the car. The woman gave him a "Who's that?" look. They seemed fine to me, apparently they were violent but I'd picked up nothing. M.J had been telling me they had the roof window open and were constantly throwing bottles out of it. The garden was tidy as was the little bit of grass down beside both houses.

"Yes I am! You don't own me!" M.J was shouting from the other side of the door. "I bloody well do! I brought you into this world you bitch!" I slammed my hand five times hard on the door "I'll give you seconds to come out or I'm kicking this door in!" I said loud but calmly. If it came to it I stood no chance, the door was solid wood and thick but it had shocked them into silence – no violence around the new guy. I'd seen the living room window open previously around the back. If push came to shove I'd hop through that "four, three, two" I shouted as the door opened I placed my foot in it and stepped forwards. Hope was in the doorway with Toby behind her and M.J was curled up at the bottom of the stairs holding her face. "Thanks for having me" I said not making eye contact with her and pushing past her like she didn't exist. She was gobbing off at Toby who stepped in front of me at his wife's comment I stood stock still with my arms by my side "move" I said gently. He didn't and it was time to try a different tack. "M.J get up it's time to go" I said. She did and I took her hand and pulled her towards the door. Hope had closed it and tried to grab M.J. I opened the door and waved her away as I walked out. M.J took the lead and got in the car. I walked slowly purely out of ego. I wasn't going to fight with anyone but I sure as hell wasn't going to go running away neither, running was Wenzel's job. At that moment when I was nearly out of the drive Toby grabbed my sleeve. I lifted my arm high above my head and sidestepped so he now had his back to me but was looking at me and still had hold of my sleeve. "Seriously?" I asked him. He knew he stood no chance and released me. I got in the car and gave Hope a wave as we left. I had no idea where we were going.

We stayed at a bed and breakfast for a week and went to tell the housing we were homeless. Apparently we needed a letter to say that M.J had been thrown out. Her parents said she hadn't been and was welcome home anytime. I went back to M.J's parents and negotiated a deal with them. I'd pop around and do the garden for them when needed and once a week M.J and I would come and do their shopping, drop it off and tidy the home for them. They agreed to do the letter. When we returned to pick the letter up it said that M.J wasn't welcome home any more because they were sick and tired of her violence. She'd become unmanageable due to her numerous mental health problems and as far as they were concerned she didn't exist. I calmed M.J down, I didn't like their tactics but fuck it, it was in fact a win for us. We'd got the letter. I had no idea how true their wording would turn out to be.

We'd moved to a cheaper bed and breakfast and money was running out, fast. M.J made a call and next minute we were offered a place to stay. Apparently her friend Paul was going away and the flat would be free, could we look after it? Well hell yes. It was an okay block of flats with only six flats in the whole building and we were in the middle on the right hand side with a fenced off field beside us. The area seemed nice it was in Beckenham which wasn't far away from where we were before and M.J said she'd known him a few years so trusted him but that he had a secret he didn't want anyone to know about so sometimes he acted a bit strange. I said if she trusted him it was good enough for me. We kipped in the living room and the week flew by, unfortunately the housing were no closer to getting us accommodated and so their was nothing we could do apart from sit tight. We agreed to pay his electric bill and some towards his rent but relying just on M.J's benefit money which back then had to be claimed on a paper book was getting more and more difficult. It was so bad I called my old social worker and asked for money. He told me I wasn't on a care order any more so he couldn't help me. However a couple of hours later sixty five pounds appeared in my account. I sent him a text saying thank you and I meant it. He'd saved us from being homeless that day. M.J said we had less and less money but I knew from the receipts it wasn't accurate. I suspected Paul was stealing from us but couldn't prove it.

It was around this time that the problems really started. I used M.J's computer to write up a C.V. I didn't have much experience but it wasn't the worst Idea in the world however when I showed M.J she started treated me like I didn't care about her at all. "You'd leave me with a strange man on my own in a strange place?" I hadn't thought about it like that at all I simply wanted to make some money instead of living off M.J. "You do know I have anxiety don't you? How do you think my Anxiety is going to be if you're not fucking here!" She stormed screaming in my face as I stepped back and I'll admit I was scared. I didn't know how to react to her, I was over a hundred miles from anywhere I knew and in my mind I'd just caused this woman an immense amount of stress because I'd got myself involved in her life and then indicated I'd walk away from her. Besides if I couldn't help her then I'd never have been able to help mum would I? They were both agoraphobic. I had to help her, whatever the cost. "I'm sorry, I didn't realise. I wasn't thinking properly I was just trying to help" I said. "You want to help?" She said. Inside a week I was signed off as her carer and she'd shown me how to make applications for income support and low rate disability living allowance because of my recurrent dis-locative shoulder. After all if I couldn't lift I couldn't work. I was amazed by how simple the process was, we had to talk to the doctor a few times who apparently M.J had a way with. He signed me off sick every four weeks for three months with no questions and then the benefits just needed a sick note once every six months. It was horrible, I wanted to work and in reality I wasn't claiming anything I wasn't entitled to in that I did have the conditions raised in the claim and I was caring for someone who was essentially disabled due to her morbid obesity often routine things became difficult and yet I felt guilty to the world because I wanted to work and felt I was capable of it and awful to me because it reinforced just how useless I actually was.

I'd been out to Sainbury's shopping for M.J as she didn't feel up to driving even though the flat was literally inside a five minutes walk to the supermarket and so I'd walked alone and carried lots of bags home. Paul was home with M.J although he wasn't due back until the evening. "Okay mate?" I asked putting the bags down in his kitchen. He didn't answer "Has M.J paid the rent yet mate?" I'd said motioning towards the bags and indicating we'd been paid today. "Yeah it's good M.J paid me but I could use electric money" He said. "Here you go" I said bunging him a tenner. I told M.J later on that I'd given it to him and she informed me she'd paid him a tenner this morning before he went out. We agreed to pay him only set amounts and to get out of his place as quick as possible even if it meant borrowing money to go private. I'd written notes all my life and had come to London with two note pads. One with all my telephone numbers in and one I'd written what I'd call notes down on. They were generally a few lines here and there about people or things I'd seen. Both of them were missing and so I knocked on next door to ask the guy there if he'd seen them in the hall, perhaps I'd dropped them on the way in? We got talking and he invited me in for a coffee. It was very dark and the curtains were drawn. It was quite cold but I had a coffee and a chat with the thin fellow who told me his name was Franklin, he wore blue trousers and a cotton shirt. He was clean shaven and looked to be around fifty years old. He rocked when he spoke and routinely rang his fingers together. The ash tray was full to overflowing with fag butts. He seemed a nice enough guy just lonely but again as was becoming routine, something wasn't right. I told him my story from Manchester to now and he told me I was right to be weary of Paul. Paul often borrows money for his Gran and has never paid Franklin back.

M.J and I cleaned every inch of Paul's flat looking for my notebooks all apart from Paul bedroom as he'd asked us never to go in there. "Fuck it, that's all that's left" I told her and opened the door. He had a single bed, a desk with a computer on it and three teddy bears on his bed. The rest of the room was littered with clothes and books. Paul was twenty seven years old, thin with dark hair and vaguely resembled a weasel. I tripped on a karate book next to the bed on the way in and started folding clothes. I found my notebooks underneath his pillows. When he got home I told him I'd tidied his room and he looked at me ashen. "Found my notebooks too, under your pillows next to your teddy bears" I added. "Oh, that's great" He said. "That it? That all you've got to say?" I asked calmly.

"Well I don't know how they got there. I don't read, I'm dyslexic" He said. I laughed "There's books in your room, you taught M.J how to use a P.C, You're not dyslexic" I said gently. I wanted him to feel bad but didn't want to push it over the top. We were staying in his home after all. "I don't know why they were there honest, look I don't care about your personal shit mate" He'd started bobbing from foot to foot, he was anxious but getting like he could start having a go as well. "I look at pictures in books I can't read" He said shaking his head at me like it was my fault. Fuck it, "Okay, well we appreciate you letting us stay and we are paying most of your bills but I'm telling you now. If you touch my stuff again I'll drop you where you stand. Clear?" I said still seated and level toned.

He immediately raised his voice "I can't read! Tell him M.J! Shit I let you stay here and you accuse me of..."I was up and stepping forwards and he leaned back and started walking backwards, I followed him like this until his back hit his wardrobe in his bedroom and then he went silent. "Nice and simple, my shit goes missing and you get hurt. Right?" I said this time changing my tone to sound like a horrible bastard.

"No, no we're good. I have stuff to do though if you don't mind?" He said looking at the floor. I stepped out of his bedroom. M.J was waiting for me in the hall and watching everything. "That went better than I thought it would" I said. Not knowing if I'd severely helped or severely screwed up.

Chapter 25

The atmosphere was becoming somewhat strained when Paul was around until one day he just walked into the living room and said "He knows doesn't he? That's why he looks at me like strange." I was pretending to be asleep on the sofa as I'd had enough of playing cards with M.J and trying to kill time until we got our own place. "No, I've not told him anything" She said whilst sat on the floor. "Well he knows something" Paul commented as I sat up. "Sup?" I asked making a show of rubbing my eyes and stretching. Paul made some excuse to go and went for a bath. As soon as he was gone I turned to M.J "What's the big secret? What is it I'm supposed to know that I don't know?" I asked. "Promise you won't say anything?" She said. "Okay?" I shrugged making a roll up. "Paul did time" she said, I laughed. "My uncle did time, my other uncle did time, my father did time. What's the big deal? Besides he doesn't seem the type. He's kinda slimy, doesn't look like he's got it in him to be honest" I said. "He likes children" She said looking straight at me. I have to say I had suspected he was a bit weird when I saw the teddy bears but I figured he was just insecure as hell. I'd never have guessed he was into kids. "That's not a small accusation M.J, how'd you know?" I said. "He told me himself" She said and I believed her. "I've been thinking. What if I go to college, not a job just college so I'll still be around to help with travel etc just not all the time and then I can work from home maybe? Then we can get enough money to leave" I said. "Go to college, with no address and no money" She replied mimicking my voice. She had a point but I suspected it was more because she didn't want to be left alone. I was starting to feel like all my choices were being shouted down or just impossible.

Paul was asking for money again. It must have been around winter because I remember it was cold and grey. We gave him what little we had left and went for a walk. A group of three girls stopped us as we went around the corner into a little off the track pathway. "Hey, you live with Paul don't you?" They were school age. "Yeah, what's up?" I asked. We got chatting and it became apparent they used to go to his place to smoke and chat until we moved in and now they can't. Paul had told them I accused him of stealing and that I'd hit him so now he's trying to find a way to get rid of us. I thanked the girls and walked back to the flat. M.J had gone and sat in the car. I rang the intercom. "Hi Paul, just bumped into some girls who tell me you want us out. Can we have a chat mate I left my keys with M.J?" I asked nicely. "I haven't said anything about you, yet" He said laughing which surprised me but didn't bother me. What did bother me was the sound of a younger male in the background laughing too. I'm going to have him I thought. I went back to M.J in the car and told her not to worry about it we'd go for a walk in the park and everything would become clearer. We were there about an hour when who comes walking down the alley towards us but Paul and a lad no older than twelve. I'd had enough and something snapped. "Stay out of my way" I said deadpan and removed my hand from M.J's grasp. "What?" she asked looking at me but still walking. We were nearer to Paul now "Just do it" I told her as Paul and boy approached. "Hi Paul!" I said throwing my arms out wide and lifting my head up and backwards as I smiled looking like I was really pleased to see him. The boy was smart and moved a good two feet away from Paul as soon as I threw my arms outwards. Paul mirrored me and lifted his head and smiled as his greasy black hair shone in the small amount of sunlight. I flicked my hips and Hooked him along the side of the jaw. His head snapped around and he fell like a sack of shit holding his jaw. The young lad legged it and Paul just lay there rolling around holding his jaw. "Right dickhead," I said leaning down. "We'll leave as soon as we can. That was a fucking tap. If you lie about me this is what happens. Now you can tell people I really did hit you." I kicked him in the gut and walked back to his flat, on the way I passed the group of girls. "Alright love? Paul's got a new story for you. This time I did hit him. Why do you wanna hang out with scum like him? Come on, seriously?" I asked them. "He's got a place" one of them said. "You can do better" I told them.

I gave Franklin a knock and told him M.J and I were off, we were going to stay in the car near her parents until something came up. Franklin invited us in and said he was going to Spain in a couple of weeks with his mum Paula. Would we like to keep at eye on the flat? Naturally we said yes.

Three days in and we'd been invited to meet Franklin's mum. She lived local and rented out two of her bedroom's to teenagers from broken homes. She had two massive dogs and she was nearly six feet tall with gorgeous long blonde hair almost hitting her ankles. She used to bring tobacco and cigarettes back from Spain for everyone and she was eighty. She'd had more operations than anyone I knew and I loved listening to her talk because it was like every part of her life she described like a beautiful adventure. She ate well and kept busy and in return she said she had no mobility issues at all. She was a legend and praised us for looking after her boy who she said was Schizophrenic. I'd heard of it but wasn't overly familiar. I had to get M.J to look it up on the internet. Apparently as long as Franklin didn't drink alcohol and took his medication regularly then he was fine she told us jovially "But don't hesitate to call me if there is a real problem and I'll get him sectioned again" she said laughing like it was just run of the mill. I was starting to think the entire world was crazy. I really liked Paula and had a ton of respect for her. "Oh and don't let that Paul lad borrow anything, he is naughty that one" she said. "Don't think you'll need to worry about that for a while, he doesn't like me much" I told her.

Franklin had no problems that week and went away with his mum to Spain. M.J seemed to calm down a lot now she had some semblance of normality around her. We even visited her parents to do the shopping and sort the garden as promised as we thought it might help to show we've stuck to our end of the bargain. Hope never spoke to me or I to her the entire time I was there. I spoke to Toby but we'd never be friends. When we'd done we returned to Franklin's flat and Paul's door was wide open. "You broke his jaw!"

One of the girls said laughing amongst the noise of several other children in his flat. Paul closed the door and I heard the lock click. "How do we stop him having children over?" I asked M.J. "Leave it the police can't stop him having kids there" She said. "I can though" I answered without thinking. "How?" She asked. "Dunno, can't sling them out but their has to be a way" I said. I wasn't happy and it was starting to churn me up that just across the hall was someone potentially messing around with children in a bad way. That somehow he was probably doing what had happened to my sister or my mum and I was sat doing nothing about it like Wenzel had done nothing about it.

I was up most of the night and so didn't wake up until gone 10am the following day. "I've got an idea give me some notes" I said. "What?" She asked "I've an idea, I'll give them back in a minute" I said. She handed me thirty quid and I slipped some jeans on and opened the front door. I walked across the hall and knocked on Paul's door. I had my wallet open with notes sticking out visible. He opened the door a hairs width "Hi mate, wanted to say thanks for putting us up. Just you in?" I asked looking around the hall and back to my notes again repeatedly. It stank of sweat and he had a bathrobe and boxers on. "Yeah" he said. "Well, can I come in?" I said moving the money like I wanted nobody to see it. He stepped back. "How's it going?" I said shutting the door behind me. "Yeah, it's alright I'll be a min" he said running to turn the porn video off he'd left on. There was a knife on the kitchen side, I grabbed it and chucked it in the fridge. I didn't want him grabbing it. "So?" He asked looking at me and wondering why my wallet was back in my pocket. "Girl says I broke your jaw?" I asked. "Well, yeah. Went hospital and everything. Dislocated they said" He told me. "Not fucking broke then is it?" I said turning Mr Nasty on him and leaning forwards. I jabbed his face and then landed a right hard "Dirty fucking nonce!" I said hooking his ribs hard with each word as he tried to push me away, left first then right. The wind went out of him and he tried to curl up on the floor as I hooked his face. He was leaned against the cupboard door clutching his stomach, his head rattled against the door and then he hit the floor as I hit him. I wasn't done. I knelt down beside him "No, kids, in, the, fucking, flat" I said hitting him hard as I could with each word. I gave him a good few whacks out of pure anger which he probably didn't deserve but got anyway. He was conscious but not fighting to curl up. He wanted to move out of the way but his body wouldn't let him. When I'd done I took a packet of 50g pouches of tobacco off the side and told him "This is for all the extra cash you had" and opened the front door making sure to let out a cheerful "Thanks Paul, see you later mate" for anyone who was listening.

I told M.J Paul was very apologetic about taking so much money and insisted we took the tobacco as a gift.

Franklin had been home perhaps four days and kept himself hidden away to the living room. When he did invite me in he was at in the corner of the living room with cans all around him. We'd been to her mothers and done a shopping run for ourselves too. "You okay mate?" I asked him as he was sat in the middle of a big leather sofa and looked so helpless leaning over a smokey ashtray. The curtains were closed again I figured it gave him comfort. "Yup, you drink a drunk Tracie?" He asked me. Then he threw his arms out and hugged me tightly. "Drink a drunk with me Tracie?" He said pronouncing my name with a W to make Twaysee. "I don't drink mate, thanks for the offer though" I said taking the can of fosters he'd passed to me and putting it back on his table. "You had your pills boss?" I asked him. "Awww go on!" He said smiling. I took a sip and told him I'd have to pee and then I'd join him. M.J put the shopping away whilst I emptied my can down the toilet and refilled it with tap water. "Good stuff this mate," I said when I returned and made a show of taking a big swig. "How many you had?" I asked wondering why the tap water was so different to the luxury of northern water. "Couple....maybe" He said pointing to an empty bottle of wine and at least seven cans. I waited until he slept and then called his mum. She explained she wasn't worried unless he started hitting himself. Apparently it's only then he becomes a danger to himself if he's not hitting himself it's not problem it's just a drink habit. I took her word for it and left Franklin to count sheep.

Franklin was very apologetic when he woke up "No worries mate, you had a drink, so what? Forget about it relax." I said. Which he did, with another can of lager, for breakfast. That's when alarm bells started to go off. How did he afford it? He doesn't work. Beautiful leather sofa, oak table, huge T.V on a nice cabinet, just been to Spain with his mum and the flat was owned outright. He always had smokes and had got through at least £30 pounds worth of alcohol last night alone. M.J and I decided as long as he was just sat getting drunk and not acting like a nob we'd let him get on with it. It's his flat and his life after all. We were both concerned about him and checked on him frequently during the next few days of his binge. His mum came around daily too and was always the same advice. "Make sure he eats one meal a day and he's taken his pills. If it escalates then call me," I think her heart was in the right place but that also she was somehow grateful the burden was off her. It wasn't helping me much though, M.J now had more reason to believe she couldn't be in the flat alone or with Franklin and so I couldn't go out without her having a go at me or saying she was having panic attacks. In no time at all M.J got to the point where she didn't want to leave the bedroom which Franklin had kindly given us when we moved in. I needed to see if I could help for my sake as much as everyone else's.

"Morning mate. Let's see if we can get some air in here shall we?" I said opening the curtains in the living room. Franklin looked at me like I'd hit him. "You okay mate? Hangover? Get some mineral water down ya" I laughed trying to sidetrack why he was looking at me so cautiously. "Close em! Close em!" He waved sliding down onto the floor and flapping his arms around. He sat cross legged on the floor waving his arms up and down "Close em!" I closed the curtains and checked the street outside as I did. Empty, I checked the windows opposite out flat and they were all clear and normal. "What's up mate?" I asked Franklin as I sat next to him on the floor. "They'll get me, all of them!" He gestured with his arms out wide. "Who mate?" I asked him.

"Them! They had me. I know, oh ignore me Tracie it's...." He tapped the side of his head with his fingers.

"It's okay mate, I know. Your mum told me" I reassured him.

"You think I'm crazy" He asked.

"Crazy? No mate, just need to relax. There's nobody outside you know" I told him.

This went on well into the evening, Franklin constantly feeling watched. He refused to take his pills but was still drinking. He'd go out in his Jeep just fine as long as it was to buy more alcohol. When he came back I had a long chat to him about drinking and driving but it went straight over his head. I cared about Franklin and he played the victim very well. "I'm fine Tracie, I'm sorry. I won't do it again. You still like me don't you Tracie?" He'd say throwing his arms wide and smiling like he wanted to hug me. He had a friendly face. It was like talking to a child even though Franklin knew what he was doing. I watched a film he'd put on. I don't remember what it was called but I know it was a horror film because it got towards night time and M.J and I hadn't slept well in days because we were worried about Franklin and we were chasing places from newspapers to try and find a place to live during the day. It was around 10pm when we heard the microwave door open and then the cutlery drawer go. I thought nothing of it until I heard lots of clattering.

"You okay mate?" I said jumping out of bed dressed in my Jeans and nakedness. M.J and my relationship had progressed physically but for the most part I still wasn't comfortable with her. It was over quickly and out of choice. It left me feeling as thought I'd helped her feel better about herself but I felt nothing for her. "She'll Kill me, wants me dead, hides all the time" He said chucking another handful of knives and forks in the microwave. I unplugged it when his hand was back in the drawer and he was too drunk to notice. "Who is mate? It's late" I asked hoping he wasn't going to say M.J. "Oh you know Tracie, You know, you're my friend aren't you Tracie?" He asked me. "Yes mate, always but this is dangerous, shall we put them back in the cupboard instead?" I asked him. I didn't dare try and move anything in case he flipped out. "No Tracie, no, no, no, she'll kill me, you be careful, you don't know" he said. I was calm but cautious, he was playing with knives and I liked him but didn't know if he'd hurt himself. I remembered Paula's words but if he came at me with a knife I was dropping him whether he had a condition or not.

"Who wants to hurt you Franklin? Tell me my friend" I offered. He looked at me like he wasn't sure if to trust me or not. I pretended I was Nigel and smiled hugely and just looked at him with all the care I could muster. I held his gaze for as long as I could which wasn't hard because as long as he stood looking at me he wasn't dicking around with knives. "M.J she wants me dead, she hates me" He said full of honesty. "Awww Franklin, M.J doesn't want you dead, M.J really likes you! Would you like to say hello? Come on she'd like that" I said and touched his arm gently. "I won't force you mate, it's up to you but she'd really like a good catch up" I said turning away and heading back to the bedroom. Luckily it worked and Franklin followed me. "No Tracie don't disturb her, it's just me" he said tapping his head hard. "Don't be silly she'd love it" I said opening the bedroom door and kicking myself for telling him not to be silly. Now he'd think I think he's silly. M.J was sat up in bed. "Franklin wants to say hello. I told him we'd love that, okay?" I said. She was pretending to be groggy. "Yeah, yeah okay" she said. I sat on the floor with Franklin and got M.J and Franklin talking and then I made my excuses to go to the loo.

I covered the kitchen. First all the sharps went in the bin bag including the forks and then I rolled it up and put it on top of the kitchen units. Then I went into the living room and bagged up his empty cans and bottles where I found a penknife in one of the drawers in the living room which immediately went in my pocket. I then went to the loo and returned to the bedroom. Franklin was sat cross-legged on the floor sipping a Carlsburg and rocking back and forwards. He was fighting his own demons and I wanted so much to be able to help him. "How does it work Franklin? If you don't mind me asking?" Through slow slurs one minute and rapid speech with elaborative hand gestures the next, he told me he used to be strong and big. He worked on the railways and earned good money. Then one day when he was in his early twenties he just knew he should leave and go walking. He remembered going for a walk but his next memory is of being near Wales on a motorway with a full beard and dirty clothes. He'd been arrested and then taken to hospital where he was diagnosed over time with several different disorders none of them were schizophrenia. The memory lapses would happen a lot and he eventually lost his job. "I was hearing them and feeling them but I was too scared to say" He told me in a clear voice which didn't sound as natural as he ever did. He glanced behind him "Do you think I'm crazy Tracie?" "No Mate" I answered for the hundredth time that night as I remembered telling Graham I never wanted to hear them because it was too real. A thought dawned on me. "Many people do though, why don't you?" He asked me. "You're you. You're not the illness and so it wasn't his fault because it's just an illness" I said. Franklin went on to fill in the rest of his story. "They said I'd broken shop windows. I don't remember" He went on whilst I tuned into him. M.J had made herself busy with an internet chat room and I'd not tuned into anyone since Graham. I could feel Franklin's agitation like he constantly had someone with him even when well. The person hated him and told him daily how bad he was, how unliked and all the bad things that could happen to him. I extended my energy focusing just around Franklin instead of on him. Beneath the surface of calm and friends demeaner Franklin hadn't learnt it was okay to have negative thoughts and so in turn he'd always beaten himself up for thinking anything negative. He couldn't accept that sometimes we'd just have these feelings and it was normal we just weren't to act on them. He'd pushed them out so much he'd given them an identity. Over time that identity became so real and so external to him it was as real to as as you or I and totally independent. Most of all it didn't actually exist anywhere apart from in his head and so was constantly alone with it. This was no spirit I was dealing with or rather Franklin was dealing with. The chemicals the doctors gave him could slow his brain and subdue his thoughts they could even increase the feelings of euphoria in the brain, they could even stop him being able to connect to this identity they just couldn't stop the identity existing in the first place and so the second he stopped taking the pills he reconnected with his negative self. Of course when taking his pills Franklin felt well and so felt like he didn't need them any more and as soon as he stopped taking them the voices came back and so he drank to get rid of them. "At least the juice tells no lies....." He'd tell me. "It's a lesser demon you know?" He asked wagging a finger at me and holding a half tilted can of Carlsburg.

Chapter 26

It was a vicious circle. The amount he was drinking might not have been the cause of his hands shaking or the hand wringing which seemed to be a tell tale sign of less medication in his system however the sheer quantities that he drank could surely kill him and from everything I knew about alcohol it was a huge depressive. Which to be fair would just make the negative thoughts he had already, ten times worse but hey I was no doctor.

Somewhere around the fifth day Franklin took a turn for the worse. I'd done a shop run and had to go back because M.J hadn't signed her prescription for Surmontil and Valium. As I'd popped home I noticed Franklin was sat up watching T.V. He was wide awake but sat stock still and staring ahead which was totally unusual for Franklin. He always seemed to have some kind of rocking or head bobbing going on, it was just his character. Something wasn't right it was as though his energy had dwindled to be replaced by something else. Like trying to hide when you've drank too much but it wasn't booze causing the problem this time. "Keep an eye on him" I told M.J as I closed the door behind me. I returned about forty five minutes later to find Franklin sat with his head in his hands and M.J was sat beside him. "Alright guys?" I said doing a Mr Happy with the massive grin and shoulder swing. The curtains were closed and Franklin's pale features shone like a slither of sunlight through black curtains as he sat on the deep red leather sofa. He was so light it barely moved under his weight. M.J however looked like she was sat on a barrel of cherries as the sofa pushed up around her more than ample frame. Franklin ignored me as M.J answered for both of them "Yeah Franklin was saying he didn't feel very well but that he'd be fine." Her eyes told me she was worried about him but then she was always worried about something. I grabbed a can of coke each from the fridge and handed them around. As Franklin took his I realised why he'd been covering his face. He'd had a shave and taken off too many layers of skin. It was red and had been bleeding.

"Shit mate what you done to yourself?" I asked him without thinking. "I'm Okay Tracie, accident" He said coldly. "Yeah, okay mate. Mind if I take a look?" I said kneeling down in front of him so I didn't appear intimidating. He glanced at M.J and then back at me. "Can you empty the bins for me M.J?" I asked her knowing that I always emptied the bins and that Franklin was feeling uncomfortable with M.J there. M.J picked up on my queue and made her way to the kitchen to start hiding the sharps. "It's okay mate accidents happen. I just need to have a look to make sure there's nothing in it or that you don't need a hospital okay?" I asked. "No, no no, hospital, no, no no!" He said waving both hands over my head. I remained motionless, I needed him to trust me and realised that if I reacted to his outbursts then there's no way he'd trust me. I had to remain calm like everything was perfectly normal. I smiled "Can I tell you a secret?" I said looking left and right as though I was avoiding M.J over hearing. I was starting to figure out how Franklin worked. He didn't care at all about himself but he did about others. "You can tell me anything Tracie, what's the matter? No hospital though, no, no" He replied gingerly tapping his cheek where the skin must have been super sore as it bubbled as it tried to heal.

"I need to look like a decent guy for M.J, If I don't at least pretend to be checking to make sure you're OK then she'll think I'm a right bastard and I'll never hear the end of it, so if you let me clear it up with a bowl and some water then she won't give me shit all day. What you say? You gonna help a mate out or what?" M.J cared about nobody apart from herself but had phases of really being depressed for no reason and I was also trying to help with that. She was hard to understand at most times but my lie had worked and Franklin let me clean him up. When I'd done I told him he didn't need stitches I also I thanked him for helping me and he shook my hand. "You've saved me so much brother you know that?" I added letting go of his hand. I wanted him to feel cared for not belittled. "My face is okay now Tracie, everything will be fine!" He said doing his arms wide bit again and cocking his head to one side as he smiled. I wasn't convinced. He leaned forwards and touched my nose with his finger. "You're a great friend Tracie!" He said then quick as a flash he punched himself in the side of the head.

I didn't know what to do and just let instinct take over and looked through beyond his eyes. I felt if I responded with fear or anger I'd make him worse. Thankfully I didn't need to say anything "I'm sorry Tracie, I don't know why I did that" he said. "It's your face mate, not mine. I'm a northerner I got a hard head" I added aiming for funny and landing somewhere closer to less serious. I laughed to hammer home that it was joke which just made me look more nervous. "Why you worry Tracie? I not hurt anyone. I don't even hurt ants!" He said.

"I know Franklin, I just worry because it's been scientifically proven that southerners have a softer skull and I don't want you to hurt yourself mate" I said. He didn't appear to understand the humour. "It has? That's why my face hurts?" He replied. "Well, yeah. That and you just punched yourself in the head mate" He did it again this time twice in quick succession. "No Tracie, no, no, no, I didn't" He said as he hit himself, again twice in quick succession. I realised he was trying to knock out the voices. "If they are bugging you mate just tell them to fuck off" I said I was still sat beside him on the sofa. He looked at me like it was the scariest thing in the world to tell them to fuck off. "They don't like you Tracie, you don't know" he replied. "That's okay mate. Sometimes I don't like me either" I said. "You don't know what they say" He said sitting down and hitting himself again before attempting to make a roll up. He'd given me an idea "Let me grab my smokes mate and I'll make us one each" I said heading into the bedroom. M.J was on the computer talking to some guy in an internet chat room on AOL. I didn't have time to care "Go to Paul's, make sure you come to the living room and say Peter has called and needs PC help. Then go over there and call Paula and get her to sort his key worker or something. He needs help and he needs it today" I said turning to leave as M.J shouted

"Wait!" I looked back trying to keep one eye on M.J and one on Franklin whilst I stood in the doorway. "What if...." M.J gave me a torrent of ridiculous events which might or might not occur which were only designed to prevent her from getting off her ass and helping. What if Paul won't help and I'm trapped in the hall outside panicking. I am agoraphobic you know? Why can he have your help and I can't? What if Paula doesn't care either? What if I go out and you and Franklin change the locks? I stepped back into the bedroom "I don't have time for this bullshit. Do it and do it now" I said before walking out of the room back to Franklin and popping Mr Happy back on my face. "I come bearing gifts!" I said standing like Jesus in the doorway with my tobacco tin in one hand and a bottle of mineral water in the other. All the while Franklin sat there punching himself in the head and my girlfriend sat in the bedroom flapping about taking the four steps across the hall. I wasn't sure who was crazier, her, him or me.

It felt good to be able to help someone for a change but I was scared too. I didn't want Franklin hurting himself or flipping out on us, which was another reason to send M.J over to Paul's place. Halfway through my smoke M.J came into the living room. "Paul called, needs me to fix P.C won't be long" She rattled off with no emotion in her voice. She was out the door before either of us could respond. I looked at Franklin "Women" I said. He laughed and then smacked himself in the jaw. I heard it rattle.

"Anything I can do to help mate?" I asked him as I sat next to him. I was leaning forwards towards the small green marble table in front of me so I could see what he was doing.

"No, they don't like you. They say bad things" Franklin answered.

"Ah fuck em, I don't care about them. I care about you" I told him smiling.

"You'll kill me, you'll send me to hospital" He said looking at his roll up.

I turned to face him on the sofa and he looked up at me. "I promise you now mate. Nobody is going to hospital. I promised you that and well lets face it. It would be pretty dumb for me to do that now wouldn't it? If you don't want to go and we send you to hospital then you'd come home and ask us to leave" I said losing the smile for effect and so he knew I was one hundred percent serious. I could tell he didn't believe me. It was time to throw a little guilt in. "I can't send you to hospital mate. If you did come out and ask M.J to leave it would kill her mate. She's agoraphobic and gets scared really easily. She acts tough but she isn't underneath mate." I added.

"Tracie, I trust you. It's them" He said thudding his cheek with a bony knuckle.

I took his hand "Please don't mate. It won't hurt them it will hurt you. By hitting yourself then well, they win don't they?" We sat repeating this process for at least half an hour. Franklin hitting himself and me trying to stop him. I never felt he'd hurt me but I was always looking for it. There was a knock at the door. I looked at Franklin like I was surprised and went to answer it. It was Paul I gave him a look of thanks figuring he'd know more about how to handle Franklin than I and so I'd just have to take a back seat to his expertise. He walked into the living room and shook his head at Franklin "So you're playing up again are you" He said taking his eyes from Franklin and scanning beside the radio where Franklin kept his wallet, change and watch. I could see where this was going, he was a manipulative sort if he could get away with it and would use Franklin's fear of the hospital against him. Paul obviously thought because I was worried about Franklin I'd go with whatever he said and so would let him manipulate Franklin either that or I was turning as paranoid as the rest of them either way the only victim here was Franklin and I wasn't having that but I needed to see where this went. Paul continued his tale of torment "So you don't want me to tell your mum and now you've gone and upset M.J my good friend. Well you'll just have to behave yourself won't you?" Paul said taking two steps closer to Franklin and to the money, simultaneously Franklin was rocking faster and had started tapping his leg wildly, fuck it, I'd seen enough. "Franklin, this is how I deal with irritating voices mate" I said leaning in and making sure my shoulder touched his. I wanted him to know I was on his side. I was there for him and somehow that touch was important. I needed to be more real to him than the voices. I turned to Paul like a stern father "You!" I shouted pointing at Paul. Franklin sat bolt upright beside me. "Fuck off. Now!" I said pointing at the door. Paul's jaw dropped but he didn't move. I stood up and he bolted. "It's okay mate he's gone." I said kneeling by Franklin with my arm resting across his knee. "Listen I gotta go tell M.J not to ring hospital because Paul's an idiot okay mate?" I said. "I didn't mean to upset M.J Tracie, I'm sorry. You believe me don't you? I don't even hurt ants!" He said looking like he was about to cry. I felt so sorry for him.

M.J opened Paul's door "Did you call Paula?" I asked her as Paul gave me daggers from behind her. "Yeah, she's gonna call the nurse" she said dismissively. "Thanks, he needs his face patched up and definite mental help" Paul had walked behind the sofa in the living room so it was between M.J and him before he piped up. "He needs a slap, he's always like this. It's just attention seeking." I ignored him and looked at M.J pleadingly as if asking her to just keep the idiot quiet. She tilted her head and opened the door for me to come in and I did. Paul looked around at me then shook his head at M.J before grabbing the phone next to the sofa. "I'll just call the police fuck him" He said. I walked around the sofa and turned the T.V off which was still blaring. "What you doin..." I didn't let him finish. "Shut up. You are being very unhelpful." I said putting the phone back in its cradle gently and turning back to him. "You're going to stay with M.J until the nurse arrives. You're not going to talk to her. You're not going to bug her. I'll tell you what you're doing from there. If you fuck her around she'll tell me and I won't be happy. You will not go to see Franklin" I didn't give him chance to answer, I turned to M.J and pointed at Paul. "If this dickhead starts you call me" and walked out. I had no idea whether what I was doing was right, wrong or what in fact all I did know was that I was more capable of making sensible choices in the best interests of Franklin than either of those two were and so I did. As the evening wore on Franklin told me tales about the voices and other episodes he'd had. At first I tried to say they weren't real and he was stronger than them. After a few hours of this I started entertaining the delusions as if this would somehow help. I recall vividly trying to distract him by asking him where he'd bought his trainers from. He told me he'd got them from an alien on the planet Mars who'd charged him twenty four rupee's for them. After twenty minutes or so of unreality he'd realise what he's said or done and then hit himself a few times to try and drive the voices out before repeating the process. By now both cheeks looked like they had tennis balls sewn into them and I mean literally sewn, two huge lumps and many red strain marks where he'd punched repeatedly. I'd had a fair few scraps and never seen anything like it. On top of the cuts from his razor this didn't make for a pretty sight. Where the fuck was this key worker? What was Paul up to? I'd talked about his past, my past, our future. I'd tried everything I could think of I'd even grabbed a clear quartz point crystal of M.J's and told him that inside it was a world where everything was safe. I'd started describing this wonderful, calm, safe world and changing the tone of my voice to replicate that of someone calm and sleepy. It worked for a short while but every so often he'd still give himself a whack.

"The sun's shining off the water and you can feel the heat travelling through your entire body, calming, relaxing, getting heavier and heavier" I'd recite from memory. I'd read it somewhere and often used it when I needed to sleep but couldn't. He finally calmed down and I'd thrown in every symbol of safety, travel, security or warmth and well being that I could imagine. "No danger can come to you whilst you hold this" I told him handing him the crystal. "It's for you, your special place. It's stronger than anything else" I said hoping he believed in it more than he did the voices. "Thank you Tracie" he said with no energy. Then he stood up and walked into the kitchen. I followed him two steps behind just to make sure he was okay. He walked over to the kitchen bin and removed the top and placed it on the kitchen side. Then he undid his trousers took his penis out and took a piss in the bin. At least he wasn't hitting himself. I watched him go back into the living room oblivious to what he'd just done or simply not caring and then went to the toilet myself, in the bathroom. Where I put his razors in my pocket just to be on the safe side. When I came out Franklin was punching himself in the face with the clear quartz point crystal between his knuckles.

Chapter 27

I was learning to stay calm pretty quickly even though my mind was going ten to the dozen. What if he kicked off? What if he hit his jugular vein and bled out? What if he got a lucky punch in, dropped me and then went to work on me with the razors? I shook it off. It was lack of sleep and dealing with an unusual situation that was all. Nothing to worry about. The victim here was Franklin not me. Franklin needs help. Help him. I was momentarily stuck in the hall whilst my mind went to work but my body refused. I just said the first thing that came into my head "What's your favourite film man?" I asked him ignoring the blood running down his cheek where he'd pierced it with the crystal. He must have misheard me "Comedies" He said. I made a mental note to get the crystal back. I stuck one of his blank video's in at random and a woman came on the screen in glasses ,she was cute and on her knee's. I turned it off and looked for another, Franklin laughed. "Sorry mate, you can watch that one when I'm asleep. If M.J comes in and sees that I'm in trouble" I said still kneeling by the T.V "She can join in!" He said and amongst the sleep deprivation, psychosis, and emotional hurts we both creased up laughing and it felt good.

A fat comedian Franklin liked was doing his thing on T.V when Franklin hit himself again. I took his hand and shook my head. "No mate, that's enough for today" I'd tried everything. I wasn't angry I really cared about this guy but if all my nicey nicey stuff wasn't working then it was time for something else and I was tired. If he went Psycho on me I'd just have to handle it. I knew drug induced people could be incredibly strong and had no doubt that Franklin's condition probably gave him the same strengths. By this time I'd been on and off sleeping for days and had no sleep at all for two. Paula kept calling the Key worker who'd been out once and said they couldn't admit him because he didn't want to go and wasn't as bad as some she'd known about. Then she'd returned took one look at him and said she'd sort it and left. She spent ten minutes with me telling me I'd done a great job and asking me questions. No he hadn't done drugs, no I didn't do drugs. Yes I was OK I was just tired. No I don't drink. Yes Franklin has drank all the many cans and bottles you see lying around the living room. No he's hurt himself I've got blood on me from stopping him hitting himself. Etc. I'd tried everything I thought Nigel would use and to no avail. It was time to try what I thought Andy would do instead. Franklin trusted me, respected me even. It was time to use that. He wouldn't hurt me, would he?

During another part of fat Comedians speech Franklin's arm moved again to hit himself and I put my hand on his wrist and held it down. "No mate" I said not looking at him but watching the comedian. "Sorry Tracie" He said but immediately tried again. I held his wrist down. I was watching T.V but I could see him in the reflection of the gas fireplace in front of us. Would he bite me? Punch me? I didn't know but had to risk it or he was seriously going to hurt himself. "If I let go will you please stop?" I asked him gently still not looking at him. "Yeah, you don't have to hold me Tracie. I'm not a baby" He replied. "I know mate but it's for your own good" I let go and several seconds passed before he lamped himself again. "Franklin, you're starting to upset me now. It hurts me when you hurt yourself." I rubbed my cheek. Let's throw a bit of Wenzel guilt in there and see if that helps. It might work, his bullshit got in my head. He hit himself again and this time I threw myself on the floor and looked at him shocked as though he'd actually hit me. "Shit man, what the fuck? Please! Stop!" I said scrambling to my feet and holding my face before sitting down beside him again. He said nothing and then started to cry. "Sorry Tracie, not me, them" Franklin opened another can and downed half of it. I was kind of hoping he'd pass out from the alcohol but he didn't. I'd already removed his secret stash and told him he'd drank them earlier in the day. He wouldn't remember anyway. I saw back and watched the T.V but kept my hand on Franklin's wrist. He kept trying to force it upwards with pure strength until in the end I just moved my hand

and let him do it. Where was that fucking nurse? I'd later find out M.J called the nurse who called Paula who agreed to take him if it was both warranted and safe to do so however because of the blood and crystal they thought he was a danger and so were waiting for a riot van with full works to take him to the hospital just in case. I didn't know this at the time, I was sat oblivious with the curtains pulled behind me and a fat comedian in front of me. "Out! Out! Out!" Franklin exploded punching his dead again and again. Little speckles of blood went on his shirt and on mine. I grabbed both of his wrists and knelt in front of him this time not fucking around with no eye contact. I looked straight through him. "Let go Tracie" He said. "no mate" I replied as calm as I could. The coffee table had budged over as I'd moved in front of Franklin and so it was now halfway into the living room but still stood up. Several empty cans were on the floor however. "Let go!" He said trying to flail his arms. "Franklin, stop it" I said calmly. He leaned forwards a little bit and my defences went up. I was ninety percent sure he was going to sink his teeth into my nose. "Don't even fucking think about it!" I shouted into his face and started eyeballing him. He relaxed immediately "what?" he asked calmly as his demeanour suddenly totally changed. I let his wrists go. "I'm here to help you Franklin. You're a mate but if you think of biting me again Ill knock you the fuck out and you will wake up in hospital do you understand?" I said not taking my eyes off his.

"I wouldn't, I didn't, sorry, sorry, sorry" He said becoming his usual vulnerable looking shell. He didn't punch himself for the next ten minutes and then their was a knock on the door. It was the nurse and I re explained everything from the last time she came and the new information since then. Then she quizzed me about my mental health etc. She saw Franklin and did a half decent job of hiding the shock from her face at how he looked. Then she sat and had a chat with him whilst he punched himself in the face. I stopped him several times which the woman said was dangerous but that I'd done a great job. I wanted to cry with relief that I was doing something right but I couldn't. I had shit to do and my mind was still partly in Franklin's head and I knew right now he'd be thinking about what was going to happen next now the nurse was here and that would be driving him crazy, well, crazier. Instead I told her the hardest two things were stopping him hurting himself and stopping him getting inside my head. She asked if I wanted therapy. I told her my father killed my mother, I've seen worse than this and walked off. She said the ambulance wouldn't be long and that she'd told everyone he could be a danger to others as well as himself and so the police would be on hand if required. Inside half an hour there were two coppers at the front door in full riot gear. Franklin was terrified and I could understand why. I asked myself what they were so afraid of? Then realised the answer was Franklin and justified it to myself that not all schizophrenics would hurt people. I hoped I was right.

Franklin didn't want the police in the flat and started flapping big time. He was scared they would hurt him. To be fair I'm northern and I was scared they'd hurt me and it wasn't me they were there for. I spoke to the nurse outside and explained. As I did so one of the coppers said "we'll bring him down" He was build like a cliff face with the same personality. I turned to the nurse "no, trust me. I can bring him down. He'll freak out on you guys. He might shout and wave his arms but he won't hurt me. Just leave him be until I have him in the ambulance?" The nurse agreed and Rambo informed me If I couldn't get him out they'd have to come in and that I should just get out of the way. I ignored him. I understood his concern but he wasn't productive at this time.

I told Franklin I was sorry that I couldn't keep my promise because I didn't know Paul had called an ambulance. That I've had a word with them and said that Franklin is fine but they need to see him in the ambulance. Franklin refused flat out "No ambulance, no doctor, no police. No, no, no." he was terrified. "I won't hit myself Tracie, I won't I promise Tracie. Look I won't hit" He said close to crying. I didn't know which way was best to go and so just blagged it. "Look mate. I agree with you. These guys are ass holes aren't they? But I've promised them me and you will go for a check up together so it's either we go together as friends or they come and get you" I felt like the parent I'd of wanted all those years ago when I went for that blood test. Just someone to hold my hand and tell me everything was going to be okay even if it was going to be a pile of shit. Franklin walked out the door with me and down the stairs. Past the cops and the nurse with his head down. The staff were pretty good and as soon as he was in the ambulance he relaxed. They took him to hospital and he stayed in for about two months. We visited weekly and we wrote to one another. Whilst he was away M.J and I managed to secure private accommodation that would accept DSS.

We stayed with Franklin until we could get all of M.J's stuff from her parents and it moved into the new flat in Bromley. During which time Franklin had another episode this time he'd hit his face whilst wearing his glasses and they'd stuck in near his temple. We weren't aware until the morning when he said he was going for a shave but already had blood on his face from the glasses. We convinced him to wait for the shave after last time and got straight on the phone to his key worker. This time there was no messing around and an ambulance came out to take him. Franklin walked into the ambulance of his own accord with no issues and I went to the hospital with him. The doctor he saw spoke to me first and then to Franklin and I left him with the doctor convinced he'd be taken care of. I got home and informed M.J what had happened and that we'd go visit him and sort out about getting him some new glasses. I'd gone back to Franklin's to sort out what I was sure would be a can filled dump and halfway through clearing everything up and putting the washing on the door opened and Franklin walked in as though nothing had happened. "You okay mate?" I asked him. "Yeah, thanks Tracie" He said as right as rain. "What happened mate? Not being funny but last time I saw you they said you were staying in a while. Everything okay?" He laughed. "Yeah I'm fine Tracie, I told them I was okay so they let me go." I just nodded. It sounded plausible and I should have expected it. I informed Paula and she asked us to stay as long as we could rather than go ahead with our move. I explained Franklin needed professional help and as much as I thought the world of both of them I could only do so much and I'd do that from my own home where we're not around Franklin constantly and can offer better, clearer help. She thanked us both.

Two days later Franklin ate his glasses frame and was admitted to have it removed and then was sectioned. We'd moved into our new flat by the time he was released. I loved Franklin like a brother but there comes a point in time when there's only so much you can do.

Chapter 28

I'd had a good year of relative quiet. We'd got our own private
accommodation. I'd even got a social worker to assist me get my
care records sent to me and we had a routine. The flat was clean
and tidy, we'd go to her mothers once a week and although it
wasn't perfect by a long shot it was a routine and that routine held
some form of safety for me.

M.J kept contact with Paul who I'd totally refused to have in the flat
at all. M.J's reason was that if anything went wrong between her
and I then he would be around as he'd always been around before
when she was at her mums. I explained he hadn't done a damn
thing about her being beaten by her mother though had he to which
she exploded. Franklin slowly stopped calling because M.J wouldn't
answer and every time I answered and spoke to him for a while M.J
would find a reason to have panic attacks. I was getting to the point
where I'd rather avoid the conflict than take her shouting. I justified
it all as manageable. I couldn't possibly walk away, Wenzel had and
that wasn't right. Men don't just walk away, they handle things and
help fix them.

 In the early days we went shopping together in the car after picking
up our money and she'd generally go to her parents okay. However
as the weeks went on she found more and more reasons to stay
inside and more reasons to panic when even thinking about going
out. To which I'd get the abuse, I figured this was a normal part of
her anxiety and depression and that on some level it was my own
fault for not being able to assist with it. After all Wenzel couldn't
help my mum what chance did I have really? I assumed the stress of
Franklin's behaviour didn't help her and add to that she'd never
really dealt with her mum's abuse it's no wonder she had issues.
Perhaps if I gave her time and just rode it out she'd be fine. I
couldn't turn my back on her and I was too stubborn. I'd get her
help and she'd become more confidant. She'd sort it out and it

would be okay. It seemed the only thing that did bring he happiness was seeing Mojo her black and white cat which lived at her mothers. She often described him as her only friend. We spoke to the landlady and agreed that the cat could move in if we could convince her parents to let him go. After a while she started to feel safe again.

She told me herself the car was a safe place and so travel was fine as long as she was in the car and the home was safe as long as she could have whatever furniture she wanted wherever she wanted. If something was changed or in a different place she got anxious and felt like her world was falling apart then she'd start shouting at me like it was my fault. She'd still shake at the door but I was pleased and I was proud of her. All the positives had paid off and I kept up my relationship pretext in the hope of leaving by making her so confident she'd be self sufficient. This wasn't low self esteem on my part I genuinely wanted her to be happy so I could say "I did it, I didn't walk away like Wenzel did" I guess in some way I was trying to rescue my mother by doing something Wenzel was unable to do. I wanted to beat him at something. I needed to prove myself.

I boosted M.J at every opportunity "You did great today, well done! Aren't you proud of yourself!" Sometimes she thought I was an ass hole other times she accepted it and eventually she started to use it and started to feel better. She sat in front of the PC as soon as she was home and that would be her for the rest of the time. She'd not move until it was time to sleep. "Coffee?" She'd ask. She never brewed up and she cooked once in a blue moon unless it was just for her. She was still on the Surmontil but hadn't taken a Valium since she'd moved in and was off her inhalers all together. We didn't play games or decorate or do anything together really, which I put down to depression. We just lived in the same place and I was her run around. Intimacy was rare by choice and somehow felt wrong. I couldn't figure out how but it was never quite right no matter who had instigated it. Her life was basically AOL chat rooms or an Online multiplayer game where she could chat to other people. I knew from experience that online she came across as the perfect person. Face to face, not so much.

My email address was a sub Email of her account because she was worried I'd run off with another woman, which to be fair I could understand her concern. I was living with Courtney when I met M.J however things started to become more noticeable like the fact that I started giving all my money to her out of choice at first, to help pay towards the Bed and Breakfast's she'd initially funded. Since then it had become habit, If I mentioned this or refused to pay her money she got aggressive. Not physically at first but shouting and swearing then throwing things around. There was always an atmosphere of something going wrong. Her favourite line was "You don't care about me!" I was getting used to it however walking the line was starting to bug me too. For instance I had a pay as you go mobile so people could call me but if I had put any money on it she'd want to know who I'd spent it calling or talking to. It became easier to simply lose the friends from the past and so that's what I did. I literally had a pay as you go phone I only ever received calls on, from M.J. What's more is she had me believing this was perfectly normal and somehow my choice.

I went on what I can only describe as a journey of self discovery, it wasn't even intentional. Through trying to help M.J with her stuff and after what happened with Franklin I noticed there were things I didn't like about myself that were getting to me and I couldn't change. It was normal to take care of the family as the man of the house however I didn't want M.J to take control of everything. I wanted to go to college, I wanted a job. I wanted friends and this wasn't possible for me. I started to get agitated and later I got angry with myself for wanting these things. I looked around me for ways to throw my head out of the rut I'd got myself into and all I could see was a smaller and smaller circle of hope around me. I looked the same place I always looked when I got low, I looked towards the past. Where was Jonathon? Jodie? Caroline? What were they doing? They always cropped up and I always chucked them back down inside because I never knew what they wanted.

Caroline had contact with both Jodie and Jonathon and said they wanted nothing to do with me because I'd gone back to Wenzel years ago and I couldn't get a relationship with Caroline because I was pissed off that she wouldn't facilitate contact and hell if she didn't care enough to help with contact why on earth would I want a relationship with her? The fact she was my sister and I'd done her my own wrongs in the past hurt even more. I spent nights searching them again online when M.J was asleep it was both a way not to go to bed and a way to have my time. I found where they lived, went to school, worked. I found that my brother had a child that I'd not known about and I broke down. Lets face it nobody that's alive cares in the slightest including myself. What did I want from life? I always wanted to know why my mother was killed. Maybe if I found out. Maybe if I got all the information together and documented it. Maybe if I wrote down everything for my family, my brother and sisters, maybe just maybe they'd not have to go through the things I had to go through to get that information. Maybe they'd have more questions that would bring them in touch with me and maybe then I'd have some kind of family? I felt the tear burn my face as I pressed and held the power button on the big home computer. It died and the silence filled the living room around me.

I told M.J the following day that I was going to look at all the things from the past. I'd make the family tree and go from there into each of their history's until I got everything then I'd document it and give it to my Brother and sisters. M.J in typical fashion said it was a waste of time and that we didn't have the money to chase dreams or go to college and do a course. Besides I have no qualifications how do I expect to be able to find anything out with no qualifications? I can't just request information about people you know. She had me believing she was right and so, I told her I was depressed and needed to see a therapist. She said that was stupid and that I didn't need it as I could talk to her. I told her I was seeing a therapist and I booked an appointment. The air in the room had changed the moment I'd put the phone down. "Are you trying to kill me!" She screamed sucking on her inhaler. "What?" I asked her "Calm down" I said stepping back as she leaned forwards into my face and took another gulp of whatever the blue inhaler was. "First you stay up all night talking to women and then you make an appointment to see a therapist! Do you think I'm fucking stupid! Do I look fucking stupid!" She was tapping the side of my head hard with her finger. I stepped back again into the hall "Don't do that" I said shaking my head. She moved forwards "aw you don't like that? Well I don't like being lied to! What do you think about that?" She said tapping my head again. I stepped back and sidestepped around her so I was back in the living room. I felt trapped "M.J You're talking shit. I was looking up stuff about my family, chill the fuck out" She sat down and started swearing to herself under her breath then routinely slamming her large forearms on the cheap woodchip desk we had.

I plain stopped sleeping in the bedroom and started sleeping on the sofa instead making the excuse that I couldn't sleep with her fan on all night which she did because of her asthma which had only spiked up again since she was so angry with me for whatever she'd decided I'd done this time. A week of this and she decided the bed wasn't helping her sleep because of her weight and so she had to sleep on the sofa. I happily gave it up and slept on the floor in front of the desk. I knew if I went to bed she'd join me but there was no way she'd sleep on a hard floor. Me however, I felt at home on the floor.

I decided if I was going to get in that amount of trouble for talking to people I'd not been speaking to then I might as well be actually talking to people and get the roasting anyway. So I got in touch with my old friend Louise and told her everything. She was naturally surprised and said it wasn't like the happy go lucky me she'd known as a kid and although I was a little weird even then I wasn't someone who'd let people walk all over me. She was right but what could I do? I figured I'd just be honest with M.J and she'd throw me out and then hey I'd get my own place or something. I was scared but fuck it, what's worst that could happen?

M.J got up in the later morning, once I'd made her food and drink I pulled a chair from the dining table and moved it alongside her pc chair at the desk and told her what a great catchup I'd had with Louise and how she was getting on with her boyfriend. I was making conversation I wasn't saying anything which was in poor taste and yet she burst into tears. "You tell me you've been up all night talking to an old friend and then you tell me you've had a great time?" I held her as she cried and explained it wasn't like that. Louise is over a hundred miles away and we were only ever friends. "I hate you! Don't touch me!" She screamed storming off. She returned with an empty bag and dropped it by the front door "I'm leaving!" she said. I'd had enough. I was sick of the arguments, sick of the borderline fighting and I was depressed myself. I'd had enough and couldn't care less any more. "Cya" I offered. "Cya? Fucking Cya! I tell you I'm leaving and you say Cya?" She was screaming and jumping up and down, the floor was banging as she did. She whipped her inhaler out and gave me the usual speech about trying to kill her whilst she puffed on it. "No, but I won't stop you from leaving. That's your choice". We'd established from some of the history paperwork we'd got through that my mum was trying to leave Wenzel. She'd actually made a phone call the night before to an aunt and said she would go and stay with her until they could sort something out with the social services. Wenzel must have talked her into staying at least the night because she was found in her pyjamas and covered in a blood stained duvet with no sign of a struggle. So no, there's no way I'd stop M.J leaving and she knew it. I would never make myself like Wenzel in any way that I could choose not to be. Hell when they said I needed glasses like him I'd grown my hair down my back to ensure I looked nothing like him. "But you're supposed to care! I trusted you!" She stormed. "You hurt me! I hate you!" She added looking for a response. I felt guilty because I couldn't help her but the realisation had hit. Only she could help her. I could try but she had to try too.

I explained to her "I do care, my mother tried to leave and my father killed her. I won't control any woman. You want to go, you go." She threw her bag outside the doorway and walked out. I watched her walk down the road on her mobile phone from the window. Oddly she didn't look back or appear concerned about being outside at all. She was back inside ten minutes. "I'm sorry, I love you" she said. I was gob smacked but chose to work with it. "Okay, how can we make you feel better so when I talk to friends you don't take it as a personal attack?" I asked calmly. "Well, maybe if I knew about her?" She asked and so I told her everything I knew about Louise, skipping the parts where we used to walk with linked arms or that I'd asked her out that third or fourth time. "Okay, if you don't talk to her I'll be fine" She told me. "What? You can't do that. I have no issue with you keeping in touch with David who's an ex or Paul. This isn't Louise's problem. It's yours" M.J was up and in my face "I pay the bills, I gave you money for a hotel, I took you in, I stayed with Franklin because of you!"She was crying and prodded me hard in the chest, I moved away. "M.J calm down" I said softly. She had fire in her eyes and I realised she had every intention of turning me into her father. It was only then that the penny dropped.

Over the next two years I wrote off to every connection to do with my mothers death. It meant I wasn't concentrating on M.J's abuse which had escalated. It meant I wasn't concentrating on how my life had turned out this way and why I was slowly turning into her father and it meant I was getting some sort of answers to why my father thought it right to murder my mother. By this time I wasn't questioning if it was manslaughter or not. I was convinced it was murder regardless of what the courts had said. I had the coroners report, transcripts, therapist letters, social services reports and even

Wenzel's medical records, I even had statements from the scene of crime officers. What I didn't have was a transcript from the courts itself as it had been over five years since the court date and so those were lost. On the telephone I was clear and confident. As far as everyone was concerned I was a fully functional person researching his mother's death for his own personal use. Away from the phone I ran around after M.J automatically and would sit in the bath staring at the wall whilst the water went cold for as many hours as M.J would allow before she wanted food or to use the bathroom. Her leg had grown to humongous proportions due to lymphodeama and it was up to me to massage cream into it morning and night because she was so big she couldn't reach. This is what happens if you allow yourself to get to twenty eight stone and you don't exercise or eat properly. I don't remember when her prodding turned into slaps but it had and I don't remember when her slaps had turned into fists but they had and I accepted it and usually closed the door until she'd calmed down. I'd find her later on having gone back to taking her Valium, at one point I told her if she was a guy I'd of dropped her already. It didn't help "Hit me!" She screamed I walked away and my compliance became automatic. If she asked if I wanted to go to her mothers it wasn't a question unless I wanted to be awake for three nights arguing about it. I'd literally said no once and she kept waking me up every time I fell asleep to continue her arguing and telling me how much I hated her parents. She was right but I never admitted it, her parents turned her into her, of course I hated them. She was quite rightly obsessed that I didn't love her because I wouldn't sleep in the same room as her. I used the same excuse she'd had me use to jump on benefits. My shoulder hurts to sleep on the bed and so I sleep on the floor. It's not personal I promise.

It was.

I always had an interest in psychology and it was my birthday. M.J had bought me a book. Diary of the warrior of light by Paulho Cohelio she'd written inside it "Thanks for everything you've done for me. You make me feel special every day. I love you" She also bought me a key ring, tobacco tin and pen knife all engraved with my initials on them. I kept them in the desk where the PC was. I didn't camp any more so had no use for the knife and didn't want the tobacco tin damaged. M.J had ballooned up to nearly thirty stone and her leg was getting bigger and bigger where she'd sat for such long periods of time. I was still ten stone flat because whenever I was angry I went down to the punchbag in the garage and let loose on that. M.J got piles shortly after her leg started to swell and spent three nights sat on the end of the bed watching T.V with bags of frozen peas beneath her. She had got to the point where she'd given up on everything. She couldn't wash or dry he hair and of course it still had to be coloured and so it fell to me. I kept giving her the positives in the hope that she'd one day catch on. I turned it into a game whilst doing her hair "I'm strong and confident", "I'm happy and healthy" "I'm bright and bubbly" etc, etc. She never followed suit. She just didn't care. My therapy wasn't really helping me, at least at that time I didn't think he was. His name was David and the guy was a diamond but I just sat there talking about the past the first few sessions and as shocked and surprised as the fella was therapists have a habit of connecting dots and sometimes those dots aren't the picture that make up the problem. In this instance he was decent enough to keep asking me what I thought the problem was instead of speculating which I did like about him and eventually after several sessions he got to the route of the problem. "How's your relationship with M.J?" He asked. I sat in silence for the remaining four minutes of the session like I had as a child and then left promising to see him next week.

The following week I noticed he worse a suede jacket as he'd had a smoke outside before I turned up. He also had matching shoes in colour but in leather. He didn't waste any time "You were telling me about your relationship with M.J?" I wasn't but it was a good attempt. "Nice shoes I've got a pair like that" I said thinking about Wenzel's shitty suede jacket and avoiding the subject of M.J. "Did you come here to talk about my shoes?" I didn't expect the directness and my head shot up. I looked him straight in the eye, he'd never come across threatening before and I'd not expected it here. I saw no threat in his eyes but we both realised something in that moment. Firstly that if I was looking for it then he now knew I'd been hurt physically before otherwise I'd not be looking for signs of it and that two he knew how to get my attention and wouldn't be messed around. I had two choices tell him to go fuck himself or trust the guy. Either way he'd brought the conversation to a head and the rest was up to me. I eyeballed him. Let's see how much balls this guy actually has if he wants to go routing around inside my head. He ignored me and took a sip of his drink then looked back at me. "I can't help you if you don't want to talk about it", "Isn't your job supposed to be to help me help myself?" I fired back. Yeah, I'm not a dumb ass who needs help. I might have no qualifications but I read. "No, my job is to see if you want to help yourself. Can you tell me why you don't want to talk about M.J?" He was good and he was getting to me. I wanted a smoke. I'm done, If you'll have me I'll see you next week. I got up and left right there. I figured before I actually dropped M.J in the shit I should at least make a go of trying to sort things out. What if we both went on a college course like together? She could see it's not all sleeping around and maybe she'd make friends and maybe then she'd get confidence and then I could leave? I pitched it to her without the leaving part. She agreed as long as I did a course with her and she picked it we could do it. So we signed up to do a British Sign Language course together. We practised online and both found we were okay. Then we went to the college and signed up. All went really well until halfway through the first lesson when M.J declared in front of everyone "She doesn't like me!" Pointing to the tutor. I apologised to the tutor and explained to M.J she was imagining things. M.J refused to go any more because the tutor didn't like her and so I couldn't go any more either. Naturally it was all my fault that she was stressed and highly embarrassed in the classroom by the tutor who looked at her and so

I had to pay for both courses because she didn't get a qualification out of it. I refused and argued with her once we'd got home. We went back and forwards for at least two hours debating and talking until She said she was going to kill herself because I don't love her any more, apparently if I loved her I'd understand her and pay for the courses and complain to the College. I naturally talked her out of taking pills and sat with her until she calmed down. I gave her all the silly answers she wanted. I'd not do the courses. I'd pay for them and I'd help her draft a complaint letter to the college.

One last shot. I said to myself one last shot before my appointment with David. I'll try and help her and myself and if it doesn't work or she goes sicko on me I'll tell David everything and he'll advise me from there. I told her I wanted to do a psychology course because I wanted to work with people who'd been through what I had, she said it wasn't possible we didn't have the money for paper and pens. I walked into the bedroom and took two thousand pounds in cash from her bottom drawer. "I know how much we spend, I know how much you save. This is spare cash, we can get it from this for less than that total" She snatched the little red tin from me and hit the monitor with it. "That's mine!" and she was instantly in depressive mode again. I'd had enough we argued for half an hour or so before I went to make a brew. She followed me in and took a pair of scissors out of the drawer. I kept my eyes on her whilst I made the brew, this was a new game and I wasn't sure how it was supposed to play out but I didn't like it. "If you leave me. I'll kill myself." Ah it was a game I'd heard before and a game I'd got sick of playing. I opened the drawer and pulled out the biggest knife with a serrated edge I could find then placed it on the side in front of her. "Here, use this those scissors are blunt as fuck" I said deadpan and went back to my coffee. She ran into the bedroom crying and lay on the bed for an hour in tears. When the sobbing stopped I went in and asked if she'd calmed down yet. She rolled over and something shone in the light. It was four sleeves of cocodamol, they were empty.

Chapter 29

I called the doctors who said take her to a hospital immediately, but of course she wouldn't go. I called an ambulance, the neighbour a little elderly man from next door called Jim heard the complaints from M.J and tried to calm her down, to no avail. The ambulance team said they'd not have the facilities to get her down the stairs in a chair or stretcher due to her weight and the layout of the flat if she wouldn't walk down and she refused to walk down despite having done so every single time we'd been up or down those stairs before, and so all they could do was inform me to get lots of fluid in her.

She loved the attention "I'm not going to the hospital! You can't make me!" I told her she was being an idiot and this wasn't about arguments or right and wrong this was about getting her the help she needed before she ended up dead. She laughed me off. I threatened to call her mother. She blanked me. I told her mother who laughed and put Toby on the phone. I told Toby who said it wasn't the first time and that he had warned me before what did I expect? I called the hospital back who said she'd be fine if she drank loads of water. I had a go at him and told him if she died because he wouldn't get someone out to her then it was on him not me and I'd find him and fuck him up. Yes it was probably the wrong way to deal with things but then I was in a bit of an unusual situation. I even saw our neighbour again, Jim and asked him what he would do. He spoke to her for an hour and she still wouldn't go to the hospital. Ironically she was scared they would sedate her.

I'd been chatting to someone called Melorna online for the past two weeks. She was a random name that stuck out on the game M.J played the majority of the time and so I'd created an account and got talking. She had a decent sense of humour and seemed as unhappy at the absurdity of the world as I was. It was nice to be able to just talk rubbish and not be judged for it. I hadn't mentioned

M.J other than to say I was in relationship with someone. However I couldn't take it any more after what M.J had done and so broke down and told Melorna everything from start to finish. I was terrified M.J might have a keylogger and find I'd told someone everything but I'd had to in case one day she did kill herself and they thought that I'd done it. Why wouldn't they? My father did kill my mother.

It can't have been more than a month had gone by with Melorna helping keep my brain in gear. I was telling David more and more but not about the violence just about her abuse in general. Melorna was a god send at this time and without her I'd never of had the courage to open up to David. When M.J came out of the bathroom in her nightdress mid morning and said "I'm bleeding." She was on the pill and had been since I'd known her so shouldn't be bleeding however she also had a supply of Tampax in the wardrobe so recommended she put one in and we'll call a doctor. She said she had but she'd gone through several in no time at all and was scared of saying anything in case she had to go to the hospital. I was talking to Melorna at the time and seeing as I could see where this was going I wanted a woman's advice. I asked Melorna who said simply "Get her to hospital." I told M.J she needed to go to hospital and she ran away into the bathroom and locked the door. She screamed out that she wasn't going and that I couldn't make her. I didn't even leave my chair I just carried on talking to Melorna. About half an hour later she came out "Clean me, I feel disgusting" she said. I was at the end of my rope. "You going to hospital?" I asked with no emotion. "No I don't need it I'm fine" She replied. "You don't go, I don't help you" I said turning back to the P.C. I didn't even see her move. She caught me twice in the temple and these weren't slaps, the second one knocked me off the chair. I stood up and raised my arm, I stopped myself two inches from her face. She flinched back and I walked into the kitchen and hit the fridge leaving a dint in it. "Enough!" I shouted. "Hit me again and that will be your face!" I said pointing at the fridge. "Now fuck off!" I added and for once I actually wasn't calm when I was in a situation. My heart was going nuts and I was shaking like I seriously wanted to tear someone in half. I sat back down as she shuffled into the bedroom crying. I had a smoke and called the hospital to explain everything including the loss of blood and trail she was leaving wherever she walked. The guy told me she needs a scan and it had to be done at the hospital, whilst on the phone M.J returned "What you doing?" She asked. "Getting you some help seeing as you won't do it yourself" I replied pointing to the phone. "I've taken pills" she said chucking an empty sleeve of cocodamol at me. I was used to her lying but never could take the chance and she knew it. This was just another form of control.

I kept the guy on the phone and checked the bedroom, there was Surmontil and cocodamol empty as well as paracetamol. He said he couldn't advise me on the phone but would send an ambulance. For the next hour Mr Polite had vanished. "Sit down, drink this" I said standing in front of her with a beaker of water. "No, who do you think you are?" She said pushing my chest. "Go on bitch hit me! I fucking dare you! I've had just about enough of your shit. You're going to drink this or I'm going to ram it down your fucking throat do you hear me?" She was silent she'd never seen me like that before and wasn't sure whether to test me or not, I wasn't giving her time to figure it out "drink" I said handing her the beaker. She downed it and I got another and another. After four I said "Right, next time you take an overdose, next time you threaten to take an overdose, next time there's one too many pills missing from that box I'm out the door, now drink" She did but my blood had started to boil "Next time you hit me, I'm out the door", drink.

"You're health is your problem not mine. I help because I choose to. I don't have to there's a difference. If you don't help you I won't help you" drink. She tried arguing and each time I cut her off. "I don't care, I've said my piece drink up" I must have said "I don't care, I've said my piece drink up" twenty times at least before she actually got it that I wasn't going to listen to her crap any more It took two days of repeating myself in this vein for her to be with it again and kept her drinking pretty much constantly. She still refused to go to the hospital and the hospital was saying a scan couldn't be done at home so the only avenue I had was that they were then indirectly refusing her medical treatment which was due to her condition tantamount to intentional infliction of emotional distress at a minimum and at a maximum endangering a human life by negligence The hospital quite rightly wasn't having any of it. However I couldn't have her bleed out in front of me and I couldn't stop the bleeding. So I called a bluff whilst I was on the phone to the hospital "Sorry Mr Daily I'm about to do my rounds unfortunately I cannot Help M.J unless she comes in." He said. "That's fine I'm calling to let you know I'll be there in the next two hours with a newspaper crew and a pair of handcuffs. Let's see how you do your rounds with me handcuffed to you because I've had enough. She needs treatment and if you don't give it to her I'll give you enough bad publicity to bring your career to an end. Your move, you've got an hour" I hung up and hoped for the best. We received a call twenty minutes later informing us that a car was being sent out with two people and a mobile scanner in it. It wasn't the norm but they'd happily make an exception on this occasion. I thanked them profusely. M.J just looked at me like she was somehow entitled to special treatment.

The medics were absolutely brilliant. They took her blood and gave her a scan. They ruled out toxic shock syndrome and said it was likely a reaction to her contraceptives which she'd apparently changed recently. I couldn't fault them at all. M.J asked me to make her the appointment at the clinic. I told her she could do it herself but I'd go with her and she did.

Melorna and I had started talking more and more about ourselves rather than the online game we were playing. I hinted at my PC potentially being key logged and she showed me ways to check if it had been tampered with. I eventually told her everything about M.J and she said I should leave. I remember clearly crying at the P.C one night hoping M.J wouldn't come in to find me upset because she'd ask what was wrong and the only thing that was wrong was that someone had validated my experience. Melorna had said "I understand you're going through a world of shit right now and it will be okay, you're right it's not normal, it's not right and you should leave." Whilst trying so hard, so diligently and so often to the point of obsession not to turn into my father I'd inadvertently found myself becoming my mother. Melorna's help was amazing it meant I had somewhere I could be me, totally me without any fake face or ego. M.J realised pretty quickly I wasn't going to do everything for her any more She started going to see a therapist I arranged for her and she drove every week and it was great because although initially she insisted I wait outside the waiting room. I could go further away and have a whole hour to myself. I used to just sit outside on the wooden bench but I was somehow more free. The therapist was really good. A cute blonde lady who got M.J to the point where she could question herself and try to figure out where he negative thoughts came from. It was a hard time for her but she was doing well with it. She had bouts of tears but it was normal tears not where she'd go into a blazing rage or anything. We eventually made it a routine to walk down the road together daily so as she got some fresh air regardless of the agoraphobia. I'd started working from home on a website that allowed me to take calls and get paid for sending emails. It wasn't great but it meant I had a reason to have time for me and I was giving advice over the phone. Graham still hadn't shown his face and my spiritual side had been dead for over four years. I meditated but nothing like used to occur with Alan or Graham. I should never have left Manchester. Not for Graham but because I was so unhappy in Bromley with M.J. I tried dabbling with Runes and had no luck, tarot, meditation to communication, self hypnosis, I'd go to the library and get the maximum books out on different spiritual methods and work my way through each. I digested them like metaphysical sponges from chakras to alternate realities. Nothing, nada, zilch. I didn't like the idea of setting myself up as a Medium. It wouldn't be true, mediums speak to dead people me I just had feelings about things that usually turned out to be accurate, well, they used to. I was trying to find out where I belonged and how much I could reconnect with something that made me feel good but I wanted to test it in an accurate and informed manner. Not one where it made money and people paid to hear a load of rubbish. I couldn't practice on people I knew and so I set up a free account and set the price to zero.

My website said specifically I wanted no information other than which of the five spreads they would like to choose from my page. Then I did my first email reading. I sat down and turned over five cards. I never used the silly little book that comes with these things I simply imagined that I became the other person and when I turned a card over I typed what I felt or saw. More often than not I forgot the reading as soon as I'd done it. In this instance I remember clearly mentioning a woman with a sore wrist but not much else. I waited for the feedback to be terrible. I waited for me to be totally crazy, I waited to discover it was someone having a laugh with me and I was so off base it was appalling. Instead two days later I got five star feedback and he informed me he was surprised because most of the people he'd been to didn't have half of the skill he thought that I had. He specifically mentioned his relatives arm. It turned out it was broken. In the end I had over 90% of five star feedback. M.J and I were getting ourselves back into a kind of order where we at least had a mutual respect of sorts. I was comfortable that she wasn't going to go crazy if I used the phone and so I called my aunt. "How's the kids?" I asked after initial introductions. These were the days before caller ID. She broke down crying, "leah's dead, sorry I didn't have your number. You missed the funeral." I used to babysit her, she was Clive's eldest daughter. I was immediately angry with the psychic side. How could I have this awareness for people about beating fear? About love? Yet not be told my cousin was going to take painkillers and fall asleep in the bath. "Nah, no, not possible. Fuck off, this a wind up?" I asked in total shock before hanging up. "Fuck you! Don't talk to me, fuck you!" I said looking around feeling my psychic self open up and me closing it back down again and blocking it out.

I played around with the psychic stuff for months. In part to try and calm my thoughts, meditation helped greatly. In other parts to see how far I could push it. What was reality? Besides it helped me calm my mind when all that was whizzing around was care placement stuff.

I'd had huge dealings with social services about my care folder because initially they couldn't find it. I told them It was probably down the salt mines with the court records in Winsford but they simply became more cautious thinking I was going to the newspapers about the several errors they had made in regard to the care they had given me. I told them several times it was purely for my use however they insisted on taking month's to reply and then missing deadlines because it hadn't been edited. It arrived over a year after I'd requested it. However with that and the coroners report I was able to piece together exactly how my mum was killed. For years I'd seen her in my head covered in blood in a white dress with numerous stab marks and her throat cut. I never told anyone but I used to see this when I was in care. I'd see it as though she was walking past my bedroom door or by my bed. I'd see it in the street or in school and as I got older I'd learnt to tell her to fuck off. My own mum and I'd learnt to tell her to fuck off because I knew she wasn't real. It worked but it didn't bring me any peace.

There was never any menace in these visions you understand just a case of her being there and the injury's my brain had concocted to say that's what she'd sustained. She hadn't. I sat on the sofa it was a blue two seater and I was chain smoking. There was a small coffee table to my left and I had the box of paperwork open in front of me as M.J passed me the envelope simply marked "coroners report". "Well, open it" M.J said. "It changes nothing" I said although my hands were shaking and the envelope was moving. The truth was it would change everything. After everything I've been through I'll finally know the truth but then what would I do? What would I live to achieve after this moment? My family still didn't care. This was just the end of my road in a different form. It had been years since we'd been in touch I was certain Jonathon, Jodie and Caroline wanted nothing to do with me.

I made five smokes and placed them around the ashtray and then picked up the letter. M.J stood in the doorway. I shook. "Whatever happens I love you mum" I said out loud. My fingers stopped working. I couldn't open it. I handed it to M.J "Don't read it. Just open it" I said. She handed it straight back and I was crying before I'd even taken the letter from the envelope. I let them fall whilst I read it and then re read it.

My mother was found prone on the floor of the Wizard Caravan site in Alderley Edge Cheshire with two stab wounds to her chest. One on the left hand side going through her ribs and another on her right going through her ribs. A four inch serrated edge kitchen knife was found embedded in the floor beside her. Once I'd looked up every medical term from why a cadaver requires the anal temperature to be taken to what prone meant. I finally put together that my mother and Wenzel were arguing the night before because Mum wanted to take the children and leave to be with our Aunt. However Wenzel in true fashion either talked her around into staying the night in that they would go in the morning or found a way to force her to stay. Either way she was found in her pyjama's stabbed twice in the chest with no foreign substances in her body and no sign of a struggle. She was beneath a duvet. Wenzel's version of an argument and him then stabbing her did not stand up. It is my true belief that mum was stabbed to death whilst she slept and cause of death although documented by the coroner as a stab wound to the chest would probably be best described as choking to death on your own blood as the knife had gone through certain arteries. I wasn't sure if I found this a relief to know or not but I can tell you now I've not once seen her covered in blood with numerous stab wounds and her throat cut any more. Not once.

I wasn't angry with Wenzel. I'd learnt a long time ago that anger only hurt me. It didn't do anything to anyone else. I did immediately look up the law though. Unfortunately it turns out that a person cannot be charged for the same crime twice and in this case he was charged for murder however got manslaughter on grounds of diminished responsibility and therefore can't be tried for Murder or Manslaughter unless there is "New and conclusive" evidence relative to the case. The courts presumedly know everything that I do. They definitely knew about the Coroners report and the phone call to our aunt. In which case they've simply bought Wenzel's bullshit as the only person able to explain it. Is it true he was stressed? Of course. Is it true he may have had anger related issues? Possibly. Is it true he didn't know what he was doing when he stabbed his wife to death in her sleep after getting her housed in a place with several caves which just happen to be ideal for hiding a body? I doubt it. I'm more of the belief that he was wanting to bang another woman, probably the one he ended up seeing at the hospital ironically and couldn't get rid of mum. When he couldn't make it look like an overdose or accident as he'd tried previously, he thought he'd kill her and take her to the caves. However after stabbing her twice he saw the amount of blood and panicked. At which point he went for a long walk judging by the rigarmortis, before handing himself in. None of which could have occurred by chance.

"Thank you, thank you" I said as the cold night air hit my face and dried the falling tears. I had my head out of the flats window and was chain smoking but somehow it helped. It stung but I needed to let go. "Thank you" I sobbed just because I knew. I was aware the new knowledge of mum choking to death on her own blood would take it's toll on me in some way. I knew I'd have to deal with that battle when it came and I knew I had absolutely no idea where I was going from here, but I knew I was going somewhere.

Chapter 30

I was sat in the bath again looking at the tiles for however long it takes for water to go cold. It was a small room and the white shower curtain was half pulled across, I refilled it. I got out when the boiler had ran out of water. I felt no better. "Going to bed" I said and fell asleep right there on top of the double bed. I awoke realising that was the first time in a year or more I'd slept on a bed. M.J was on the sofa and hadn't woke me up to get me to sit with her in case her asthma plays up or hadn't asked me to move so she could put the fan on. I appreciated her for that. I put the computer on and fired up my favourite online game, Runescape and then told Melorna "I got the coroner's report"

We chatted for hours and over the next few weeks I learnt a lot about her. She was originally from Texas and had three sons plus a controlling ex. She is also more direct than I am and twice as sarcastic. We got along like a house on fire.

Martin M.J's brother popped in. He weighed about ten stone less than M.J but was still the same small round shape that she and her mother was. He just had stubble and a shorter haircut which was black instead of red. He smiled more and seemed genuine enough to be honest. He was with a much older woman and had a couple of kids. I always made the assumption he was compensating for not having a mother figure at home but hey I could talk, right? He also played Runescape and got along OK with me, we didn't talk much but we were friendly enough. Today he'd brought us a new monitor as he'd got a new one. I unplugged our old one and set up the new one which worked perfectly. I then got the chair out I used to stand on before jumping up into the loft. We had a strip light up there but I needed to run the extension lead up to get it to light up and so I jumped up and plugged it all in. I climbed back down and picked up the big old square monitor. As I stood on the back of the chair and balanced the monitor forwards over the lip of the loft entrance, I slipped and somehow managed to catch the cable from the light fixture around my neck. It was a complete accident but I was now swinging by my throat with a heavy monitor on top of me. I dropped the monitor and clutched my throat. I panicked and kicked the door because I couldn't breath, to no avail. I knew I had to remain calm and could feel my world going blank. So this is it, I thought as the curtains started to close. No white light, no tunnel, no family coming to visit fuck all just darkness, thanks guys thanks a lot. I let out one more kick before I knew I'd be out when I felt myself lifting up into the air and then dropping to the floor gasping for breath.

Apparently Martin had heard me kick the door and seen me dangling and so lifted me upwards. I was kneeling on the floor. All my visions, all the psychic stuff, it amounted to nothing. I stood up still gasping "Fuck you!" I screamed and laid into the cupboard door beside me. "Fuck you!", "Fuck you!" I said over and over again as I just lost it. Lost control, lost everything. I sat rubbing my neck on the sofa for the next hour until Martin left. I shook his hand and said thanks before he went but otherwise I hadn't moved. I knew I wasn't myself since the coroners report. I'd done the essentials like shopping and creamed M.J's leg but I'd not cooked or hoovered, hell I'd not even washed apart from sitting in the bath. I was getting a rough beard and just didn't care. I stopped the online work and got back on benefits with my shoulders. I didn't care about me and despite Martin's help I felt nobody else did either. My teeth hurt and I needed a few fillings but fuck it, I deserved the pain. I was useless and I couldn't help M.J or myself. I grabbed a coke and sipped it. Out of nowhere my body exploded, my hands were shaking, throat sore, numb tongue and heart was moving eight hundred miles an hour. I clutched my throat as the world seemed to spin endlessly "What's up?" M.J said looking shocked. "Can't breath! Can't breath!" I said sticking my tongue in and out rapidly and pacing the flat. "Choking!" I said over and over. I checked my can of coke, it was fine. I tipped it into the sink. It was just coke. I paced from the bedroom to the living room window the full length of the flat and couldn't get away from this feeling of dread. I called the emergency doctors "help me, I'm choking." I said. The man was brilliant and stayed on the phone with me explaining how I couldn't be choking as I was talking just fine. To see my doctor in the morning as it's probably just panic attacks. I was wild. "Panic! My father killed my mother, my uncle fucked my dad up and I watched my granddad die. This is not fucking panic ass hole. I know panic and this isn't it! Help me!" He asked to speak to my partner and so I put M.J on. Whilst I looked at her bewildered how she could possibly be the sensible one all of a sudden whilst I bounced up and down in the corner waiting for my throat to close up she got off the phone to the fella who had just reconfirmed to her I was fine and I should see a doctor in the morning. "Check my throat?" I asked her. She ignored me and played Runescape "There's a fucking tennis ball in my throat will you check it please?" I asked her. "Nothing there" she said. "Fuck off nothing there, I can feel it" I stormed back and forth. I must have done this for hours before I plain collapsed.

I had no idea what was wrong with me. I'd not chose this. It was out of nowhere, instant, no warning what so ever and was like someone had dropped me into a pit of hungry crocodiles. I was terrified and felt totally as though I had no control over it. I didn't want it so couldn't have created it. Who wants panic attacks? It made no sense what so ever and I flat out refused to believe it. I sat explaining to my doctor "No pills, just get rid of them" I said. "Can I ask why you don't want pills?" He asked me. "Sure my mum was on anti depressants and they slowed her down. She turned to drink and ended up dead. My mate had bad side effects on pills and turned to drink he ended up sectioned. M.J gets very depressed and has pills that she sometimes overdoses on, no thanks doc not for me, I'll take hypnosis?"

"Sorry hypnosis isn't available on the NHS I'm afraid how about acupuncture?" He said.

"No, no needles, I don't like sharps" I said. I left with the advice of "Get some sleep" and come back in a week.

I was due at the dentist for this tooth. Her name was Helga and I'd seen her before she was usually pretty good. I wasn't worried we were forced into going as a kid where they took photo's of our teeth in care and mine were always bad so I knew the drill. "Hi Doc, filling please" I smiled. She was a nice lady but had a screechy voice when she spoke. I couldn't place where she was from. The only issue I'd ever had with dentists was requiring a female dentist because occasionally I felt trapped and needed to sit up. I felt stuck with a male and concerned I'd lash out where as I knew full well I'd never hit a woman and so it was safer for me and them if the dentist was female. If a guy hurt me I'd drop him but with a woman I'd simply walk away. She got her hands washed and had done all the x rays when she came to give me the injection. I sat in the waiting room for ten minutes and as my cheek went numb my anxiety increased. I realised not only was my cheek numb but so was my tongue. I sat there pushing my tongue in and out repeatedly like before so much so that it hurt. I couldn't breath and ran outside trying to be sick next to the dentists front window. There were people inside watching me and people walking past as I stood there trying to make myself sick and heaving. M.J had come with me and said I'd be fine just go back in and get on with it but I couldn't I was terrified. Not of Helga or even of having the work done but from the moment she'd put her hands even partially over my mouth it felt like I was choking and I'd freaked out. I promised to make another appointment and went home.

I hadn't eaten solids in a week and was drinking very little. The less I drank the more raspy my throat was and so the more I thought I had a problem and so didn't drink. The food was just intolerable. I tried chewing a piece of bread and just couldn't swallow because every time I tried it felt like I was choking. I felt weak and like nobody would understand me. I told Melorna everything from the care system until my present day. Including M.J. I even told her I killed my granddad, albeit by accident but the guilt never left me. She not only stuck around she also helped talk me through some of the hardest times in my life. I didn't believe I'd get through it. I wrote to my doctor and requested therapy. I'd still not eaten any solids when the therapy came through six weeks later.

Chapter 31

She was a good looking girl, tall with shoulder length blonde hair
late twenties. She'd come around to see us for an initial assessment
on account of M.J's agoraphobia and knowing due to being with the
same doctors if I left her alone she'd freak out, M.J did most of the
talking and every time panic attacks or anything relating to anxiety
came up M.J was off on a tangent about how she had the worst life
ever, her mum abused her and nobody knew what it was like apart
from her. I let her get on with it, to be fair to the therapist she tried
several times steering the conversation around to fear of choking,
generalised anxiety and eating disorders. Eventually I explained how
it came about for me and that I still wasn't convinced it as panic
attacks but that I freaked out whenever I felt something either was
or could be lodged near my throat. I noticed she loosened her scarf
and then kept subconsciously touching her throat every time I
mentioned it. It wasn't long before she was clearing her throat
every few minutes. I had to stop talking to her and accept the
therapy just in case she ended up with more issues than I did. I
brought it up that she may be empathising but it probably wouldn't
help her to over think it. Me the great hypocrite, she did say she
was newly qualified but would put me forwards to see the person
she'd been training with. As soon as she'd gone I called the doctors
and cancelled the appointment. I wouldn't get fixed by someone
who couldn't take a problem with the throat without internalising it.
What's going to happen when I start talking about my past? She'd
fall apart. I made another appointment at the Doctors.

I'd sat in the waiting room for forty five minutes and was getting
irritated. I wanted a smoke but they dried my mouth and made my
anxiety worse. Eventually it was time to go in. "Mr Daily you've
refused the offer of therapy I see?" He said before I'd got sat down.
I explained the situation as I sat opposite his big heavy desk, his
monitor was to my right and there was what looked like an in tray in
front of me. He offered me acupuncture again if I wasn't willing to

take the antidepressants which were on offer. "Look Doc, I'm needlephobic and you offer me acupuncture? Give me a break. I need something to help me eat and something to remove the panic attacks. You're the Doc you tell me. How do I eat? I just want to be able to eat comfortably again" I told him. My stomach had stopped churning about two weeks ago. Now it was just varying degree's of pain but mostly from the tooth which was getting worse. He gave me two weeks worth of ensure plus vitamin drinks which are basically a meal in a carton I drank them inside four days. It simply felt so good to have something heavy inside me and they were thick and filled me up. I felt great once I'd taken them, I started to try eating food with the theory that if I could down Ensure drinks then I could surely manage Soup? I was on Ensure plus vitamin drinks and Tomato soup for over three months before I could stomach crushed up wotsits on top of the soup. I hated meal times. Each time I sat down I was back there in front of Wenzel and he was dishing out the abuse. I couldn't hear him or see him as such but I was back there in my head none the less and the feelings were exactly the same. I explained this to my usual therapist David which wasn't even supposed to be treating me for the eating disorder and he said it was a form of Post traumatic stress disorder. I didn't even realise it could come out that much later. Another therapist would make the connection that the panic attacks started when the needle had been put in my mouth and it was sharp. I didn't do sharps because according to her I associated needles with knives and because my mother was stabbed by my father apparently I'd subconsciously made a connection there. Someone else said I'd had a crisis of faith in that as soon as I believed that there was no after life when I fell from the loft then I started to deteriorate and refused to eat. I argued that point staunchly, I hadn't refused to eat! How dare they? My body was doing something I didn't want it to do and had no control over what so ever. It was terrifying and I hated and made active progress in trying to remove it. How dare they blame me? I'd seen more than most people, I'll admit I didn't know everything but

I surely knew that?

My teeth deteriorated rapidly from just fluids and I needed several fillings. Most times it hurt and I'd started taking soluble cocodamol to numb the pain. I was taking them every four hours and found before the time was up the pain was back. One of my teeth had such a hole in that it was so brittle I knew if I pushed down on it then it would break. It was just a matter of when and how, of course M.J disagreed and told me everything was fine. Maybe it was, maybe I was just losing my mind entirely however the dentist had agreed to see me but I'd told her no work to be done, no needles. I just wanted to know what needed to be done altogether. After the appointment she said she'd refer me to the hospital because I needed four teeth removed and three fillings. I had a meltdown in her office. I wasn't going to be put out at a hospital, hospital's meant needles and I wasn't going anywhere near that.

My doctor had progressed to giving me a month's worth of Ensure drinks at a time and a good year had gone past. Well, a year had gone past as years go it was probably one of the worst to be fair. I still wasn't eating properly and that hospital appointment, well I'd cancelled that easily enough. I had taken to sitting down in the church every few days. Maybe I'd find an answer there? I asked If there was a God quite a bit and got no answer. I swore at him and then laughed at myself for swearing at something I don't believe in. What an idiot, to this day I don't know what that church was called but ironically it would play a large turning point in my life later on.

I'd walked to the pharmacist with my headphones in. I'd taken to listening to hypnosis at every opportunity to try and keep me calm. I found Dr Barry Weiss many lives many masters was a brilliant CD and helped me sleep a lot especially on nights where I'd woke up panicking several times. However today I was listening to some guy rattle on who didn't seem that interested in what he was saying. Morning Scott I said as usual. It was known as Scott's pharmacy but I knew full well the guy wasn't called Scott, He was a nice fella though and it was our routine. "Sure you'll be okay?" He said looking at the forty two cartons and my tiny frame, plus M.J's medication on top of that. I smiled "Yeah mate no worries" I knew they'd be heavy and it would be hard work but I also knew they were my only source of food so I'd get them home if it killed me. I got four steps from the counter and dropped the lot. I fell forwards into the door and knocked my head and turned around to find four of the cartons had split open onto the floor. I broke down on the spot and just sat there crying. What the fuck was wrong with me? That's my food. I need that! My brain was telling me to get up. To work shit out. To stop these customers staring at me. To clean my mess up and I just sat there watching the raspberry Carton drip away into the carpet. A tiny part of me laughed inside because I didn't even like the raspberry one but I'd of drank it anyway because it was food. I stood up and apologised as I attempted to scoop the cartons into the box. Scott saved me and told me he'd have them delivered. I helped clean the floor despite him telling me it was okay, I couldn't leave it. I had morals no matter how low I'd got. I took ten Cartons in a small box so I had food and the rest he delivered and he delivered every month after that too bless him.

It was bugging me that parts of my care folder were blanked out. They'd arrived in two huge boxes and I felt on some moral level as the oldest and the only person working to find out the truth I should have been allowed to get exactly what happened regardless of who that information related to. Of course I understood about freedom of information and the Data protection act, of course I respected privacy and peoples human rights. However on a human level I felt it was my job to protect Jonathon, Jodie and Caroline and I'd done a piss poor job of it so why shouldn't I be allowed to know everything? Who could it hurt? What's more I didn't trust social services there was rumour that I could have something called Oedipus complex which apparently is where I have an automatic distrust of any authority figure including but not limited to government bodies, schools, bosses, hospitals and pretty much anyone with more power or control than I wielded. I thought it was bullshit but couldn't deny I found more negatives in social services than I had positives. I couldn't deny I'd met more bad therapists than good ones and school was a total disaster for me because of the teachers and so I blamed social services and presumed they were hiding something. Had they been involved with us before mum was killed? Yes, but the reasons were blocked out. They were involved before I was sent to live with my nan apparently because Wenzel said he couldn't cope with mum's condition and so we moved to be closer to Alan and Pats. I guessed it was probably fake to get a bigger property. They were involved again before Caroline moved in with our Aunt's this time I presumed was more to do with Wenzel than anything although the reasons were blocked out because they solely related to Caroline. I called her and asked her, naturally she didn't want to speak to me and told me nothing bad had happened with her and Wenzel before hand. She also happened to say I should get my head out from the past and start living in the future as Jonathon and Jodie already wanted nothing to do with me did I want her to go the same way? I told her to fuck off. She didn't know what I was going through, I'd not told her. Hell I'd not spoken to her in about three years. I'd speculated Wenzel had abused Caroline and then scared her into keeping quiet I presumed he'd then killed Bernie to keep her quiet. Better to go inside for murdering your wife than as a paedophilia right? However Caroline said it wasn't true and it was Leslie that had abused her. I had no reason to doubt her and couldn't bring myself to ask what happened. Perhaps he'd dropped me on my head as a kid? It would at least explain the panic attacks.

I added temporary tooth fill to my chemist list and bunged some more orange stuff around my mouth which I'd learnt turns hard quickly but does stop the exposed nerves playing hell with me. I was still taking the cocodamol every four hours for fear the pain would kick back in and then I'd run around the flat doing my choking bit again. Vicious circle, what I didn't realise is I'd gone from having panic attacks to panicking about having my panic attacks. As Susan Jeffers would say I was fearing my fear.

Respect to M.J her therapist came out of the office after seeing M.J and approached me. "I know you're having a few issues, if you want to speak to me you can." She was gorgeous and if she wasn't seeing M.J I'd of jumped at it like a shot but I wasn't going to get involved with that and thought it was bad form for her to even mention it whilst she was seeing M.J to be honest. "No thanks, you're doing great with M.J she's made wonderful progress. Just keep doing that and you'll be doing me a massive favour" I said. "You've helped her a lot too" she whispered which was nice.

I didn't realise how low I'd got until I realised I was fantasising about suicide. I'd not attempted it but I'd thought about it a lot. As much as the faith thing did bother me I had this underlying reason not to attempt it and that's where my faith saved me. I didn't believe we continued after death, I knew it. I knew and still know today that we are here for a purpose. Whatever that purpose may be I don't know but I knew I couldn't actually die as much as I might have wanted to and bottom line as much and as angry as I was with the spirit side I knew they're real and if I did kill myself I'd just have their bullshit to deal with and my own when I come back and do it all over again until I learnt to handle it. I didn't like it any more than I liked how the dentist worked. It hurts and it's scary and it's horrible and intrusive but you know what, it makes you better and it makes you stronger. I don't like it but I understood it. I know at times I was that low and then asked myself "Would you have chosen before your life started to go through all the shit that you have been through?" I probably would out of ego or plain stubbornness I know myself and I guarantee if my options were live ten lives and go through something negative in each life or have ten lives and get all the bullshit out of the way in the first one I'd take option two every time. Maybe we are just in the bullshit life right now? Maybe we are just that stubborn, that determined or that stupid to have taken it all on in one go. Maybe I'm wrong and maybe those weren't the options. Maybe the options were "You can go through all of this or you can give it to someone else to go through but someone is going through it and has to learn it" Hmm we all know that person at work who does nothing all day and gets paid for it. We all know the poor sod who gets all the work dumped on them because they're positive and pro active and appear as if nothing phases them and we all know there's a third type of person and independent confidant person who takes extra responsibilities because they think they can handle them and sometimes can and sometimes it's harder than we initially envisioned and maybe, just maybe we are the third type. Have you ever met anyone who's been brilliant to your life for no benefit to themselves? Someone who went above and beyond the call of duty to help? I wonder if we chose those people before hand in case the going got too tough. I don't believe in destiny, I don't believe in the blueprint theory, I believe totally in free will however I can't deny that some things, not all but some, they happen for a reason. Besides I couldn't kill myself and had to find numerous ways to talk myself out of it. If I killed myself Wenzel had won and there's no way I'd let that sack of shit win, I'd out live Wenzel and I knew it, what's more I wanted him to know it too.

Chapter 32

I'd changed my glasses because I didn't like how they made me look. I was stood in the small white bathroom a place I'd called home for about three years, M.J's flat. The bath to my right the sink in front of me with the mirror above it and I stared through my expression. I looked just like Wenzel with them on. My long hair did nothing to hide the similarities I looked at him looking back at me and felt sick. "I hate you, I hate you and if I ever see you again I will kill you" I told my reflection flatly.

That night I tried tomato soup. I managed a quarter of it and it was the best soup in the world. M.J gave me bread and I fell apart crying "I can't eat it!" I lay on the floor with tears rolling either side and kept clogging my eyes no matter how many positives I put in when it came to it I still couldn't eat solids. The nightmares were back too. I was trying to sleep on the floor and must have nodded off because as I awoke there was a figure by my feet. I lifted my head to speak and it lay across me stealing my energy. It felt like it was pulling all my feelings into it. I felt myself disappearing "Get off!" I fought it but it was stronger. I imagined myself turning into a tiny light and slipping away from it and at that point I woke up gasping for breath. "Bastard!" I shouted looking around "Tried to kill me, bastard!" I later realised it was nothing more than a message from my subconscious. When push comes to shove I'll fight before I'll ever quit. I don't want to die. Not all of the dreams were bad. I'd been to my twenty seventh dentist appointment with Helga just trying to sit in the chair and let her do the work. She'd kindly promised to work with me as long as it took and I thanked her for it but still ended up walking out before I'd even sat down most times and on those times I'd talk worse to myself. I'd hate that I couldn't do it yet again and it would make me more reluctant to go next time. This time I'd gone alone and still couldn't manage it. I'd told M.J I'd failed again and was going for a walk. I turned my phone off because I knew she'd call me and knew she'd expect me back inside an hour. I stopped in the church on the way home the radiator was warm and it was quiet. I needed to feel good, perhaps if I could tune into the energy's of the church I'd be healed? I laughed at my own joke. I sat there an hour and felt nothing but the memories of people who wanted to be saved from themselves. I left feeling worse than when I went in, at least all those people I could tune into had something. They had the belief in something stronger than themselves that would take away or help them with whatever problem they were facing. I didn't even have that, I believed in something stronger than me but my something was panic attacks. Who am I? Why am I here?

I went home and sat in the corner with my headphones on and I closed down totally, grounding exercise and visualisations closing all chakras until there was a perfect nothingness which would allow me to sleep. I fell asleep. A hummingbird came into view, nothing else just a motionless hummingbird in the air leaning to the left slightly in magnificent colours It remained there doing nothing for a few minutes and then vanished. I woke up refreshed. "I'm going out" I told M.J. "Where?" she asked me. "Dunno" I told her and I didn't I just knew I felt amazing, the vision whatever it was had sorted me out.

It was important but I didn't know why or how just that amazingly through not caring about anything any more I'd awoke feeling great. I was in pain still I just didn't care that I was in pain. I was hungry still I just didn't care that I was hungry and I couldn't eat still I just didn't care that I couldn't eat. The day was sunny and I bounced down the street towards the town centre. I felt good enough to smile for the first time in ages, "I have nothing" I told myself smiling "How the hell did I make that a good thing?" I asked myself again laughing. "You've got nothing to lose" I felt Alan say from my right hand side. "About time you showed up" I sent back "Been busy lad, how you holding up?" He said. "Yeah, me too" I replied. I knew in that short exchange that they'd been trying but due to my mentality and physical state they couldn't get through. We simply weren't on the same wavelength He was right though I did have nothing to lose. I walked into the citizens advice office, then the doctors and then the social services. I wanted therapy and I was going to get it. "Doc your last therapist was hopeless I want a real one." I told him. They couldn't provide a different therapist due to, yadda, yadda, yadda, "Send me to one then? It doesn't have to be here does it?" I asked. He refused but social services had put me on a waiting list which was a result. I left the doctors and went to the library still on a high from Alan turning up. So the doctors and social services and citizens advice were making me fight for it, what was new? I've been fighting for years. I smiled at myself and bounced up the library steps and turned left to head towards the main library and stopped dead in my tracks. On a stand at the top was a white book underneath a sign that said poetry. On the cover was a hand drawn bird painted blue which had exactly the same colouration and shape as the one in my dream. Okay it wasn't a hummingbird but it was the same bird. I had to have that book, it was Leonard Cohen's book of longing. I looked again at the sign above it, poetry. I was never interested in poetry and walked on leaving the book on the shelf. It must have meant that I should draw or something. I used to as a kid and found it very beneficial until Brenda made me stop doing it. I got a selection of books on Astral travel and hypnosis and picked up one on drawing animals, on the way out I picked up the Leonard Cohen book and chucked it with my pile.

I was trying to draw at the round wooden table when M.J approached having changed somewhat this past year "want a brew?" She asked me knowing I'd not drank a brew in months. "No" I replied continuing. "Sure?" She asked, "Yup" I answered. "Well I'd better make one then if you won't!" She said. Maybe she hadn't changed after all. I ignored her it was daily routine for her to kick off about something. I was past caring if I was guilty of not being at her every beck and call. Past caring if I was a good person or not. Like my father or not, could help her or not, I was nothing so whatever I got was a step up if it was good great if I was a bad person then at least I was something and something was better than being useless. I constantly talked myself into corners over analysing everything.

I scrunched up my drawing and chucked it on the floor with the pile of others. "What is love?" I titled the next page. If we are all responses from our brain and merely respond to outside stimulus with pre programmed learnt thought patterns not one of us can know what love or anything else truly is. It's an idea, a feeling an undefinable illusion placed within us by out brain to escape a poorer feeling just as illusionary and just as false." I went on in a similar vein until I'd filled several pages and finally got love down to a chemical imbalance in the brain. "What about love of self?" Alan said vanishing as soon as I'd felt his words. "Fuck you" I laughed inside. M.J put a coffee down in front of me. I didn't know whether to be happy she'd made me one or angry that she'd not listened. I ignored it and grabbed an Ensure carton off the side. Part of my chores were to start M.J's car for her every night because she was worried it wouldn't start if she didn't. "I'm going to the car" I told her.

I was sat in the car with it running as the punchbag lay sideways on a storage unit in front of me. It was dark and I didn't have the energy to train. I flicked the headlights on more out of habit than anything and saw five hanging men dangling from the ceiling by their throats. I knew they weren't real. I turned the headlights off. "I'm not going" I said from inside the car, I flicked the lock down on the door anyway as I shook a little. I knew I was speaking to myself and knew in some part I was talking to a lack of sleep, poor life choices, lack of food and that whatever I'd seen was not at all spiritual and just my mind messing with me. I knew as much as I'd seen them briefly they weren't there and were in no way real but still I blamed the idea of a God. "You can scare me all you like, take my family, my teeth, cause me pain, you can beat me until I'm an inch from death. I'll get back up. Fuck you" I said opening my carton. I'd downed half of it when I flicked the lights back on to see a woman solitary and alone dangling this time with her head half cocked spinning around slowly. "You're not real" I said as I got out and stood in front of the car. She vanished, I was hallucinating I knew the difference. I returned home "That was quick" M.J said "Yeah, can't be assed" I answered. I grabbed my pad "every brick is one" Alan said from somewhere behind me. It made perfect sense in that moment. I turned to M.J "If you could change one thing from your life what would it be?" I asked her. "I'd be happy" she answered. I put my headphones in whilst she ate her chicken and bacon. "I'd eat" I thought.

I remembered my first time at David's I was in the waiting room designed especially for younger clients. I could tell by the blue walls for healing, positive health magazines and children's toys all tidied up. The receptionist was bubbly, her name was Porsche. David wasn't long and shook my hand. It was relaxed, he had thick forearms and a quiet voice. We went through to his office and I have him the usual spill. "I'm here about panic attacks I started having them last year. I fear needles and choking. I don't know why it started but you should probably be away my father killed my mother in 1993, my grandparents died in front of me when I was 9, my family was abusive physically and mentally and I grew up in care. I don't think they are relevant to the panic attacks but you may make connections during our sessions. Any questions? I'd made at least two therapists cry just at that point without going into any details so was ready to expect anything with a new therapist and in all honesty most weren't that good. David however was a good guy and spent numerous sessions going over my past however found no clue as to why I was having panic attacks. It must have been our fifteenth session or so when I finally opened up. "M.J doesn't like me seeing you, she's violent, it's never anything bad or over the top it's mainly slaps but she does punch occasionally. I'm fine it's not a big deal. It's never enough to make me snap. I told her I'm not going to stop therapy but right now I don't want to talk about it but thought you should know" I'd not looked at him the entire time. I'd just looked out the window, he's a bloke he'll probably just take the piss I thought. He didn't. "I don't love her, I never loved her I made a mistake, I was just trying to stop her turning into her mother" I said shaking my head. Then he threw a question at me that changed my attitude. "Do you think you're like your mother?" He asked me. I hadn't thought about it much. Interest in the psychic side, yes. Stayed long after I should have left, yes. Panic attacks, yes. Hell the only two issues I didn't have were drink and accepting prescription drugs. M.J may have been turning into her mother for sure but whilst I was fighting turning into my father I'd become the spitting image of my mum. "Better to be her than him I guess" I told him. "What about you?" He asked. "What about me?" I replied standing up. Session was over but he'd made me think.

I started to see it everywhere. "You don't leave me!" M.J would shout during one of her rants. Something she'd love to say to her mum but couldn't. "I can't do it!" Meaning she could but she wouldn't because her mum wouldn't like it so anger is the only thing she had left to use to control, so by being angry at me she felt in control. Just like her mother had felt with her. "I'm my own person I don't have to go out, I'm fat nobody likes me, you won't even stay home you're always with David!" Meant she couldn't get her own way so she'd make believe I was controlling her just like her mother had done to her when she wouldn't take responsibly for her actions. All the while I just let these things either get to me without me responding or go over my head until one day during a row about me being at the library for too long she over stepped the mark. "You're just like your father and you can't stand it can you? I'm going to therapy, I have friends and parents and it pisses you off!" Unfortunately that did it and something inside me changed. I could feel myself tuning into Wenzel as I had when I was a child to pre empt his next move but this time I wasn't doing it to save myself. I was doing it to unleash unholy hell on her. She wants Wenzel, I'll give it to her. "You want to know what you're problem is?" I asked her calmly. "Seriously?" I added knowing what would come "Yeah, tell me!" She stormed. I took several seconds to piece it together and then went off like a steam train my only mission to make her see all her faults in one foul hit. She'd either change her ways or fall apart either way I didn't care. "You're mother beat your father in front of you. You hated it and loved your dad swearing never to become you mother but you were a kid. Not responsible and wanted her love and a normal family, Instead she used you like she used your dad and when you stepped out of line she beat you too. Daddy who you love so much did fuck all! He let it happen!" By now she had turned pale and was stepping backwards "Stop it, no," She said as I continued. "When you did finally break free of the bullshit you chose violent partners, people who'd love you like your mum did. News flash darling, not one of them gave a shit!" I screamed as she covered her ears. "Your brother ran off with an older woman to feel some resemblance of motherly love, he became the emotional equivalent of your dad. Not only do you act, smell and move like her you're the fucking spitting image of her. Now I've taken your shit for two years plus. Two fucking years and now I'm ill because of it!" She had backed herself into the bathroom and was sat on the toilet sobbing and covering either her eyes or ears depending on how much I was screaming at her. "You're wrong, she loves me, you're wrong" she said. "Really? Where was loving mummy when you were unconscious because she'd hit you too hard?", "Where was daddy? Why didn't he stop her? He loves you, right? Because he's a fucking coward M.J! That's why he'd rather see his kid get knocked around by his wife than tell her to stop. You're mum's an ass hole and you're dad's a coward and an ass hole" M.J looked defeated, a look I'd never seen her have. "I may have no family darling but that's a step up compared with what you've got. I'm not jealous I'm fucking privileged It's obvious my dad's a twat but you can't see through yours can you? You can't see it because you become what you believe you're supposed to become. You can't see what you're actually worth, you can't say "I love myself" can you? Don't try tearing my life up princess I grew up with a fucking professional he did it every day of my life, your bullshit act is nothing new" I walked back to the computer and told Melorna everything. It was several seconds before I got a message back. "Good, it needed to be said" she sent back.

Chapter 33

"I'm leaving" M.J said. I hadn't even heard her come into the hall I was so used to throwing my mind somewhere else I'd done it automatically and was totally engrossed in Runescape. "Okay" I said not interested. "You won't stop seeing David?" She said. I glanced at her "nope" I replied. "If you don't I'm leaving" she said. I took the landline phone from the receiver and handed it to her. "Call your mum, if I'm right about what I said she won't have you back because you'll be too hard to control after you've tasted independence. If you want to go back to being a slave you go ahead darling" I said returning to my game. "I will leave you know" she said making no progress with the phone or the door. "The choice is yours stay or go but if you stay I expect you to stick to therapy, no excuses and sort your shit out. I'm terrified every time I go to the dentist but I still go." She called her mother who refused to take her back. Her exact words were "You've made your bed you lie in it." M.J hung up and went to cry in the bedroom. I felt like a right bastard. I left her for an hour then went in to see her. She was lower than I'd ever seen. "I'll stop seeing David if you stop the violence" I told her as she lay crying into a pillow. "I hate her" she said referring to her mum "I'm sorry, I'm sorry I was violent" she said sobbing. I rested my hand on her shoulder "do you mind if I take a Valium?" she asked me. It was the first time she'd ever asked. The first time she'd even considered that her actions affected other people. "If it helps and you need it then yeah, I know this shit's hard. Trust me, but you can handle it" She took a pill and passed out shortly after.

She went to therapy religiously which dragged up more and more issues. She stopped seeing her parents because she said it hurt too much. She called them every week sometimes to chat and sometimes to question why they weren't the parent's she expected them to be. Why they didn't get her help for the agoraphobia or why they were violent to her but not her brother? She over thought it but like anything viewed from a distance it was quite simple. Her mother was abused by her mother and her father did nothing to stop it and therefore she thought it was normal and did it herself ad infinitum. M.J's mum didn't like girls just as my nan hadn't according to her they were there to cook and clean. Boys to earn the money and girls to take care of the boys. A girl was more a threat to a woman's position than a man was.

I kept my end of the bargain as I sat opposite David. "I think we had a breakthrough, this is the last session and she's doing well. When she's better I'll leave her. I never told you this but she said if I leave she'd kill herself." I shook his hand and he kept hold of it and looked me in the eye. "You're strong enough you know. You'll go for it" he said releasing my hand. "I hope so" I replied not looking back.

M.J had come across an article online about a website called S.A.M.M support after murder and manslaughter. She said it was previously parents of murdered children and they help people who have problems after going through bereavement of murder or manslaughter. "Load of shit, bunch of sob stories" I told her not looking around from my drawing. M.J said it wasn't and might be useful. "Look it's mostly mercy killings of the dying spouse and the fifty year old kid wants some publicity. I ain't interested" I replied. "just read it" she said. I had a look through their site and it seemed they were the real deal. It appeared that everyone there working for them was actually bereaved through murder or manslaughter. Was it possible there was other people out there like me? I doubted it but hey I'd give them a ring and see what they could offer me. I spent an hour that day on the phone to a lady called Daisy who told me her story of how a driver had killed her baby girl. I took to her immediately and opened up. Afterwards I asked her the question that had been eating me up inside. "Are there more people like us?" I asked. She invited me to a meeting to train to listen to others talk on the phone. M.J hated the idea and made hundreds of excuses as I'd have to go to London by train. "What if I panic?" she said. "Call your mum" I replied.

"What if we have a leak and the flat is flooded?" She said.

"Call a plumber" I replied.

"You bastard you don't care you'll be miles away anything could happen to me!"

"I'm going and that's it" I replied.

She woke me up several times during the night with similar questions and examples of what could possibly go wrong to prevent me going or make her panic if I wasn't there. I was wise to her ways and I'd set an alarm on my phone as well as the one on the alarm clock. Sure enough the alarm clock failed to go off but my phone woke me up. I was still having my own issues so downed a carton and chucked two in the rucksack. "Call if you need me not if you want me" I told her and headed out the door. Five minutes up the road I turned my phone off and it was the most free I'd felt in years. Two long bus journeys and I was in London. This time I wasn't concerned about the big buildings. I was going to meet people. A thin guy was sat on the step crying, he had jeans and a T-Shirt on but was partially blocking the building I had to enter. My hand accidentally brushed against him as I went up the steps and a vision hit me. It was of a woman picking up keys by a rack of coats in a hallway, she was a cleaner. As soon as it hit it was gone, a woman walked past me and spoke to the guy crying. I introduced myself to the guy who looked like he used to be very strong but had been hit by the emotion train, twice. It turned out the woman who came out was Daisy.

You okay mate? I asked him "Keys gone, last time I lost them I got broken into I lost everything" I turned to Daisy who knew about the readings I used to do on account of during our conversation she'd asked about my faith. "Listen, this is going to sound weird but keep him here. His keys are safe he'll be fine shortly" Daisy said okay and smiled. I wasn't sure if she thought I was a nut or what but ten minutes later a cleaner handed them in to reception. Turned out half of the S.A.M.M crew had stayed over at the hotel last night and his keys had fallen out of his coat. I was in a room with maybe thirty people. Some obviously knew each other and most of them were woman with only five or six guys present. We were seated around several tables with a whiteboard in the middle whilst Daisy explained why we were all here. From the unemployed to policemen and lawyers, every single person in that room had lost someone via murder or manslaughter. My shoulders relaxed and a great warmth spread through me. All these people had made it. Some were strong and confidant, some were still on the path but all of them were living proof of survival and the ability to achieve. They had jobs, children, families and I was overcome with a sense of pride. If these guys could all do it so could I. If they deserved love then so did I and the ultimate reality hit me.

"I would not treat any of these people the way I'd treated myself these past fifteen years or so."

Daisy discussed P.T.S.D. Loss, bereavement, grief, shock and what S.A.M.M can do for people. She discussed her history and how it affected her. She told us stories about others and we heard from several of them as they shared their life and I was inspired. I went from knowing I had nothing going for me because I was just "that kid in care" to knowing without a doubt I had everything to commit to life for. I had experience, I had the history, I had years of therapy experience behind me. I had the ability to be confidant and by god I was a survivor not only could I do well for me but I could make a difference! Daisy gave us a guided meditation and I thoroughly enjoyed it considering I'd never done anything outside of the home before apart from that one mediumship circle.

I turned my phone on during the trip home and instantly M.J Calling flashed up. "I nearly had the police looking for you! We have a leak I told you this would happen!" She said sounding exasperated. I could hear her smoking at the window. I stood smiling into the sun. "I dropped my phone just got the damn thing working again" I explained. Turned out when I got home that she'd unscrewed the pipe beneath the sink, ran the water for a bit then put it back on. She'd denied it of course but I knew she'd have to prove a point. I cleaned the leak up and made the first coffee I'd had in forever. "I'm going to college to be a therapist" I told her not asked her. "What? You? You can't look after yourself let alone anyone else" she said all stern and agitated. "Exactly, college will help teach me and give me something to do" I said writing up my feelings on the S.A.M.M meet. I called Daisy "I loved it, you are an amazing person. I don't want to be a listening ear. I'm a doer not a listener. I'm going to college if I pass psychology I'll go to university and if I pass that can I work exclusively for S.A.M.M?" I asked. Daisy laughed "It would be voluntary until we sorted something out but if you do all that then yes we'd be happy to have you" I hung up playing with the idea of breaking down thought patterns I'd always heard Mans laughter when I thought of manslaughter. I needed to change that, I needed to change my negative association with Wenzel laughing at me because he killed my mother because then I felt angry and that anger was constant. I couldn't change the situation but I could change how I thought about it. I decided to use a similar vein of how Nigel helped me with the visualisation but I'd use a memory technique "Make a new stand leaving all unnecessary garbage here to enter reality" It was vague and a bit clumsy but I could try it. I stood in front of the mirror because it was no use preaching it if I couldn't get it to work on myself. I looked at him looking back and me and I smiled. "I'm not Wenzel, I'm Tracie" I repeated "Manslaughter" over and over each time making myself smile and forcing my body to relax. I felt stupid as hell but I did it every day three times a day and after two weeks manslaughter had a whole new meaning. It meant "I'm moving on"

I grabbed a bag of wotsits crushed them down to nothing and sprinkled them on my soup.

Chapter 34

"That will hurt your teeth" M.J told me as she stood over me. I was at the P.C trying to concentrate on anything apart from eating but I was determined to eat. "If it hurts, it hurts" I told her as I started to shake. "You'll panic, here have a carton" She said turning back around and heading towards the fridge. "I'm going in the bedroom, don't disturb me for an hour" I said walking away. I put Red dwarf series one episode one on and took a mouthful of soup. I immediately ran to the bathroom and spat it down the toilet shaking badly. "Argh! Go on, stop me!" I screamed into the mirror. "Do it!" I said angry as hell and realising it. "I'm calm and in control" I repeated from habit and my body slowly began to calm itself. I repeated it ten times and then another ten for good measure. Whilst I watched Red Dwarf I ate all of my soup and wotsits and I loved it, it took time and I forget the amount of times I ran to the bathroom or stopped myself from running to the bathroom but I felt full. I walked to M.J who was on the P.C in the living room and dumped the empty bowl on her desk "Don't ever tell me I can't do something, I'm not you" I said heading to the kitchen.

I ditched a handful of carrots in the juicer and drank them down. "Well done" M.J said not turning away from the computer. "Thanks" I said grabbing a Biro. Over the next six months I slowly moved food into my diet. On one occasion I sat for over an hour trying to eat half a piece of toast, each time I swallowed I panicked and had to repeat my mantra's or visualisations until eventually regardless of the sweat and tears, I did it. During this time my rotten tooth broke off which hurt a lot. It probably scared me more than it did hurt me and the tooth was grinding slightly onto my cheek. I used a nail file and rounded it off and kept eating. It was going to hurt whether I ate or not, I was going to panic whether I ate or not and I was going to have all the irrational thoughts about choking on my tooth or food whether I ate or not and so I made a choice. I could live my way for as briefly as that may be or I could live letting the panic attacks beat me every single time. Each time it came back to the same thing. "S.A.M.M showed me there were others out there like me. If they could beat this then so could I." I went from a twenty eight waist to a thirty six, I went from Soup and Ensure plus vitamin drinks to Pepperoni pizza that I'd added my own chicken strips, cheese and bacon to and that was my breakfast and tea. For dinner I'd have a sandwich, I still couldn't eat standard crisps on account of my teeth but I could manage wotsits and had them with my sandwich sometimes. I still panicked when I thought about the dentist, maybe my brain did translate a needle as a knife, maybe I just hated a numb tongue, maybe I was just moving too quickly, it didn't matter the why, it just mattered I was eating.

I was sleeping well again, eating well and had panic attacks down to once or twice every three days and that was enormous progress. I noticed I only panicked at home or at the dentist. Was this because I didn't go anywhere else or because of my lifestyle? It was time to change that. I found a pair of my jeans in the wardrobe from when I was a smaller waist and held it up next to the ones I was wearing these days and I was immediately disgusted with myself. This wasn't me, I didn't care about looking amazing but I was never a big guy and I felt fat and horrible, I looked at M.J and remembered her mother and brother. No way, I wasn't turning into that but I wasn't going to stop eating how I was either. Now I could eat I needed to keep eating. M.J had some one and a half kilogram weights, I don't know why as I'd never seen her use them but when she found me stood in the living room jogging on the spot with a tin of potatoes in each hand she offered me the weights. I started slow with ten minute increments of just jogging and throwing jab then cross. Each time I threw punches I gave myself positives. "I win", "I can eat", "I eat well", "I'm strong", "I'm calm and in control" whatever it was it didn't matter as long as it was positive. Inside a few weeks it was a daily routine and I'd added crunches, sit ups and squats. At the weekend I treated myself to bag work allowing myself to go into fits of laughter every time I opened the garage door because I'd learnt to praise myself for every tiny little thing and not only was I happy for my successes, I was happy because of my failures too, each failure meant meant I was strong enough to try and that I wasn't a quitter.

It was cool in the garage but I was warning up from the shadow boxing and sidestepping around the bag as though it was a real, living breathing person. Jab, cross "I'm fast" I told myself internally, Jab "I'm happy", thud "I'm strong", I'd changed in my relationship too. Any negativity from M.J was met with "Okay no worries if that works for you great!" I wasn't being sarcastic or rude but I was through letting people dictate my feelings. I was going to be happy if it killed me.

I signed up for college to resit maths, English and I.T. I should have done it at school and hadn't. English was never a problem for me and yes M.J had plenty of excuses for me not to go. It didn't matter I was doing it whether she liked it or not. I wasn't responsible for her condition or how she felt about what I did with my life. She was responsible for that and that's how I should have been seeing it from day one with everyone. However because of my mental training from past experiences and because I was reluctant to take an active part in how I should treat life I became docile and allowed myself to be controlled. Not any more, I completed a two year course in less than a year, I spent the rest of the two years gaining extra tuition in maths from a wonderful lady called Julia who spent more time on me than she probably should have and helping the other return to learn crew some of which had some sever disability's or memory problems.

Initially my brain wouldn't accept the pressure of maths and I got ratty with myself very quickly. I felt under pressure as I had in care and blurted out random answers or tried not to answer for fear of feeling wrong. The fact was I just didn't understand the maths Nobody had taken the time to teach me in a way that I could understand. Julia spent hours showing me. I'd kicked the psychic side away because I needed to concentrate on me but occasionally it would appear. It was last lesson of a term and I was paying attention to a large division sum that Julia had given me at my request whilst the others either caught up on homework from other lessons or sat chatting. It was a lovely relaxed atmosphere but I once again found myself concentrating on something logical and listening to others at the same time and so my mind kind of wondered whilst I did the sum. "Whoever guesses the right amount in the box can have them or share them out" Julia said placing a box of sweets on the table. I didn't care about the sweets as I was concentrating "76" I said and carried on working. Naturally I won and the sweets were handed out, I declined, the caramel would have played hell with my teeth and chocolate just hurt no matter what.

I loved college as it allowed me to be away from M.J for long periods and I'd started going in earlier and earlier. M.J had noticed it I knew but I didn't care, I wanted the space and lets face it we'd been over for at least a year. I'd run to the college just to count it towards my training which helped. I didn't know what I was training for but knew the adrenaline was my friend. I'd arrived early this day and so sat at the front reception waiting for the main hall to open so I could head to the library. The receptionist smiled at me as I went to sit down. I touched my name badge so she could see I was a pupil and sat down. She was cute, nice smile and light eyes, unique hair it was all over the place and short but curly. I kept watching her on and off as she answered the phone in a chirpy singsong voice, it was no secret I was drawn to her. Several people went past her and said "Morning Pam" and so I had a name to connect with the face. She'd just finished a call when she moved sideways and knocked a pen off the desk and moved back to pick it up. That's when I noticed she was in a wheelchair, electric. She used a ruler to try and get the pen and I heard her mutter "Shit." I laughed and approached. "Hi, can I help?" I asked. "No, no it's okay" she said not making eye contact.

"Sure" I asked noting that she was wearing a blouse with a black cardigan and a black skirt. She looked smart and professional. "Someone will get it later" she said looking at me. She had blue eyes. "I'm Tracie" I said. "okay can I help you?" She asked. "Nope" I replied heading back to my seat. I was still an hour early.

The following day she was on ground floor reception "Morning Pam" I said sitting near to the desk where a row of seats waited. "Weren't you upstairs yesterday?" I asked pondering about the sudden change. "Yes" she replied. "Work both receptions then I guess?" I asked. "Yes, when needed" she replied. She wasn't impolite but she was hardly entertaining any sort of conversation either. "Well you're obviously good at your job then" I commented, she ignored my futile attempts at conversation for a further four days. I'd wait for the remainder of my time to vanish as she answered calls and then I'd say "See you later" as I went to lesson to which she'd reply "bye" out of politeness. Maybe it was me but I saw in that moment with the rule someone who'd never let life get to her, someone who'd always keep going no matter what it took and I wanted to understand he more, besides she was cute and that never did anyone any harm. I was in English and helping a lad called Moses when I was thinking about how to get Pam talking. I wrote out twenty positive quotes off the internet and each day I said morning and dropped one on her desk. She'd read it and put it in her bag. We didn't speak, a few days of this repetition and she asked me what course I was on. We got talking about became friends, she was a nice girl who volunteered at the local charity shop when she wasn't working and I looked forwards to seeing her in the mornings I was at college. I'd got my panic attacks down to about once a week. I was in a good place and I told Pam about M.J.

Pam and I met up outside work several times and spent a few hours chatting over coffee and cake, neither of us being big drinkers we preferred a decent cafe to a bar any day. Pam said I should leave M.J and she was right, "I'll be going back up north if I leave M.J, I don't know anybody down here " I said. "You know me" Pam said smiling. I did know Pam and I knew she had enough problems of her own without me putting my shitty life on her. Besides was I really strong enough to leave M.J? What if she did kill herself? Could I handle the knowledge that I'd caused that? Should I do what's right for M.J or what's right for me? Would Pam really put me up if I did leave M.J? Would I be able to face Pam if M.J killed herself? I was torn between everything. Before we left the cafe Pam slid a piece of paper over the table but said nothing. One one side was her address and telephone number on the other was the first quote I'd given to her. "If I believe I have the ability to achieve something, I gain that ability even if I did not have that ability to begin with." - Mahatma Gandhi

A few days and another cafe later I'd been out and spent some of my money on a gift for Pam, just for listening to me ramble on. She'd pecked me on the cheek as I'd put it in her lap. I didn't think about the consequences, I could do this. I could leave M.J.

Chapter 35

I'd got to the point I literally just had maths left to complete and so the lesson was down to three times a week. I'd filled my time with training but today I was physically drained, as I got out of the bath the door went, it was David a friend of M.J's and his girlfriend a cleaner he'd picked up at work. I said my hello's with a towel around me and headed to the bedroom to sort myself out. M.J hadn't told me to expect visitors and besides they were friends of hers not friends of mine. I stuck a game on the playstation and made myself busy whilst they chatted in the living room. M.J came into the bedroom and stood in front of the T.V. I paused the game and looked up at her with a question in my eyes. "David's here" she informed me. "Yeah?" I replied. "Well, you going to say hello or not?" She asked. "Hi again David!" I shouted through without getting off the bed "Hiya!" he replied. I smiled at her and waved in her general direction to get out of the way of the T.V. "I'm not moving, my friends are here. I want you to talk to them" she said. "Your friends, not mine. We ain't together darlin. They ain't my problem. You invited them" I replied. "Not together!" She screamed and took a swing at me. I moved my head out of the way just in time. "You don't care do you?" She said. "No, not at all to be honest" I replied. "Now if you don't mind" I added making that move out of the way gesture again. "See David this is what I have to live with!" She shouted looking down at me. Enough "You want me to go in there? You should know me. If I go in there and he starts with your bullshit I'll lay him the fuck out. I've never hit a bird and for that you should be damn grateful but he starts I'll drop him. Now go play with your friends" I said shooing her away, although I was still seated and the motion would have been comical had her and I not removed one another from eye contact for at least thirty seconds and so now it was just tense. She broke eye contact and left the room, less than five minutes passed and Derek and his girlfriend left the flat "Bye Tracie" David shouted, fuck it, I was pissed off "Come again anytime, good to see you!" I shouted back in my best

Mr Happy voice. I chuckled to myself and carried on with my game. "We need a chat" M.J shouted from the hallway. I ignored her as she entered the room and leaned down next to my ear "we need a chat!" She screamed. "I fucking heard you!" I replied. "Well?" she asked. "Well what?" I shot back. "Are you going to talk to me?" she shouted marginally less louder than previously. I blew the head off a villain and he dropped like a stone. "No, there's no we here. You need a chat. I don't and seeing as there's no we here we don't need shit. I'm happy playing my game" I said matter of factly. "After all I've done for you! That's it?" She stormed. Maybe I could have handled it better, maybe I should have but the truth remains I was done being scared, done caring and done worrying. "Yup, that's it! I won't disturb your depression if you won't disturb my happiness, I'm happy nuking bad guys, you're happy being depressed so if you don't mind" I did the shoo thing again and got a punch in the head for my trouble. I stood up out of reflex "Hit me again?" I said. "You'll what?" She taunted hands on hips leaning forwards into my face. I walked around the bed and opened the wardrobe door. I grabbed the rucksack I'd had packed full of clothes for months. "What you doing?" she asked. "I'm leaving, I told you. Hit me again and I'm off" she was stood in the gap I'd need to walk down between the wardrobe and the bed. "Well?" I asked waiting for her to move. "Well what? You just expect me to let you leave? You said you loved me!" She bellowed. "Yeah well, I've said a lot of dumb shit in my time luv, you gonna move or what?" I replied now fully dressed. "No! Fucking make me!" I dropped the bag and walked over the bed and around her. Fuck the bag I'd get it another time when she'd cooled off. Despite her obesity she was fast when angry and blocked the door by the time I'd reached it. "Do you love me?" She asked head cocked. Her eyes were telling me this was dangerous territory, more dangerous than I'd seen her before and yet I'd have no idea what was going to happen later on. She was ready to explode and I'm semi claustrophobic so didn't like feeling trapped. I don't use lifts or car washes so was starting to feel stuck. "Sit down, lets' talk about it?" I gestured towards the bed but she wasn't falling for that one. "Do you love me?" She asked not moving and still blocking the door way. "No, I don't love you, happy now?" I said doing the hand gesture thing for shoo. She didn't move so I just started walking forwards and as I did she stepped back. As I kept walking she kept stepping backwards and at no point did we touch until she put her hand on the front door lock and stayed stationary. I reached to open the door when she shouted "No, you're not leaving! You love me!" It was an order not a request and I realised just how pathetic she'd got. I matched her pathetic argument with one of my own. "No I don't and Yes I am!" I'd got the door open about an inch before she slammed herself into it. Tried opening it again but it had at least twenty stone of weight holding it closed "move" I said. "No, you're not going" she said. I'd had enough and morals or not I felt trapped and she was moving "Move or I'm going to move you" I said. She took a swing at me. I took her wrist and shoulder and turned it against her then stepped forwards one maybe one and a half steps pushing her off balance and backwards enough for me to get through the door. She was behind me within seconds "I hate you!" She screamed. "Tell someone who gives a shit darlin" I called up the stairs as I left.

Now what? I got my mountain bike out of the garage but I only had my wallet, my phone and my keys on me. No money in the bank because I'd given it all to M.J and just eight pounds left on me. I wore boots, camouflage jacket, trousers and a T-shirt. I didn't even have a coat on me. Fuck it, I'm a survivor. I was cycling towards Pam's place when I saw a Texaco garage. I picked up a bottle of drink because it was refillable, bin bags because I could use them for shelter, bedding or holding items and chocolate out of hiking habit. I might need the sugar even if it kills my teeth. Then I tried my credit card, I knew I had a credit limit but I'd never really used it, I'd be okay for a while it was one thousand five hundred pounds. I took my five silver rings off to punch my code into the pad when a hand took my rings from beside me. I turned to face him "Mr Daily?" A copper asked me. "Yeah, can I help you?" I asked trying to read his eyes. "Do you know about the pushing and shoving incident with M.J?" He asked. "Yeah she wouldn't move, I asked her several times and she wouldn't budge, I tried to leave and she took a swing at me so I moved her. What's the problem? She alright?" I asked. "Come with me sir" he said. She's done it I thought. She's fucking killed herself the selfish bitch. Then I felt guilty, "She alright? She said if I leave she'd kill herself" I told him. Great now I look like a murderer. He wasn't alone a smaller copper was waiting outside and followed behind me as I sat on the kerb "Wait here" he told me ignoring my question. Small cop looked jumpy "Relax I aint going anywhere, you've got my rings" I told the little fella. He ignored me sizing my rings up. I could see him considering ways to drop me if I tried to run. I knew that look I'd had the same one many times myself. I looked off into the distance keeping my body language relaxed despite my head going south. "She dead?" I asked the big fella when he returned. I was still sitting down. "No, we have a van coming for you" he told me. "A van? What's the charge" I asked remembering Clive's advice about six minutes too late. "Assault, you said you pushed her and she said you hit her she's got bruises" He looked at me disgusted. "I've never hit a bird mate and I didn't hit her either" I said still sitting. "I'm not your mate" he said wagging a finger at me like admonishing a naughty child then her turned to nervy and had a chat with him. If he wasn't a cop I'd of chinned him. Fuck it "Figure of speech officer I didn't realise you guys were so easily offended, won't happen again" I was looking straight ahead again. No threat. He ignored me. The boss turned up "Hi mate what we got, this him?" He asked gesturing towards me. He read me my rights and told me I'd be put in a cell and then questioned. He seemed a decent guy right up to the point he grabbed one arm and the big copper grabbed the other. "I should inform you I have a recurrent dislocative shoulder, if you put pressure in the wrong place you'll pop it out of socket, I'm happy to walk you don't need to restrain me" I said. The boss nodded and the big guy let go. I got in the van.

It was tiny in the back "Oh and I'm claustrophobic" I added sitting on my hands. My shoulders touched the metal either side of me. If they replied then I didn't hear them as the door slammed shut.

Immediately I was back in that car as a child with Wenzel and it scared the hell out of me. I threw myself outside on my skateboard with my granddad behind me telling me how well I was doing then pushed myself further out and I was in care at Brenda's on the wall sat next to Louise in the snow. It was cold and I was free and then bam I was in the back of a police van and then I'd throw myself out again mentally to escape the confinement. My brain was going eight hundred miles an hour and trying to rescue itself over and over. Thankfully I have a strong personality and managed to keep a grip on it but it went around and around for ages the last vision before pulling up outside the police station was of M.J, Courtney, mum, Alan, and Pat as snow cones in the road and I was zipping between them on my mountain bike. I was sat on the back step of the police van waiting for a custody officer to take me through "Any chance of a smoke?" I asked the copper. I didn't want his I wasn't that type of guy. I had a tobacco tin in my back pocket which had made my ass go numb in the van. He let me roll my own "Thanks, what happens now?" I asked. He looked at me like I should know. It was probably my northern accent. "You'll see when you go in" he said Definitely not my next best friend then. "Fair enough" I replied. I felt like that kid again having to read everyone body language. Nervy was less, well, nervy when at the station. He was my build with freckles. I was in a car park where all I could see was a door in front of me and cars around me, no hopping off out of this one I'm afraid. I was taken in and then stood in front of a desk which I immediately leaned on and told to stand behind a yellow line which I did. "Name?" The bald fella behind the desk asked. "Tracie Daily" I replied. "First name?" He asked looking at me as though I should know how his form is set out. "I just said my name's Tracie Daily"returning his glance. "Don't get smart with me son!" he snapped. I'd be surprised if he was five years my senior and judging by his attitude I wasn't overly surprised that he couldn't handle smart. I answered his questions and was given a book to read and then I was put in a cell by nervy. "He always this happy?" I asked him. He tutted. Apparently I'd upset desk jobs lackey because he slammed the door and poked his freckles into the food slot. "Button for drinks, you'll be seen in the morning" he told me walking away. I pushed the button "It's six o'clock why can't I be seen tonight? There's plenty of you here" I asked. "No solicitor until morning, want a coffee press the button, breakfast in the morning" He said before the slot closed. Fuck it, I pressed the button again. "Coffee please" I said grinning ear to ear. Fuck it it was childish I know but I needed to find some semblance of control I could have. I wasn't going to be stupid but I sure as hell wasn't going to roll over.

I read the book then read it again at the parts which applied to me. The flap opened "If you rip or, eat it or deface it in any way including dropping it in the toilet it's fifteen pounds for a replacement" The shutter didn't close, but the face vanished. Apparently whoever had been watching me reading the book cross legged on the floor had decided I was a twat and now expected either an answer or an argument. I stood up stayed two feet from the door and extended the book so it lay on the hatch. "I've read it, thank you" I said keeping my eyes on the hatch. Freckles appeared momentarily as the book vanished and the hatch closed. I pressed the button "Coffee please" I needed a piss and had no choice but to ignore the camera watching me. There was nowhere to wash my hands.

I started remembering my martial arts and scouting days. What could I use to my advantage? Knowledge, how? I couldn't do anything about anyone wanting to give me a kicking in such a confined space which was my fear. However I could maximise my chances of using it wisely if push came to shove. I stepped around the room without actually going into Kata's. I could roundhouse once if I needed to but not twice and only depending on where I stood. If shit turned bad I'd have to judge by the inch whether to comply or fight and lets be fair I'd had nothing to lose I'd already lost everything by now so fuck it. I wanted out more than anything so complying was certainly the aim. Coffee arrived in a second Styrofoam cup and I let it cool whilst I sat cross legged and meditated.

The key to good meditation is to allow all conscious thought to float by ignoring them. "Well, how you gonna get out of this one dickhead?" I let it slide through a hole in a metal door and drop onto the floor. "Well I always knew I'd end up inside but this Is ridiculous" I flicked it into space into another planet that exploded into a thousand pieces leaving nothing but darkness. "Just like your father" I blew it into a bubble and blew it at Brenda and Jim's home watching the building shatter. "Typical Macc lad couldn't even get a job before getting a record could you?" I taunted myself and willed the thought to leave me. "I'm not my family" I told myself. I'm not my father, I'm not a killer. I felt like one. I felt guilty because M.J was depressed. Guilty because Alan was dead because I'd tripped him and guilty because I felt by not helping M.J beat her agoraphobia I'd somehow let my mother and myself down. I opened my eyes and looked at the tiled wall beside me. I knew that road out there. I'd walked it at least a hundred times and not once thought about anyone stuck in here. "You're not stuck. You're going through a process of change. It's your room, you're safe space, your toilet and your bed" I told myself turning them into positives but realising I was detaching by talking to myself in the third person. Not good. I closed my eyes and my inner self stepped out and through the wall. I found a bench that I wasn't sure was real or make believe and sat on it watching the world go by.

I woke up still sat cross legged my chin had fallen to my chest and it took me a good few seconds to realise where I was. I sighed and pushed the button not bothering to smile. "Coffee please" I asked the young lady that appeared. "Sugar?" She asked. It was obviously late as the staff had changed and I heard a couple of drunks going through the whole "name?" process I'd been through. I hoped they didn't put them in here with me. My coffee arrived and I made it last as long as possible. Then pushed the button "What time is it mate?" I asked. He was grumpy. "Night time, get some sleep your solicitor will see you in the morning" the shutter slammed shut. Ass hole I thought. Maybe it's because I called him mate? I smiled to myself. I had one thing going for me. I'm a survivor whatever happens I'll never quit. I've beaten worse. I thought making a pyramid out of my three Styrofoam cups. One of my nails was a little bit longer than the others and so I used it to cut a small square out of one of the cups and then decided to entertain myself by flicking it back into the top cup of the pyramid. "I'm calm and in control" I said each time I flicked the polystyrene my mantra was one I used when my panic was bad and I knew I had to keep it up. I'd sat at M.J's with a Biro and blank paper and done a small circle and then another and another no bigger than a keyboard o until I'd filled the entire page. "I'm complete", "I'm calm and relaxed" "I'm healed" I repeated each until my mind blocked everything else out. Two days later the page was full. I got through numerous pads with this method and it helped. Flick, missed, flick, missed, no sense of humour some polystyrene I laughed at my own joke and a thought occurred to me "Wherever you are and whatever you're doing give it 110%."

My nail and I went to work cutting squares into the Styrofoam I made three smiley faces in the cups and there was just enough room to place them on the little shelf thing side by side. So when grumpy opened the hatch he'd be faced with three smiley faces. I ditched the little squares in one of the cups and pressed the button. I stepped back from the door three paces with the cups on the shelf. He opened the shutter, did a double take and grunted. "Coffee please!" In my best sing son happy go lucky voice. Inside I cracked up laughing. Maybe I'd brightened his day. Maybe he'd piss in my coffee. I didn't care, fuck it. I'd found a way to keep me sane and make my experience unique. I drank my brew imagining I was in a five star hotel and lay down to try and get 110% worth of the sleep I needed to think clearly in the morning.

Chapter 36

I didn't pay much attention to the Omelette and chips breakfast in the yellow Styrofoam packaging I just ate it. I was in survival mode and didn't know where my next meal was coming from but if it was anything like this meal it would be a child's portion that was at best half cooked. "You can make a call" the officer told me as I went for a medical. I told the doctor about my shoulder, my parents and the depression in vague detail. I declined the call I only knew M.J and Pam. I wasn't calling M.J and I wasn't worrying Pam. I was given a duty solicitor and was finger printed and a DNA swab taken before I was questioned. I explained for over an hour the same thing I'd explained before and I knew nothing of the law. They told me I could accept a caution and not go back to M.J's despite the flat being a joint tenancy or I could be held and go to court. "What's a caution?" I asked. "You admit you pushed her and agree not to return to her place and it will stay on record for five years but you'll be free to go" He said in front of a lady officer. Fuck it I had no plans to be with M.J anyway and so I accepted. I should have chosen court, I should have got my own solicitor. I should have found a way to go online and look up every single thing about the situation I was in because my world was about to get much, much worse but no, I accepted the caution.

I remembered what I'd read in the book though so when bald desk man returned my rings and money but kept my house keys I asked for a copy of my interview. "It can't be done now you'll have to come back in a few days" he said looking at me shocked. He was less impressed when I said "no sorry the book says the same day as the interview, I'll wait if you don't mind?" I naturally expected him to exert his authority and he did "You'll have to wait in a cell then" he said smiling. "I will but actually I don't considering I've accepted the caution therefore the crime is spent and I'm no longer under arrest" I didn't give him chance to reply. I was already walking to my cell. One of the woman was ready to leave with her bag and coat when desk guy nodded to her to signify she had to copy my tape. I am a lot of things and I've made a lot of mistakes but I am honest. I'd never hit M.J and If I had then I'd have the balls to admit to it. I'm not Wenzel, so after being treated like I was a woman beater that small victory in making these clowns do some more work felt good. I wasn't just going to lie down and take shit. I'd had enough of that game. Around an hour and a half later the door opened and I was handed my cassette. "Time to go" he said. I was relieved as hell but wasn't going to let him see it. "So soon? I was just starting to like the place" I replied. "This way" he said motioning me to the hallway. I winked at desk guy on the way out. I stood outside looking up at the sky as the eleven am sun hit my face for a whole two minutes. I felt dirty, I felt guilty, I had a record. I was as bad as Wenzel and even though I'd technically done nothing wrong I felt the only way for me to go now was further down. I fought with the idea that the world was crazy and then settled on no, it's probably just me. I had to check, I walked to my right and found a noticeboard and beside it was a bench. I sat down smiling "Thanks guys, thanks for not leaving" I said putting my head in my hands and crying. I immediately stopped myself "No, not now, not here. I won't let the police see me break or M.J think she's won" I won't, I won't quit. I can break down afterwards, somewhere else. Not here, think Daily think! What now? They'd taken my keys and I wanted nothing to do with M.J before so I certainly didn't want anything to do with her now she'd had me arrested, for assault? I'd not mind if I'd of chinned her but I hadn't...my mind went back to the interview and I'd told the woman honestly. "I am glad you guys picked me up. If you guys had picked my father up my mother might have still been alive so I get it. I understand but you know what sometimes you get the wrong guy and this time that's what's happened. If it was my father you'd have saved my mum but it's me and I've never hit a bird" Her reply was "Have you ever had thoughts of killing M.J?" That bugged me. "No" I replied looking straight at her and holding her gaze for two seconds before continuing about how I'd got her into therapy. It was over and the interview was complete. I'd never have to go through that process again I told myself.

I called Louise, she'd been there for me as a kid. I'd been there for her numerous times when she drunk. Okay we hadn't spoken In three years but she'd see me right. If I could hitch-hike to Cheshire I'd stay there until I got on my feet. I was certain of it there's no way she'd let me down. "Hi Louise, long time sorry. Look I don't have much battery and nowhere to charge my phone. I've just left M.J and I'm homeless lots to tell, police are involved if I'm honest. I'm also a bit of a mess to be fair. Any idea what I should do from here?" I asked her not having the guts to ask for a place to stay but knowing she'd help. I'd started walking to that nobody could overhear my conversation and because I knew exactly which way Cheshire was an it would take me forever to get there so wanted to start moving now. "Wow that's awful, You've got nowhere?" She asked me. "Literally what I'm stood up in duck. Just need a place to bed down to get my head straight. Any ideas?" I asked more directly. "No none sorry, give me a call when you get yourself sorted though!" She said cheerily. I managed a heartbroken "Will do" before hanging up and burst into tears near college. The tears burnt my cheeks. I had nothing. No home, no money apart from a fiver. No clothes, Nowhere to charge phone. No family, no friends. I stood there until I was empty of tears, people walked past as I stared at the sky. I didn't care and neither did they. "Why, why?" I kept asking the sky, "What did I do? Seriously? I've been beaten, abused, cut, thrown and verbally abused with not one arrest. I've defended myself against two knife attacks and won. Not one arrest. I push a lass out of the way who's preventing me from leaving the flat and I lose everything? I felt a little voice I'd never felt before. It wasn't Alan "Quit, go on. This is the third time you've been homeless now. You're not worth anything. Nobody loves you. You're useless. Quit" They were my thoughts and I was very familiar with them. I was back to the same thought patterns I'd had daily when I was with Wenzel I'd treated myself like that for twenty years. I considered it, I looked up at the college with it's high tower. How do I get up there? I knew partially as the library was up there. As soon as I thought it I looked up at the sky. "You're right" I said out loud. "You're right, I've lost everything," I started sobbing "I've lost everything and I'm probably not worth much" I bent double crying and holding my stomach as it cramped, it was a force to stand straight "But I'm me. I know what I am and I'll never give up" The tears burnt my cheeks as I turned towards college but I was scared I was scared if I went into college I'd find a way to get up that tower. I went from sad and lonely to fuming in seconds I stopped and looked back up as college kids passed by me "I'm still standing! Come on! Bring it you worthless piece of shit! Strike me down! Is that all you've got!?" I was on fire inside and out. The sweat was pouring from me. "Come on! Father killed mother! Uncle abused sister!" A woman looked at me as she went past and I laughed "Ha! Father's a nut job! Grandparents dead! Self harm and depression! Arrested and homeless three fucking times!" I started laughing like a maniac "Is that all you've got!? I'm still here! Kill me! Kill me! You can't fucking win!" I stormed through college like I was on a mission and explained to Phil my IT tutor why I wasn't in lesson and what the situation was. Phil was incredibly helpful and allowed me to use their phone to call the citizens advice bureau and get information on what to do from here. Phil said he'd get me free dinners if I could prove I was on income support. I declined, I couldn't prove shit as M.J had all my paperwork. Besides I wasn't owing anyone anything any more I had a credit card I'd use that, they were a big company they could take the debt. I left and walked the mile and a half to the library where I emailed Melorna and changed all my passwords. I explained everything and remember clearly ending with "I totally understand if you don't want to speak to me any more, nobody else does. I can feel everyone looking at me like I'm a criminal". I booked into a bed and breakfast on my card and had a shower. What I'd do if my phone died I didn't know. It was late when M.J called me. I ignored it, She called again and again I ignored it. The third time I answered it. "What?" I asked. "How you doing?" She asked me. "Fine, you were out of line, you had no reason to do that" I said. "Fuck off! You hit me! You beat me! You raped me!" She shouted.

"What!?! I asked.

"You fucking know what! You deserve whatever you get! Who is she?" She demanded.

"What do you mean raped you? I never laid my hands on you?" I was gob smacked, hurt and upset as well as worried I was losing my mind.

"That's not what they think" she said laughing.

"Who's they?" I asked.

"Who is she and I might tell you" she said.

"Who is who?" I asked.

"Your new girl. The one you've been fucking whilst with me!" She yelled.

"I'm not with anyone, look it's obvious you're not well. In fact you're fucking twisted but either way. I need my charger and clothes and my paperwork then we can go our own ways. Yeah?"

"I'm twisted!? She's there now isn't she? You'd have never talked to me like that before you were good. Kind what happened to you? Bastard!" She said hanging up. What the hell?

I went to Penge and bought a phone charger, notepad drawing the cash from my credit card. I got bin bags as the police kept mine and topped my phone up. I bought a rucksack for eighty pounds and it went everywhere with me despite only having two Biro's and a bottle of water in it.

I saw Pam and explained everything to her. She invited me around for tea next week to meet her family which I felt was awfully trusting of her considering what I'd just been accused of. I told her I'd have to tell her parents everything, at least part of what got me into this mess was lying from the outset. I'd said I was a different age when I met M.J. I'd said I owned my own home. I'd set a lot of shit which just wasn't true and so how could I expect anyone to believe me about anything else? No more lies. If I was to meet her parents then I'd have to tell them everything.

The homeless persons unit wouldn't help me as I had no benefit letters so couldn't prove who I was. I called Daisy from S.A.M.M who said if I had any problems with police or anything to get them to call her and she'd sort me out. I also got her to write a letter to say she knew me and was happy to confirm I am in fact who I said I was. Unfortunately they wouldn't accept that letter it had to be a benefits letter and without access to the flat I couldn't get it. I was getting nowhere and I'd been in the bed and breakfast over a week. I kept getting calls from M.J and was ignoring them. I'd never felt more lonely, I missed M.J but not in the sense of missing her just in the sense of missing someone being around. It was weird I really didn't like her and was pretty upset about what she'd done even though I knew she was crazy but I wasn't vindictive. I just wanted to get on with my life and needed my paperwork. I was stuck and couldn't see a way out. I called the Samaritans "Look. I'm not suicidal and I don't know exactly what you do but it's got something to do with suicide right?" The woman said yes and went on to explain that they are basically there to listen to anyone who's having thoughts of harming themselves. I explained I wasn't but I wanted to tell them a story. I told her about everything leading up to this moment and I hung up. I balled my eyes out. I'm pretty sure I made enough noise to wake the entire building with my sobbing and it went on for at least two hours. I felt no better afterwards but at least I'd been through a part of the process. I called them back and said thank you to a different woman. She said she'd try and pass the message on that I'd said thanks and I could call again whenever I needed. It was useful in ways but offered zero support otherwise. I was still homeless and I was still in the shit. Without the credit card I'd of been screwed. My head was slumped over my full English when a man in his mid fifties came downstairs folding his newspaper. "Good morning, Ah beautiful day aint it!?" He said pointing to the sun coming through the window. I wanted to grab him and rake his face across my plate of tomatoes and mushrooms. Slam him repeatedly into the window whilst shouting "Why, are, you, so, fucking, happy!?" I was angry with my life, big time. Of course instead I looked up sighed to let him know I didn't give a shit and said "yeah". He must have heard me balling last night. "It's a magical day. One where anything is possible" he smiled. I looked at him like shit on my shoe as he opened his paper. I looked out at the sun, it sure was pretty. "Thanks" I said leaving the table. "What for?" He asked folding his paper. "The chat, just...thanks" I said as I headed off he called back. "We can talk more tonight" he said. I ignored him. I wanted nobody's charity.

I made the most of that day by ploughing into getting housing help, maybe it was that old guy, maybe it was pure bloody minded or maybe I just had no choice. I went to the police station and told them everything. They said it wasn't their problem and I should get a solicitor. I'd never had one and had no money. Luckily a woman queuing to be seen slipped me a phone number when she left. "They'll help you" she said. I hoped she was right. I checked my email and Melorna had replied! I was over the moon. Not only did she still want to talk to me she'd also replied with a ton of legal information she'd found online. More so she'd replied with a comment that really helped me see sense. "Give it a rest Tracie she's what thirty stone? I'm sure if you had tried to hurt her she could have dropped you no problem" It wasn't the "no Tracie you're not the type to hit a woman" that I was looking, for but at least it meant she believed me and that meant worlds. She was brilliant and kept me sane as I emailed her every day from the library.

Apparently the police had no right to request I don't go back to the property as it's a joint tenancy and as I wasn't under an injunction. Melorna was right of course but I still wasn't going back. I didn't want to be arrested again. I needed proof that I was a good guy. I got hold of David who provided my therapy notes which stated M.J had a controlling nature and I had a fear of leaving because of her threats. Then I got copies of these silly online questionnaire things people do online that M.J had sent her friends list including Melorna which stated clearly "I love my boyfriend so much he's always there for me even when I'm kicking off."

I called my credit card to check the balance and found I had just two hundred pounds left. I explained everything and they gave me a break down of the charges and incurred debt. Turned out I had more on my card than I thought, M.J had done some Christmas shopping as well and bought her parents some gifts. I asked them to send me the breakdown in writing and then I signed on Facebook to see if I could find any old messages that would help my case. I had a friends request, it was M.J. I screenshot it and bunged it in a word document then sent myself and Melorna copies. Then I blocked her. I called the number the lady gave me and it turned out to be a free legal advice line. They talked me through how to get a police escort to remove my stuff from the property and so that's what I did. They needed a list of the things I wanted. It was pretty simple I wanted my guitar, my paperwork, my charger and my Paulho Cohelio book warrior of light. She could keep the P.C and anything else I'd bought I didn't care. I just wanted the basics and a clean break. M.J was home when I turned up with a policeman and two policewomen. They said they'd talk to her first then I could get my stuff what did I want? I explained and they said they'd go in and get them I could wait in the hall. I agreed. They got my basic I.D but nowhere near the amount of paperwork I had got there, M.J told them she couldn't find the charger. The policewoman asked me to come in with her which I did. I immediately pointed to the charger on the table when M.J ran out of the bedroom claiming it was hers and screaming. The policewoman asked me to wait in the hall which I did. I said she could keep it but I still needed the guitar, clothes and book. The clothes were already in four black bags so I took them outside and was waiting for the guitar and book when a policeman came down with the book. He told me she'd said she bought me the guitar as a gift and as a matter of law it was hers. I told him "She's full of shit but she can keep it. This will prove everything" I opened the Paulho Cohelio book to find she'd ripped the front page out of it. I shook my head in disbelief as a motorbike pulled up behind me. I sat down on the bin bag and asked one of the policeman what happens now? He said he thought I'd arranged for a lift or something. A man tapped me on the shoulder and asked my name. I said "Yes" and he handed me an envelope and left. I opened it and nearly fell apart. I was due up court as I was being accused of over one hundred and twenty different accounts from damaging goods, threatening behaviour through to rape. From the first time we were in a bed and breakfast and she alleges I've told her not to talk to anyone through to present day when she claims she was raped over a hundred times. I half fell and half sat down. A policeman sat beside me "are you okay?" He said. I asked for a smoke and handed him the papers. "What you want me to do?" He asked. "Read that" I said holding my hand out for a lighter. His other policeman friend came over. "Anything new?" He asked. "Usual shit, poor bastard" he said looking at me. My cab turned up and they helped me load it up. The woman behind the wheel looked a bit concerned but the copper smiled at me "He's okay, we were just helping him out" he said. I didn't have the energy to nod. I was in shock. "Sure you want to know?" I asked the woman when I was halfway there. "Yeah" she said. I turned my head to look at her and then looked away. I felt bad and knew she'd see me differently the instant I told her. "I've just been accused of a hundred and twenty four accounts of abuse most of which were rape" I said. "They should have told me" She said looking nervous and clutching the wheel a bit tighter. "They should, I agree but I am innocent" I said meekly. "Do you want me to get out?" I asked her genuinely. "No dear, you told me. You didn't have to" she said. "But don't be offended if I stay in the car when you unload okay?" She added. "No worries" I replied figuring I'd have to get used to not being trusted now as well. I unpacked at the B&B who told me I couldn't put that amount in my room but could in their shed but it had to be gone as soon as I could. I agreed and gave the cabby the only note I had from the ATM which was a twenty. "Keep it" I said pressing it through the small gap she'd left by the window's edge. She was nervous enough already. She just wanted to escape before the woman beating rapist did anything to her. I felt really, really sick. This was beyond reality.

I'd asked Pam to meet me in Bromley in a place where I knew there were C.C.T.V Camera's and she agreed. "This is the last time I'll see you Pam" I said. "Why?" She asked looking upset. "Same reason I asked to meet you here in a public place surrounded by camera's. I don't trust anybody any more I won't be alone with a woman. Thanks for not hating me, thanks for listening but I have to go" I said. She leaned forwards to hug me and I jumped backwards. "Cya Pam" I said as I turned and walked away. I wouldn't let her see me crying.

Chapter 37

"Sorry Mr Daily It doesn't matter that you've got I.D technically you've made yourself intentionally homeless, you still have a home with M.J" I couldn't believe it. I'd sat there at the homeless persons unit all day waiting to be seen and if you've never been in one of those places you're lucky they are one of the most depressing places in the world. I used to go there every Christmas to drop toys in for the kids in care because it was also the social services office and I knew that kids without much could go there and they'd let the parents take a toy or two each for their children and without fail every year I'd given them something. I wasn't expecting anything back but I was expecting them to recognise my good will and at least try to help me with the homelessness situation. Hell I knew four of that team by name before today's meeting.

The B&B agreed I could leave my stuff in their shed for a week but my credit card had ran out now and I had nowhere to live. The B&B kindly offered me a room for the night guessing my predicament when the card was declined but I couldn't accept it. I had a tiny bit of dignity left. I wasn't giving it away. I headed from the housing office to Mario's where I'd become a regular for my usual sausage in batter. Mario was cool he was a big Italian fella who did handgun shooting in his spare time. He legally owned a side arm. We rarely spoke but I overheard a few of his conversations. His dad ran the chip shop and cafe a bit further down the road. A big fella with close cropped hair cut and a friendly smile, every now and then he'd throw in a bap or extra sausage at no charge. Today a group of lads were in and they were already half cut and heading to the pub afterwards. "Oi Dickhead gimme chips!" The tall one said slamming his hand down. Mario and my eyes met briefly. I nodded, he'd got it. If shit turns bad he either wanted me to get help or help him. Either way I wasn't moving, this was my local and they'd been good to me. "Alright lads, what we havin?" He asked. Words were exchanged as the two smaller lads grabbed cans from the fridge and filled their pockets. I took my plate up, fuck it. "Coffee please Mario" I said and turned to the lads "and don't forget these boys cans" I said pointing at them. They said nothing, I went back to my table and sat down as I pulled out my notepad and pen. I wasn't writing but if it kicked off I wasn't scrapping there were too many of them. I wanted my pen handy. At least if I got nicked I had food and a bed. After gobbing off at Mario for a minute and grabbing their chips they stood leaning on the counter hurling insults at him. I walked over and stood next to the lad closest to me "Show no fear, confidence creeps them out" I remembered Karl looking through Phil when I was in care and it somehow gave me confidence. One of the lads got pushed into me "What?" He said as though I was the problem. I just looked at him for a couple of seconds stood in front of him then sipped my coffee without taking my eyes off his. He was about a second from it going in his face when the tall lad said "come on guys lets go." They left and I sat down "on the house" Mario said nodding to my coffee. I nodded back at least someone liked me.

It had been a while, I don't know how long but my feet hurt, I had no money, I'd been walking around all day, emergency housing and social services wouldn't help me. Even the emergency grant place wouldn't assist. I didn't exist. My socks stuck to my feet and it hurt like walking on a bare floor. I had less than a quarter battery left and I truly didn't know how the phone had lasted so long. I headed to the church as I knew they had a radiator and it might keep me warm. I figured I had enough battery for one call, two at the most. It really was my last hope otherwise I was just going to sit in the church and keep warm until a priest threw me out. What do you have? I asked myself. I knew I could build on that. I knew I could steal a knife and make a bivouac, I knew I could light a fire and steal food. I'd love to say I didn't because of some moral standard. The truth is however I didn't because I didn't have the energy, no will and didn't know the area well enough to get to a forest with what energy I did have. This place wasn't like up north. In Macclesfield I can walk an hour in any direction and find the countryside Down south I can walk an hour in most directions and find nothing but more big buildings. I rummaged through my pockets to see what else I had that could help me and found a piece of paper. It was the free legal advice line the woman at the police station had given me.

I called and explained everything to the guy on the phone starting with "I have no fixed abode and my phones about five minutes away from death I'm at the church in Bromley next to the big Churchill building" I couldn't fault the guy on the phone he was brilliant. He took notes and then promised to call me back. "I don't have battery" I told him. "Where are you?" He asked and I repeated the address. He said if my battery died to just stay there. He called me back inside ten minutes and my phone died halfway through whatever it was he was saying "Shit!" I said inside the church hallway. I looked through the chapel door which I tried and which was locked. "Fuck you" I muttered under my breath and leaned against the radiator then slid down the wall. Now what? I had visions of being pissed on by a homeless guy as I awoke beside the church and hoped it really wouldn't come to that. About twenty minutes later a suited man entered the hall, he was smart, clean cut and spoke in short sentences he was very clipped and direct. He reminded me of my uncle Karl and he wasn't taking any shit. "Tracie Daily" he said looking down at me. At first I thought he was a cop then figured he was too well dressed then figured fuck it who gave a shit? "Yes" I replied instantly regretting it and hoping he wouldn't pull out an envelope and accuse me of another hundred allegations. "Come with me" he said, "and you are?" I asked. His demeaner changed "Mr Lee Black of blah blah solicitors I believe you're homeless, I got a call from yaddayadda at free legal advice line" He asked me some questions and then asked me to sign a form. I read it, "Last time I signed a form in front of a solicitor I ended up with a criminal record, okay so it was only a caution but I dunno mate" I said honestly. His response tickled me. "Ask yourself what choice do I have?" He had a point. I signed it and he gave me an address. "What's this?" I asked wobbling foot to foot my heel hurting. "That's where you sleep tonight" He said. Tell them I sent you. They're expecting you, you'll be okay" He said with an unwavering stare. I had the feeling this guy believed everything he said unfalteringly. I was shocked, half an hour ago I didn't have a pot to piss in. Now I had a solicitor and he was trying to help me and somewhere to sleep. "You be okay?" He said looking down at my feet. "Yeah, I'm good. I'll find it. Thanks man, thanks" I said. It was along a main road. A set of rooms that looked like they used to be offices. I had to go through a door to enter reception, a black lady was there called Stephanie and two guards with more people in a room behind her. "I'll show you to your room and we'll have a chat tomorrow" she said. "Can he show me?" I asked pointing to a guy who looked switched on. "It's okay, I don't mind" she said standing. I'd clocked two camera's as I went in. "Am I on camera all the way around?" I asked her. "Don't you like camera's?" She asked back obviously used to the question. "It's okay there's none in your room" she added. "You don't understand luv, I feel safer on camera. No offence, I've just been accused of a hundred and twenty four things that I didn't do because I was alone with a woman." I said.

She stopped and looked at me. I took three steps back and stood myself in front of one of the outside camera's. "I trust you. If it makes you feel better I'll come back when you're at your room" She said. "Okay" I replied nodding to the camera and knowing switched on guy would be watching. I walked several paces from Stephanie until we reached the door. She gave me a key which I took at arms length and went inside. She followed me "You're safe here" she said. "I know" I replied. "Please, on camera when with me" I said slumping my head. She stepped back outside into the line of sight of the camera "Toilets are down there. Make coffee in the kitchen" She said closing the door. It was a large room with a bed and bedclothes, a T.V a huge set of joining windows covered by long curtains and best of all a roasting hot radiator. My shoulder was killing me from being tense and carrying my bag. I lay against it and flinched. I didn't realise how much pain I'd been in. It took me ages to undo my boots and get them off but I didn't care. I got undressed totally and put my trousers back on. Then took my underwear and socks to the kitchen. I didn't know if It was communal or not because there were doors at either end of the corridor but I wouldn't be long and I had to risk it. I also didn't know if I was on camera or not but I needed this. I washed myself down in the sink then drenched my boxers and socks in tap water, gave them a good squeeze out in the sink and slung them over the radiator to dry. I did the same with my T-Shirt and I'd tied my boots together and slung them around my neck. If I had to get out in a hurry I'd have my boots if nothing else. My feet hurt on the cold tile floor, I made a coffee in an old cup, there was no milk so I just bunged eight sugars in. I sat in bed with the duvet around me and tried to think about positive things like how lucky I was to not be homeless tonight. It got me thinking about college and I remembered I had a pad in my rucksack. I got my English homework out and started doing that. The task was to write a story about your life. I wrote about Christmas at M.J's and how her mother would inch the table up so the Christmas tree stuck in my back until it bent. Then they'd fall asleep after stuffing themselves with chocolate. I'd wrote in red because it was all I had. I explained in the writing where I was now and why I didn't have a blue pen. Then I looked at the Black T.V capable of giving so much out and yet sat doing nothing. I felt like that T.V. Totally reliant on whether someone else could help me be active or not. I balanced my pen on the door handle and placed a sheet of paper on the floor beneath it. If it fell I'd hear it. I fell asleep listening to the endless stream of cars going past. Each one sounding like it was saying "gone" as it whizzed past. In the morning I was told by Stephanie who I'd seen through the plexiglass reception window that I'd get a "on your feet parcel" or some similarly designed gift from the rich to the poor. I just nodded. I didn't want hand outs and I'd been given my own room until told otherwise. I didn't know anything about where I'd be when I returned. I headed to college. I was early and Pam was on reception.

I said my "Hi's" and she blanked me. Can't say I blamed her, Julia my maths teacher went past me several times. "Tracie? You're not due in until 9:30am why are you here so early?" She asked. "I'm chatting up the receptionist" I joked. She laughed, Pam didn't. Sod it, truth it is then. "I'm homeless luv, It's warm here, that's why I'm early. At this point she did something which I respected but I was so embarrassed about at the same time. She pulled her purse out and took out ten pounds and handed it outwards. "No love" I said waving it off. "I got myself into this mess I'll get myself out of it, thanks though" I said. "But... what do you have?" she asked me. "What you see is what I've got" I said holding up my tobacco and my phone "but I'm not taking your money" I added and walked away. "If there's anything I can do?" She called after me. I could feel her sympathy and it hurt my pride. I liked her, she'd done the right thing. I sat in college an hour when I heard people talking about a college therapist. I left my lesson to go to the toilet and signed up then and there. I was told she'd give me a call when she was free.

Stephanie had to give me an interview where I had to answer questions mostly about whether I'd had drink or drug related problems or whether I got angry easily, self harmed or had ever attempted suicide. She told me mine was an unusual situation and that I'd make it. I presumed she just said that to everyone. I'd refused to interview unless a guard was present and he'd stood in the corner the entire time. "I won't hurt you" she'd said as soon as I'd gone in. I wanted to believe her.

My new room was the same as the other one but a lot smaller and with a cooler radiator. I was happy just to have my own little bit of space that I could sleep in. I had a single bed with no covers or anything but I couldn't complain. It was off the floor and their was a cupboard as well as a sink and a T.V with an in built VCR. I was told I could cook whatever was in the box and anything I bought myself. My rent was eight pounds per week and my first week was free if I got a place within that time. I was torn between realising the similarities between Wenzel's half way house and being happy. I had a box of unknown contents from someone who didn't know me. I called my solicitor who got me out of the meetings as long as I agreed to see Stephanie weekly at a minimum. It was a deal, I was okay with Stephanie just didn't fancy a group of junkies and alcoholics deciding I was their new best friend. I unpacked the box trying to think positively, "Wherever I lay my hat, that's my home" I sang softly. I had two shelves both were damaged but had a small built in wardrobe with a shelf on it. The Tinned food from the box went in the wardrobe and my Rucksack became my pillow. There were tins of all descriptions mostly of stuff I didn't eat, a tin opener, fork and spoon, a plate and right at the bottom my hand touched a warm sheet. It was wool around four feet by four feet and knitted in coloured patches. I held it to my skin the cold still biting me. I left the box where it was and cried. I cried for all I was worth because I had a sheet. "Thank you, Thank you" I said over and over as I curled up against the wall on my new dirty mattress. I fell asleep with the wool against my face before 5pm and didn't wake up until after noon the following day, the door was knocking. It was Stephanie asking if I was okay as they hadn't seen me in twenty four hours. Apparently their was a check in system and if nobody saw you then entire building came searching.

I got therapy at college almost immediately. Her name was Angela, she had a nice smile and was very friendly. "Hi, and how can I help you?" She asked. I'm not sure you can. I thought to myself. I was very aware of being alone in a room with an attractive woman. I looked around the room in some vein attempt to stop myself appearing uncomfortable. Their was a two seater sofa and a small desk. A small table between the sofa and a chair where Angela was seated. I went to stand by the window so I could see out and wondered if the car park camera could see me here. I was hoping it could. To be honest I was totally speechless, how could I tell her about my past and then hit her with everyone M.J had accused me of? She was such a dainty little thing I didn't suppose for a minute she'd be ready for the type of material I was going to dump on her. I asked her about seeing a male therapist. She cocked her head to the side and smiled prompting me to continue. I'm not sure how she made me feel so at east but she made me feel relaxed. I'm sure she wasn't copying my body language. I figured if I just told her a little bit then I could judge for myself whether she could handle it or not. I explained about being homeless and ran over having anxiety attacks vaguely and I was here simply because I needed to talk about it all, that was all. I explained how I got from Manchester to Bromley omitting all the violence but including M.J's controlling mentality. Angela praised my college achievements and asked if I'd like to see her again or someone else. Naturally I agreed to see her again but told her straight I was nervous as hell. As soon as I left that room as far as I was concerned she could accuse me of anything and who'd doubt her? How would I prove my innocence? "Do you really believe I'd do that?" She asked me genuinely. She was a kind person I could see it in her eyes but I was me and I was used to people turning. "See you next week" she said as I left.

I saw Pam as I got downstairs. "Fancy a walk after work?" I asked. "Yeah, okay" she said tapping away at the keyboard. I was up court for this injunction in a week and I wanted to say bye before I got it put in place. I knew nothing of the law. If she wanted an injunction she could have it. I wanted nothing to do with her anyway but was still gutted that she'd felt the need to make these stupid accusations.

I was at Pam's parents and trying to praise myself for getting past my fear of being with a woman when it came to Pam's parents, Pam or Angela. I was surprised when I entered Pam's house and found the lights switches were all lower down. High tables so her wheelchair could fit anywhere and her parents had made the garden accessible too. It was beautiful with lots of foreign plants in they'd had their downstairs space turned into Pam's bedroom with an en suite disabled access bathroom. It looked great. They were a good family and treated me well. I made myself scarce at mealtimes at first not wanting to feel intrusive and feeling like I didn't belong. The more I saw how great they were together the more I craved family. Pam's mum was called Tracy too, she did all the cooking and cleaning for Pam with a smile on her face and used to take her out wherever she wanted to go if she needed help. She was her mum, therapist and friend. Andy was no different just quieter. He sorted the bills and the house but was just as caring and protective of Pam. I felt I was living a lie. I'd had two meals with them and told them nothing apart from that I was at college and wanted to work. Pam had a sister called Lucia. I hardly saw her, she was able bodied, Good looking blonde girl and outgoing. Rarely home she seemed to have a fieriness about her that I admired but didn't want around me. A "here is my opinion whether you want it or not" type attitude. The more I got to know Tracy and Andy the more I knew I had to tell them. The more I got to know Pam the more I realised that beyond the bubbly nature she was very, very depressed. To this day I cannot pinpoint why, at work she was an amazingly positive young woman and yet at home she was a complete mess. Her dad informed me she'd use lies like we would potentially progress to a physical altercation and therefore where we might get angry to extremes she could lie to extreme. I didn't think much of it and even understood the theory behind it but to be fair I was keeping some pretty hefty secrets of my own it's not like I could judge. Initially I was told Lucia was jealous of Pam because she had a boyfriend – me. However over time it became apparent Pam wouldn't hesitate to get her own way. Lucia wasn't jealous of Pam, Pam was jealous of Lucia, Lucia could work, had a job and led a full life. Pam was stuck between loving her as a sister and hating her because she could do the things she couldn't. I felt sorry for both of them. It must have been hard loving a sister who would routinely turn on you no matter what you did for them.

Andy was in the back garden when I told him. I simply handed him the accusations "I'll leave immediately if you want me to and I understand completely if you never want me to see your daughter again" I said. He read through them and I told him my story from moving to Bromley until now. "If you get charged. Don't come back here. Otherwise you're welcome here anytime. We like you and Pam loves you. You're good here" He told me. I couldn't have respected him more. If I'd of been in his position I'd of kicked me clean out.

Court day came in no time, I'd practised speech after speech after speech like I was in a review meeting as a child. Whilst Pam was watching music channels I was reciting answers in my head and following them up with further questions and then answering them myself. I treated it like I was playing chess with Wenzel, whatever move they threw at me I had to have a better one. Andy offered to take me to court and I declined. They'd fed me most nights as I was coming straight from college to see Pam, as much as I kept telling myself nothing could happen with Pam and I it was no secret we'd become an Item. Everyone knew including the staff at college, I'll never forget her mum asking me "So what do you say when people ask you about Pam?" "I say she's my partner" I replied to which Tracy let out a "Awwwwww," People's perception's are exactly that – there's, "I don't care what people think about me and Pam as long as they keep it to themselves if it's negative" I added." Tracy seemed to understand. It was hard not to fall for Pam, she'd been there when others weren't and I had this overpowering feeling of wanting to be needed and needing to be understood and, or accepted and I was totally confused. I had no issues with her physical condition in the slightest and was convinced I was in love. That said I had nobody and was convinced the lies M.J had spun like thick cobwebs were about to cling to my face and choke me. Having Pam around fuelled my desire to not feel guilty and fuelled my belief that I had a purpose. If a disabled lass trusts me, I must be okay, surely?

As it stood I'd accepted this injunction without a solicitor. The guy making the decisions had actually asked me if I was sure I didn't want a solicitor and I'd agreed I didn't need one I wanted nothing to do with M.J and so had no reason to object to the injunction. I didn't realise the implications and again the guy making the decisions said "are you sure?" I said yes. I just wanted out of the same room as her as quickly as possible. If I'd known anything about the law then I'd of got me a solicitor.

Unfortunately by accepting an injunction the person making the claim has certain rights. In this case when they make a further accusation about you whether you've done anything or not you get arrested immediately and asked questions later as a pose to asked questions and then arrested.

I found this out the hard way. The first time I was at home when the door went at seven am. I answered the door half asleep and was immediately bundled into the back of a police van. I was allowed five minutes between answering the door and being in the van with cuff's on to get my gear before we left for the station. When I got to the station I was told M.J said that last night I was seen outside her place in Bromley with a rucksack on. I'd spent the majority of the night at Pam's including another time a few days later that she said I was outside her flat. I had three witnesses who were happy to state this. It was at this point I started writing down my every move. From the minute I left the flat, who I saw, what time I saw them, what time I left and if I had free time I tried to spend it in public places where I could be observed on camera so I could always be found out to be telling the truth. Twice they called me whilst I was at college and in lesson to which tutors informed the police I had been there all day. Once I was picked up from college because she'd made an accusation about me whilst It was during my lunch hour. I was exactly where I said I'd been which was with two friends and some animals in the animal section of the College. Most often than not they'd take me in and my solicitor would turn up and explain the situation and they'd let me go again. However sometimes M.J made an accusation late in the day and they picked me up in the evening which meant staying in a cell the night until my solicitor turned up the following day. I soon learnt who was a good solicitor and who wasn't. Either way I was always released without charge because they had no evidence but had to pick me up because of M.J making an accusation whilst I was under an injunction.

They never charged me because they had no proof I still only had on my record that initial caution which would be spent in around four years. Why? Because I was innocent. However one day amidst all the mess of juggling college, getting arrested for no reason whatsoever and getting on with my life I went to the bank to hand a cheque in. Part of my injunction was that I wouldn't go in a certain distance of M.J or where she lives or contact her in any way or ask anyone else to. All of which I happily signed off to. However as I entered the bank M.J and her dad were leaving. I was listening to headphones and stepped to one side well out of the way of the walkway and removed my earphones. M.J saw me and walked past, her dad saw me and walked past. I knew this was going to bite me in the ass but there was nothing I could do about it. I went to the bank and then went straight to where Pam was volunteering to tell her I wouldn't be around that night as I was just about to get arrested. She was getting to the point where she understood the process and so I headed off to the police station to explain the situation. Apparently M.J had alleged I'd approached her in the bank and stuck two fingers up at her. I requested the police get the C.C.T.V from the bank. They refused. I left as the police said they were not going to arrest me and I went to my solicitor and explained to them. I asked them to get the C.C.T.V from the bank which would prove my claim and she said she'd sort it out and not to worry. It was shortly after that I got told I was going to court for breaking the injunction on that day I saw M.J in the bank. With all the accusations if I was found guilty I was looking at Jail time. Naturally I was gutted but I was getting quite used to being gutted.

Chapter 38

My solicitor was sat in a big room. She'd refused to question me although I'd asked her to she said she couldn't. Apparently there were other cases going on and we just had to wait our turn. I guess I presumed we'd go into another room and everyone would be waiting there but I was wrong we were all to wait in the same room together. M.J came in and immediately pointed at me "There he is! Rapist! Hide me! Hide me!" I remained seated as she was led away to a quiet room with her solicitor. I kept my eyes on the table in front of me. She was playing a class act and trying to get a reaction. When she was gone I glanced at my solicitor. She said nothing. My barrister turned up, he was a fella with cerebral palsy. I recognised the condition immediately because it was what contributed to Pam's paraplegia and was a condition two of my close friends had. He hunched when he walked "You're lucky they didn't choose a crown court. Most they can sentence you to here is five years" He said. It didn't help. "You think I'm going down? You think I did this?" I asked him honestly. He shook my hand "Not allowed to talk about it" He said. What was wrong with these people? I was on my own. I'd been quizzing myself for weeks with every little thing. M.J might make up, Blow out of proportion or alter to get me into trouble. I was ready but I wasn't perfect. I needed a persona, A confidence, a niche. Something to tune into. Who did I know that was clever? Confidant and could twist words easily? My father. No way! I told myself. I'm not going to lie. I'm innocent. I never hit, raped or abused her in any way. Okay I might have said some harsh shit during an argument but that's about it. Yeah but can you do what Wenzel can? I asked myself. At that point I saw myself as an eight year old child making eye contact with him as he spun me around the room by my arm in a painful lock and I threw my mind into him. Him looking at me enjoying the pain, he knew he was untouchable, could I have that control, that confidence, I hated him and I hated myself but I needed that confidence and he was the only person I could think of who'd get me the words and clarity of them without stuttering, without looking nervous which I knew they'd interpret as guilt. To get through the next hour and if I did get set down for something I'd not done who better than Wenzel's mind to sink deeply into to survive it? I just hoped I'd have enough strength to find myself again afterwards.

I stood up and looked around the room, I own this room and I own everyone in it. I thought. "Sit down" my solicitor said. I ignored her for a few seconds, she may speak when I tell her. I thought "I'm nipping out for a cigarette" I said hearing my father's voice, his polite sing-song words that told you what was happening, instead of asked. I smoked outside and walked back down the halls. My barrister had followed me in case I ran off. "Relax, it'll be okay" He said. I smiled at him "It'll be better than okay" I told him. I was walking back in before I'd finished the sentence. We were called up and M.J took the stand claiming she was religious. Lie number one. She swore on the bible. I ignored her and kept my eyes to the corner of the room M.J started softly and when explaining anything about me she stamped her feet and panted. I didn't react. Then she worked herself up to shouting again and again I didn't react. The judge asked her to explain calmly and clearly. The case was to see if I'd intentionally broken the injunction. I hadn't. It peaked on whether I could be expected to know M.J was in the bank at the time I walked in. However M.J ranted about all her accusations from times she claimed I attacked her to rape and apparently how my eyes had burnt red when she was leaving the bank and she thought I was going to attack her then. M.J's dad was in attendance and could have been a witness as he was at the bank that day however he refused to give any statement. I respected him for that. He knew his daughter as well as I did. The judge asked M.J why she had seen fit to add me on Facebook after applying for an injunction. M.J claimed she was dyslexic and didn't know what she was doing yet she'd read the oath just fine. Finally my barrister got up and asked about an account where M.J claimed she'd seen me through her window at a day that I was at college and had proof for. Within minutes we established that M.J possibly saw a man with his back to the window in the rain with a grey bag on his back, apparently the man left after ten minutes of standing motionless in the rain. We also established M.J doesn't like being questioned as when my barrister asked "Do you love Mr Daily?" Her response was "No rapist, yes, yes I do, what a stupid question I hate him" to which my barrister replied "Do you want to hurt Mr Daily?" M.J simply exploded. "No! Why would I? He's not important enough to hurt! Liar, you loved me!" She was asked to calm down by the judge and I was called up. I answered everything calmly after taking the none religious version of the oath and I didn't look at M.J the entire time I was on the stand. I made eye contact with the judge and looked from her to the corner of the room and back again. I'd heard M.J's lies a hundred times or more in my head so her accusations were not phasing me any more although I made a shocked expression each time they were brought up. I gave answers which always included a positive way in which I'd assisted her or helped her to assist herself and where I couldn't I explained the reason why I couldn't be guilty of such things for example Wenzel being overly controlling and therefore I couldn't be. I went on further to explain the hardest questions were those where I couldn't provide an answer. How can a person prove they didn't do something? If something has happened there is generally some sort of evidence. If the event hasn't then there is none. The judge commented "That doesn't always mean the event didn't occur" to which I replied "which is why I'm at a loss trying to prove my innocence, the first I knew of them was in that big list of papers I was handed other than the bank event which I immediately went to the police station about as soon as I'd informed my partner and asked police to get C.C.T.V footage, as I knew from M.J's previous accusations that she'd certainly make another one here and it would prove I was nowhere near her. If I'd known she was in that bank trust me I'd of wanted nothing to do with it" I was seated as there were no further questions. The judge rambled on in legal jargon I didn't understand.

I was just waiting to hear "Not guilty" I didn't just want to hear it. I needed to.

Instead I got "no action to be taken as there's no evidence to support parties request for conviction" I'd zoned out still waiting to hear a not guilty. Instead the judge looked at me and said "Will Mr Daily be requesting compensation?" My solicitor looked at me and the shock on her face told me everything I needed to know about her beliefs. I didn't know how it worked. I presumed M.J would have to pay me and that meant seeing her and I didn't want that" My brain wouldn't work and the only way I could express myself was to look at the judge and say "What?" "Do you want compensation?" She asked me again. "I want to go home, I want to be left alone" I replied. It was signed and I left. I went straight to Pam's workplace. "We won. I'm going to see your dad" I said giving her a hug.

That night Pam's brother and his little boy came over. The young lad played with Pam and wanted to play with me. I kept sending him away until I went to speak to Andy outside. I lit a smoke and we sat side by side on a bench in this beautiful garden "How can I play with this kid?" I cried. "After all I've been accused of? I didn't do it but....the accusations? Who'd trust me around their kid?" I asked. "His dad doesn't know" Andy told me. "Thanks, but that's not the point man. If I was the kid's dad I'd want to know so I could make my own mind up" I said. "You're innocent" he told me. "Yeah, until when? Until the next time they arrive" I chucked my pad to him "I write down my every move, when I go in I'll write that I spoke to you and I'm now around Pam. When the police took my phone they asked who the kid was in the picture." I broke down "It's my mates daughter for fucks sake" Andy touched my shoulder, I went in. No sympathy. I won't accept it. I'm stronger than that I thought. I made my excuses and left.

My time got taken up with college where I was now doing a higher course in psychology, history, higher maths, English and IT in the hope of going on to university. I wanted to become a therapist and help people like Angela, Nigel, David and countless others had helped me. I needed positive people around me and Pam wasn't it. Her sister had been looking after her as her parents had gone away when I got a call "Get here now she's tried to kill me!" I was twenty minutes away and ran there all the way. When I arrived everything seemed fine. Lucia was calm and opened the door just fine and was polite. Pam had no injuries, wasn't out of breath and was sat watching T.V just fine. "You okay?" I asked Lucia. "No, She's lying" Lucia said. She went to Pam and told her a few home truth's and then got upset herself. I sat with Pam for an hour and then left. During that hour I told her I didn't have space in my life for any negativity or silly drama's. I couldn't handle the stress and I'd had enough to last a lifetime. We'd split up twice before over silly things because I'd taken them as controlling mannerisms or because she'd said stupid things which I didn't like and presumed would lead to complications either way I knew I couldn't just be around her as a friend because I did love her. I just couldn't be with her. I told her we were done and that I couldn't see her any more I'd not been arrested in over two months which for me during that past year and a half was amazing, I had therapy, I was doing good at college and I was surviving. I got a breakthrough with a place to live. A studio flat ground floor in a place that had a bit of a reputation. I was okay though nobody bothered me. Maybe it had calmed down or maybe it was because I kept myself to myself. I didn't know but it was nice not to be in trouble.

Angela was brilliant and I actually started looking forwards to our appointments. She fought my corner in letter form when I'd gone through all the crap with M.J. Angela was more than a therapist though. She was someone I trusted and that was rare for me, more so considering my past. I knew I had to do it this time properly or I'd never move on. I had to tell her everything. She laughed with me, cried with me. Polite, friendly and professional throughout. I'd be lying if I said I could recall each session or even what she did for me.

She's the type of therapist to get in your head. Twist all your thoughts upside down and inside out. Make you question everything and then guide you to believing all the positives. At the end she'll tell you she did nothing. That you did it all and you'll walk away believing it wholeheartedly. I went into those sessions a homeless broken man accused of countless crimes with my own demons to fight and rotten teeth. I left each session more and more determined to change the world, to make a difference, just for me, because I wanted to, because I deserved it. Money wasn't just a negative tool people used for control as I'd grown up believing. I deserved a job and was more than capable of it. I wasn't a failure because my education sucked. I was a champion for learning anyway. I wasn't guilty because someone else said I was, I was strong because I'd fought back in the right way, without violence, without losing my mind. But we still had things to resolve. I had to tell her about my granddad, I'd killed him. My guilt lay there. I deserved every inch of punishment I dealt myself because I killed my granddad and therefore was as bad if not worse than my father. I told her the story knowing full well she'd see me differently. Knowing she'd hate me. Knowing I was useless. When I finished she smiled, not a little oh you poor thing smile, not a I'm pretending to be happy but I'm really wondering what to say smile but a whacking big genuine grin. "Well done" she said tipping her head forwards slightly and fixing me with her eyes. Her hair fell forwards and she pushed it back subconsciously. I looked at the table "Thank you."

I'd woken up at home shaking after a nightmare where I was trying to find Alan and whenever I finally make it to the room he's in I wake up in bed and cycle repeats itself until I start to notice each time something in the room is a little off. I'm more afraid each time I wake up and find that I'm still asleep and then I do actually wake up for real and I'm wondering if I'm still asleep? Is Alan dead? I downed some cold water and held the living room door open. "I'm sorry Alan, I'm so, so sorry" I sat on the edge of my bed and held my head in my hands and then started to shake. This time however I didn't try to calm it. I needed to feel this, my heart pounded and adrenaline was flowing through me like wildfire "No" I told myself out of habit. I knew what came next. "You're not ten any more" I told myself in an attempt to calm down "feel it!" I yelled inside my head. Immediately I was back in front of nan's sofa and I'd flung it over like it was nothing as my arms were alight with strength of the adrenaline. I was back on the bag at Winsford boxing, back in Nigel's session hitting Clive, Cycling from Jonathon and Jodie's in care, Stood in front of Wenzel as he counted down from five to one and then Alan sat listening to Woman of Gold and crying because his wife was dead and I flipped. "I'm sorry!" I screamed kicking my table over. It broke. I grabbed the mattress and it got slung as did each part of the divan base which landed on top of a borrowed laptop and smaller table. The chair beside my bed was in pieces where I'd wanted to destroy every bit of hurt I'd felt inside. "I'm sorry I couldn't help you!" I cried, "Pam, I'm sorry I'm not your best." I was half growling half just making random guttural sounds where my stomach was churning with anger and sadness of a hundred different emotions I'd never allowed to go through me. "M.J I'm sorry you're not sane!" I punched the door to my airing cupboard hearing the thud and seeing Alan hit a door when I was a child. I unloaded, no technique just pure aggression. I didn't stop until my wrist gave way. I left two holes in the door and looked around the flat for something else to break. Half because I felt bad I'd broke the door and half because my wrist stung and that just irritated me all the more. Tears stung my face and I wiped them away to find blood. Apparently I'd managed to split two knuckles as well and I was bleeding. I called Angela and slumped on the floor of my kitchen "I'm sorry" I said bawling and catching my breath. Angela spent an hour explaining about anger and pain and how it had all come together, how normal I was for getting it out in a controlled way, not the brightest of ways but a controlled way. She had a point and she considered it a breakthrough. I wasn't sure, I was still sad, I still hurt. I was still guilty. I'd lead Pam into a relationship and walked away once I felt strong. The fact I actually loved her meant nothing to me. I'd really upset her by walking away, taken away perhaps her only chance. Was I to blame for her unhappiness? Fuck it. I unloaded on the wardrobe whilst Angela was on the phone. Then apologised for being violent, apologised for being me, apologised for being a waste of space useless bastard and then I stopped in my tracks. "I'm talking to myself like Wenzel again aren't I?" I asked more to myself than to Angela. "You tell me" she responded. She was right, not only was I to tell her I had to tell the rest of the world as well. This is hard, but it's beatable. I'm not going to be Wenzel or my mother or talk to myself like he did any more I'm going to sit here and get upset until the bullshit's gone. The pain is gone and then I'll get up. When I'm better. I thanked Angela who checked I was okay before she went and then I hung up. I was okay as well. It was becoming evident I'd reached a new turning point in my life where I had no family and no real friends. I knew people at college but they weren't friends. They didn't know anything of my past. I realised I had to make an effort at this life thing and it was going to be hard. I looked in the tiny round mirror I'd bought from the pound shop whilst I was in my bathroom and sat down on the floor. I was there maybe five minutes just thinking when my electric flicked off. I had seven pounds to last me two days. I was okay for travel as I had a full oyster card and plenty of food in because I always bought too much out of habit. If I was made homeless what would I eat? I always had biscuits, Weetabix and butter in the flat because if shit turned bad I'd eat them. Now I had a choice, I still had hot water as it had been on since this morning. Ciggarettes or electric?

As I sat in the bath in the dark with the ember of my roll up dimming. I got upset again, not because of the electric situation. I was still chuffed I had a roof over my head, but because I'd been apologising to everyone else earlier and not once had I apologised to myself. Not once had I said "I'm sorry I treated myself so badly, I didn't deserve it. I didn't deserve years of guilt, Wenzel's beatings or mum's alcohol addiction. I didn't deserve to have my family taken away or have M.J lie about me" When the water ran cold I got dried and grabbed my sleeping bag, got inside and hunkered down in the bathroom. It was the smallest room of a studio flat and therefore the warmest. Last thing I remember was staring in my reflection and telling myself to forgive myself for every wrong I'd done. I punched the mirror. It broke.

Chapter 39

It was Christmas eve in early two thousand. I was lonely, I thought of every other person out there with family. I was grateful for the roof over my head, my freedom. My friends and my character. I was happy in every way other than being lonely. Which for me was enormous progress. Where were they? What were they doing now? With who? It had cropped up time and time again and I'd blotted it out like a bad bit of ink. Still there scratching away beneath my perfectly tippexed page. Still eating away just invisible to anyone apart from me. I remembered those days with a stick and dustbin lid where I'd play swords and shield with my brother and wondered what it would be like to spar with him today. Almost all physical affection, I had to accept I did so through contact sports. Never able to admit It felt like caring to have a friend run into me at a hundred miles an hour knocking the wind out of me in rugby or karate with my friend Nigel, swords and shields with Jonathon. I found his email address and mailed him. I discovered rather quickly that he didn't want to know me at all but he did want to know the past. Why had I not been around? Why had I been so distant? Naturally he'd heard more made up stories about me from over protective carers and people as I had heard about Wenzel. The difference however was simple. I wasn't a danger to anyone but who would believe that? I had gone back to live with Wenzel after all.

A year later after answering a lot of questions we arranged a meet. "Where?" He asked me as I'd travelled the hundred and fifty eight miles by train and arrived at Macclesfield station. A lot had changed, cars weren't on bricks and people coming and going had left bags further away from themselves than I remember them doing as a child. There was only one place that seemed suitable enough to meet my brother after all these years apart. Besides it was also the only other place I knew by heart where I could check the entire area before he got there in case their was family I really didn't want to bump into. "Mum's grave" I said. He was there inside forty minutes.

I'd knelt next to mum. "Long time princess, I did it" I said in my leather jacket, black jeans and cotton shirt which was also black. "I got everything. I gave it them. We're back together. I love you mum" I held a tear. "I can't promise how this will go but I can promise I tried. I've done all I can. Rest well mum" I heard a car pull up above me and knew he'd be ten minutes. He'd done the same as I had, he'd checked the area first to make sure I wasn't with other family members we didn't want around. We were both trying to trust each other, trying to become the family we both knew and felt we were and yet we were also both Macc lads who grew up with Macc rules. I was alone and so was he. A tall man approached me as I was knelt down. He had vaguely ginger hair, wider shoulders than I and was very tall. He'd later tell me he expected me to stand up and be taller than him. He'd got our uncle's height and was wearing ripped blue jeans, a dirty T-shirt and had an unkempt beard. I didn't care. He was a grafter, a survivor and most of all, my brother. I stood up and hugged him. It was brief, neither of us knew what to do. We'd never been shown. "Good to finally meet you bro!" He said his northern accent much thicker than mine. "Long time man, looong time" I said. If I'd called him bro then I'd of fallen apart. "You checked the area didn't you?" I asked. "Yup" He laughed looking around. "I'm alone" I said "Me too man, me too" He said. I took a look back at mum and walked off in the direction of the car with my brother. Who I'm still in touch with to this day.

I'd forgotten all about it as I'd not been arrested in ages but the police requested I attend the station to pick up a phone they'd taken from me when M.J accused me of calling her,of course the phone was clean. I had a couple of months until the injunction was up and in that time I had two calls from the police asking where I was, both times I was in college and they didn't come to pick me up they asked to speak to someone who could verify that and I put Phil on the phone then they left me alone. There is no letter when your injunction ends. You don't get a gold key that says you're free from her harassment or a call to say if she makes any more accusations they won't just pick you up they'll actually have to ask her to prove it first. There's none of that and so the fear stays with you for a while even though you know they can't just take you. I was in a much better place but I was still waking up if mail came through the letterbox, I was still by the door as it hit the floor in case it was someone coming through it and I was still envisioning it being two police officers with some ludicrous accusation, however getting my phone back helped. It was somehow like someone had said "Here's your phone, sorry mate, our error" Of course the apology never occurred. That's not in the style of the police and it's certainly not in the style of M.J.

I actually make friends easily and college had become routine. I had a group of about eight regular friends that went out fortnightly with. It was nice, just being myself but routine things were beyond me. I could tell them how to get their own place from being homeless with no paperwork. I could tell them how to beat fears and phobia's. I could explain what a debt relief order was and how to obtain it. However I was no good when it came to "who'd you like best on Britain's got talent then?" Or "It's awfully wet out today isn't it?" I didn't care and was no good at pretending to care. I couldn't give a toss about such mundane conversation. I wanted to know about people, their loves, hates, fears and successes. I didn't give a damn whether they liked hot or cold weather.

With Angela's help I'd become much more confidant in my abilities yet I still didn't know who I was, what music I liked or felt stable enough to set my home up as a home and why was I training? It made me feel better but it wasn't leading to a fight so what was the point? I let the art therapy or self work as I'd started calling it slack and I'd stopped meditating. Before I knew it I was taking the late night parties home with me. Just a small bottle of baileys of a night and then within weeks I was getting up hungover, going for a run and picking up more on the way home. I'd just survived, I'd won at everything and who cared? What did it change? One night I fell off a

P.C chair and cracked a rib because I'd drank tequila too fast, straight. I'd called Melorna who was in Florida whilst on a bus in U.K to ask her where I lived. Then I'd passed the phone around to people on the bus, apparently they thought it was hilarious. The more people thought I was funny the more I drank. The more people said how much of a laugh I was when I'd had a drink. The more I drank. It numbed the pain and I believed it made me more likeable. It didn't. It wasn't long before that circle of friends turned into two friends. One was Melorna and the other was Tim. Melorna had seen me through everything from the start of M.J's charade and Tim I'd met at college. He'd seen a few of my adventures and watched me go from a confident caring individual to a drunk inside six months. He called me nightly trying to get me to stop drinking. I told him to fuck off. What does he know? He'd still call and always would as would Melorna. I wanted to leave this place and drink allowed me to temporarily do that. It also left me depressed and wanting more. Melorna and Tim tried everything, tried to discuss anything that might be a trigger or reason for my drinking and then one night they both called me inside the space of an hour each with a very similar message that amounted to. "I'm sorry, I can't watch you do this to yourself any more I'm off, call me when you've been sober a while" I laughed "Yeah, I'm funny me, fuck off then" I hung up on both of them as I sat cross-legged on the floor surrounded by cans of Carlsburg. I watched Steven Seagal films back to back and finished my drinks. The following night I did the same only this time, nobody called me.

I'd got half way through a crate of twenty four on the third night when I paused the DVD and looked at my reflection in the heater on the wall next to my T.V. "What you doing to yourself lad?" Alan's voice but my words. I punched the heater, I punched the reflection. "Fuck off!" I'd dented my storage heater. My hand hurt. "Wanna fight! Fight me!" I laughed at my own joke as I made mouth moving shapes with my thumb and finger using my hand as a puppet. I was losing it and knew it. I jabbed the reflection and then just unloaded on it. I was sweating by the time I finished with the heater and my hands both hurt but I wasn't quite done. "Idiot!" I shouted picking up what was left of the crate and half staggering to the bathroom. I threw the lot into the bathtub one at a time by jumping up high and slamming it down into the bath. "I'm not you!" I screamed remembering my mother's drinking and how much it hurt me. "I hate you!" I said to her "Who are you?" I said to me. I didn't know who I was, I sat on the floor with empty cans around me in the dark. The next day I went for a run and bought a bottle of Baileys home. I called Tim and he didn't answer. I called Melorna and she didn't answer. I opened the Baileys and smelt it. "No, no more" I said as I tipped the lot down the sink without taking a mouthful. "I don't drink" I told myself. I was three weeks sober before Melorna would talk to me and she spent the next year drilling me about self worth. She helped me get my music sorted out so I knew what I liked, we literally went through genre after genre, song after song and redesigned my flat so I knew what to put in it. It still wasn't a home but it was liveable and I at least liked it.

I got a breakthrough with the council and was offered my new flat. It was beautiful and I loved it it's own balcony and a little old lady used to live in it. I bought a cowboy hat on the town and called Angela. "Guess what!?" I said "What?" She said sounding excited. "I've got keys!" I said. "Yay! Well done you!" She was genuinely pleased. "I'm walking through town in a cowboy hat!" I said and we both laughed. I decorated and my circle of friends grew again. I just had my teeth to repair and I would be fully functional. Another year past and I'd got back into meditation and spiritual circles. I didn't drink at all and didn't do readings for anyone either, paid or otherwise. I started actually trying to write poetry instead of just writing my thoughts and feelings down to rhyme which is how I best described how I felt inside. The only way I could combat the stutter and allow my words to flow without visualising them was to make them sound similar I never intended to share it. I was convinced the operation for my teeth was going to kill me. My dentist had done me a big favour and refereed me to the hospital.

I took all my history paperwork and dumped it in a giant cardboard box. I wrote "Burn this" on it in big writing. Then I gave my mate my flat keys. "If I don't come out, burn the box. The rest is yours" I had no family save my brother and we weren't regularly in touch. I called Angela on the way to the hospital. I was terrified but I needed to do this and needed to tell Angela. "Whatever happens you gave me the tools to have the confidence and strength to do this. Whatever happens it's my choice to go so whether I come out again or not I want to say Thank you and I'm ready for it." I hung up. I had got myself completely ready to die. I believed it wholeheartedly. I took the needle and felt the anaesthetic go up my arm and into my shoulder before I screamed involuntarily. "You're not knocking me out! Come on you bastards!" before darkness hit me. As soon as I was out it felt like I'd woke up. When in actual fact it was over an hour later. My work had been done and although drained I was otherwise fine. I'd had five teeth out and numerous fillings. My nurses name was Joy "rest" she said as I sat up and swung my legs out of bed. "No, I need to walk" I told her muffled from a swollen mouth. I stood up, swayed and then sat down before I fell down. Joy was a big girl, blonde and in her forties. "I did it?" I asked. "What dear?" She asked me as I bust into tears. All those years of fear for less than five minutes work. "I did it, dad killed mum, needle is knife, knife means death" I said as tears leaked all over both of us as she held me. "Aw OK dear." I text Angela simply. "It's done, Thank-you". What more could I say?

Over the next two years I quit college and started volunteering at the British Heart Foundation. I trained Jute Kune Do and boxing with my friend Lee twice a week or more. I loved the work it was furniture and electrical store and my main job was to compact warehouse vans with furniture. I had the stamina and determination to do it. The rest I'd have to learn and within six months I was running a team of fifteen people. I loved it but my mate lee had hit some trouble at home was now staying with me for a while. I helped him get his own place, he was a natural boxer and had a very unique personality. If something entered his head he just said it no matter how raw it was. I was convinced he'd become a professional boxer from the amount of times I'd thrown everything I had at home and hit nothing but air. Other times I'd be convinced he couldn't get closed enough to even hit me and next minute I'd be on the floor. He was a natural and I was honoured to be his training partner and punch bag. He cracked two of my ribs one time and that was an accident. I hate to think what he could have achieved had he been serious. When he got his own place we saw less of one another purely because I was working a lot and then one day I got a message online. "Lee's dead" When I'd finally got the the bottom of it I discovered he'd been hit by a train. To this day nobody knows if it was an accident or not. The nickname he gave himself was Sharpshooter and in my mind he'll live forever. I had to make an enormous choice however, I could dedicate my life to researching everything to do with my friend who I loved dearly to find out what happened that day or I could get on with my life. I knew Lee and I knew he'd want whatever was best for me. I remember being on a bus up London one time when this fella wouldn't get off the bus and the driver had to stop. We'd been held up for a while and it was a night bus so Lee and I went to see what was wrong. Well the fella turned on me and I stood in front of Lee so he wouldn't get hit. Lee pushed me back and stood in front of me. We both continued this silliness several times until we both started laughing at either one of us trying to protect the other. So I knew what Lee would want but I also knew If anyone could find out, it was me and didn't I owe him that?

I couldn't take it and threw myself into work. I knew the affects of murder and manslaughter, maybe it was just an accident maybe it wasn't either way Lee was dead and you know what. Once you're dead, you're dead some thing's are easier left that way and this was one of them. I chose to get on with my life. I ran warehouses for

British Heart Foundation furniture and electrical stores In Bromley, Croydon, Old Kent Road, Mitcham and Camberley. I was finally fully functional. I had a good job which I earned and deserved, a nice home, great circle of friends and a string of on off relationships. Since Pam I'd pretty much given up on girls for anything serious. I had them over for company now and then but otherwise I was happy being single. I never saw me settling down. Who wants that? I'd been through enough already. Despite my great awakening to my own independence and confidence. I still didn't think I belonged in any orthodox family and that's how I liked it. I had several girlfriends but nothing that would ever amount to anything, exactly how I wanted it. I'm very private in ways when it comes to my time and my home and very open when it comes to helping others or using my past to assist others. No more, it was time to live just for me.

Chapter 40

I was introduced to Ellen by my friend Tim. He liked her and had been flirting with her for months. We were in a pub "Hi I'm Tracie, get you a drink" I asked? She had brown eyes her hair was long. She had a butterfly tattoo peeking from beneath her black lace sleeve and pale skin, definitely attractive. "No thanks" She said cocking her head and holding her drink up. "How you doing?" I asked. "Fine thanks" she said again smiling but cold as Ice. "Well I tried" I thought and sat talking to Tim for two hours. The music became louder as the night went on "dance?" I asked Ellen holding my hand out "you can dance?" she asked obviously believing I couldn't, she was right. "Tell you what, you teach me to dance and I'll teach you taikowondo?" I said having had a couple of lessons from another friend a few weeks before but not really taking to it. I didn't think "Go Ken Ryu or Jute Kune Do" would have the same macho ring to it and I wanted to see how that hand of hers felt in mine. She laughed. "You do taikowondo?" She said. Bingo, something I actually could do. "Yes" I said smiling. "Go on then" she said pointing to the dance floor. "What....here?" I asked. She smirked and walked away. Dammit.

My friend Melorna had come over from Florida to visit and it was brilliant after knowing one another only via the web for years to finally get a grasp of who she is face to face. I introduced her to my friends and we all went out for a party. Tim had invited some others that I didn't know and amongst those was Ellen. Melorna and Ellen hit it off straight away and ran off together to another pub for girlie chats. Irony or what? It was very late when Melorna got home "have fun?" I asked her a little pissed off that she'd come over to see me and disappeared with someone I didn't really get along with but still. She was staying with me because it made more sense than paying for a bed and breakfast so I wasn't going to kick up a stink about it. "Yeah, Ellen's a good girl you'd like her" she replied. "Ellen's a cold hearted lass, besides Tim fancies her" I replied. "Cold eh?" Melorna said. "She'd not accept a drink with you anyway" Melorna added as my eyebrows rose. Challenge accepted. I messaged Ellen when Melorna returned home and we got talking but only ever via text. Then I got an offer of work in the Camberley area for two weeks which turned out to go on for just over a month. I accepted and asked Ellen to dinner to hear the good news I had. I liked her, she was definitely sensible which was more than could be said for the usual type of woman I go for. I tried keeping myself at a safe distance because I could see she was a genuine girl. She wasn't like the others and I'd certain she'd run a mile if I put my past onto her. Who wouldn't?

That month in Camberley was brilliant. I worked an enormous warehouse all day and spoke to Ellen on the phone of a night. We were soon flirting. I couldn't help it. When I returned I continued a days work in Bromley and then saw her immediately after work. In the pub with Ellen I realised for the first time ever I wasn't looking around over my shoulder for trouble to appear. I wasn't cautious nor was I jumping if a glass broke. Somehow I'd changed and Ellen had my full undivided attention and she was stunning. I asked her if she'd like to go for a picnic with me and she said yes. We went to five arches bridge in Sidcup meadows by a church I'd been to a hundred times or more usually at night and in a panic ridden state. I'd never been inside. This time I was back there again living a totally different life. It was beautiful hot day and I set out sandwiches and drinks. We'd just sat down by the lake when the heavens opened and we both got drenched. We were soaked to the bone and had smiles through to our core. We jumped in puddles and acted like children It was good clean fun. I was wearing black trousers and a tight black shirt and everything clung to me. We went back to my place for coffee and talked all night, she went to work and then came back and we talked all the next night too, literally all night. I told her everything and she told me a lot about herself too. Neither of us ever believed we'd be the kind to settle down. Her because she didn't feel she'd find anyone who'd love her for her and me because trusting anyone was just too painful. I'd switch off long before love happened and it wasn't fair to someone I love for me to do that to them. We remained friends and saw one another at least three times a week. Ellen came to watch a film one night, we ended up watching both My sisters keeper and Seven pounds. I was dying to put my arm around her but didn't. She got up to make a coffee and stood by my kitchen window looking out. The sun was shining over her neck and travelling through her hair. I had to walk away before I held her. We got chatting and Ellen got to telling me about her feelings regarding men. Unbeknown to her I'd written down how I felt in poem form. I'd also written "Don't tell her" On the back just in case I felt that stupid when I was around her. As she sat telling me all the reasons she didn't feel she'd settle down. All the reasons she felt someone wouldn't love her. I knew I had the power to change that belief even if she walked away she'd know someone cared for her and therefore know someone else would in the future. I had to risk it. "What's this?" she asked as she was curled up on my sofa as I stood in the middle of the room one arm out holding the A4 sheet. "Just read it" I said. She did and then she left without a word.

She called two days later and we met up "okay, let's make a go of this" she said sounding just as cold as when I first met her. She'd moved in within six months and it was the happiest I'd ever been. I had to try and make this permanent. I bought an engagement ring on my lunch break and it was near Christmas. I was sat in a local cafe with the box open on the table, the ring was just staring at me. Everything is perfect why ruin it by asking her to marry me? What if she says no? I didn't care I loved her and it had to be done properly. I told Ellen I had to work late and went to see her dad. I'd only met him once before he seemed a decent guy. "Okay mate, thing is....well let me hit you with this first..." I told him I didn't do drugs and that I didn't drink hardly at all, I told him my father killed my mother and I have a bit of a past but I love his daughter and I'd never intentionally hurt her. I'd understand if he said no but could I marry her?" "If she wants to marry you and you make her happy then that's good enough for me" He said. We chinked glasses and I had a beer with him. It was boxing day and I'd spent Christmas at Ellen's parents with her two sisters and Ellen's nephews. It had been great they were a welcoming polite family with no ridiculous expectations and no control issues or violence. I'd told Ellen I was only staying the one Christmas as I don't do families I like my own privacy, but these guys were great and I really liked them. Boxing day came and I was nervous as I'd chosen today. A day when her family were together because she said family was the most important thing to her. I stood up in front of her mum and dad, her sisters, her nephews and her brother in law and took her hand, she stood up. "There's one more gift, you said when I met you family was the most important thing to you which is why this is the right place to do this." I knelt down and opened the box. "Ellen, will you marry me?" I asked her on bended knee. "Erm....okay!" She said throwing her arms wide and waving them around with a mixture of nerves and excitement.

It was a day off work and Ellen had sat up on the bed to get a drink of a coffee I'd made earlier when a thought hit me. I say thought but...something was different with Ellen. I saw the arch of her back and at the bottom a little blue dot was hovering around. I placed my hand on her back "Hey babe, wouldn't it be weird if you were pregnant?" I said. "Yeah, it would be but I'm not." She replied. "A little girl, brown hair and eyes, virgo." I said leaning back on the bed but keeping my hand in place. Ellen looked at me with an expression that said "you're serious aren't you?" I didn't need to reply. I looked at her and she understood. She took a test and yes it was positive. A digital test that read 1-2 weeks. We held onto one another and cried tears of joy for an hour or more. I was totally amazed and ready for this. Chuffed we'd have our family and totally terrified that I might not be a good enough father. Over the next four month's I digested every parent and baby book I could find. When she kicked, because I was convinced she was a girl. I'd lay on Ellen for hours and talk to her or read. We had a scan and a girl was confirmed. We were both delighted. Then she stopped kicking and Ellen couldn't feel her moving any more I was more scared than I'd ever been but refused to let on to my wife. We got checks and monitoring at the hospital at least three times a week due to low featul movement. I gave up work, I had to be home with my future wife and child. I knew the extra money would of helped us but I'd never of forgiven myself had something happened and I not been there to help. The warehouse guys had a few pieces of advice. "You'll write? Poetry and fiction books? You're a dreamer aren't you?" I didn't care. People too weak to follow their dreams shouldn't stop another from following theirs. I forget where I'd read it but amongst the years of positives it had stuck. Besides it wasn't a debate my wife and child needed me. My choice was made. We had daily monitoring in later months and then twice daily and each visit I told Alan, the spirit world and even prayed to God "I'll go through it all again. All of it. Just let her live. Please" I still wasn't telling my future wife how I felt. "She'll be fine baby, she's half northerner. I love you. You're doing great!" That's what I was telling her. Then we saw a second specialist who examined the notes and Ellen and told us our girl was healthy and so we didn't know what to believe but it was August and a month before out wedding. The doctors said we didn't need to have more monitoring just to wait for a happy birth.

Melorna flew over from Florida and I'd asked her to be my best man. How could she not be? After all she'd done for me. I worried about her speech though. I wasn't bad with words I'd spin that shit off the cuff and make it pretty and I'd tell the truth. Melorna though, she'd just tell the truth and that worried me. "Well Tracie's been through a world of shit, more than once I dragged him out of it but hey he's fine now" wasn't going to put me in good stead with Ellen's family which are good decent people. Not like the people of mine and Melorna's past. When we say their was a punch up at every event we went to we aren't saying it to sound egotistical we're saying it because it's the truth. We've learnt not to hide the facts as someone else will use them against you. I need not have worried. I stood with Tim and Melorna as the guests arrived. I could say none of my family were there and that would be an accurate statement although it wouldn't strictly be true. You see all of my family were there. My wife carrying my child, Tim, Melorna and my friends. All the family I'd grown to love and I won't deny that truth. I turned from facing the alter and was faced with over a hundred people I barely knew, my friends and a handful of Ellen's family I'd come to admire and respect and then Ellen and her dad walked in and two things happened simultaneously. Ellen had taken four steps towards me and I couldn't speak. She looked amazing, long hair cascading and twirling down her back and shoulders. Deep brown eyes flickering mine and a beautiful white dress. As she got halfway down the aisle I saw the briefest flash of black and white photograph go off in my head and heard "Congratulations lad" and it was gone. That photo was every snippet of my past and the voice was Alan, clear as a bell. I knew then things could only get better from here on in.

Chapter 41

We were in what had become our flat watching season five of Sons of Anarchy when Ellen got up off the floor to go to the loo. I'd quit smoking and I'd only been stopped for two days. I went to the kitchen and put the kettle on when Ellen returned "I do believe my water's have just broken" She said so calm and relaxed as though it was the most natural thing in the world. "That's great, you okay?" I asked grabbing the bags we had ready to go and looking around for my spare smokes simultaneously. We stayed in hospital a night and she was induced in the morning. Ellen was amazing throughout the short four hour labour. She only had gas and air and held my hand for at least eighty five percent of it. Our midwife was a thin brunette lady who mostly felt comfortable leaving us to it. She was always to hand and we couldn't have asked for better. She guided Ellen through the delivery of our daughter as she gave a light thud into the world. She had a full head of her mums dark hair and was a tiny five pounds thirteen ounces. I'd cut the cord and She was placed on Ellen and then I took her and sat with her. I was amazed. My beautiful little girl. We'd done it. A midwife came in and I didn't care. I couldn't hold it and didn't want to. I burst into tears staring in wonder at our precious child. "We did it" I told Alan. "Thank you" I said to the spirit side. "Awwww" I heard the midwife say as she carried on about her business. I glanced at Ellen and hoped my look conveyed it all. "Thank you I am complete" She was born 23rd September 2013 ten days after we were married. She is bang on the Virgo/Libra cusp and has her mother's beautiful eyes and my beautiful personality.

I started writing this book just before my daughter was born, I'd received a "write your own autobiography" Book as a gift from Ellen when we were joking about my past. I wrote it out initially by hand and later typed it up. It's taken me seven years so far and they've been the happiest seven years of my life. I am a completely different person to the man I was ten years ago, aren't we all? I don't need to instil the positives and care into myself on a daily basis any more. I don't need to question whether I'm a good person or a good parent.

I'm too busy loving and caring for our two amazingly happy and precious girls. Our second was born on 30th January 2018 and weighed 7lbs 6 ounces came into the world kicking and screaming through a fairly traumatic although short labour of four hours. She has my hair, my looks and my personality. God help us all. Due to complications she was handed immediately to me and I went straight into dad mode with cleaning and cuddling. I wouldn't recognise until later on just how like me she really is, she has my eyes and you know what? They're beautiful. She's perfect and my family is whole.

Seven years to complete and a lifetime to discover, I can say with hand on heart knowing everything that I've come through, everything that I've experienced. If I had to live it all over again from day one to get the result I have today, I'd do exactly that.

Thank you for reading and sharing this journey. I hope it's proved useful and please, please share. You never know when there's a person out there that can benefit from someone listening that little bit more.

If I've learnt anything it's this.

"
If I have the belief that I can do it, I shall surely acquire the capacity to do it even if I may not have it at the beginning."

— Mahatma Gandhi

—   Tracie Daily.

Printed in Poland
by Amazon Fulfillment
Poland Sp. z o.o., Wrocław

54475378R00181